The Complete Guide to
BATHROOMS

Updated 4th Edition

Design • Update • Remodel
Improve • Do-It-Yourself

COOL
SPRINGS
PRESS
Home and Garden Experts™

MINNEAPOLIS, MINNESOTA

Quarto is the authority on a wide range of topics.

Quarto educates, entertains and enriches the lives of our readers—enthusiasts and lovers of hands-on living.

www.quartoknows.com

First published in 2015 by Cool Springs Press, an imprint of Quarto Publishing Group USA Inc., 400 First Avenue North, Suite 400, Minneapolis, MN 55401 USA. Telephone: (612) 344-8100
Fax: (612) 344-8692

quartoknows.com
Visit our blogs at quartoknows.com

Cool Springs Press titles are also available at discounts in bulk quantity for industrial or sales-promotional use. For details contact the Special Sales Manager at Quarto Publishing Group USA Inc., 400 First Avenue North, Suite 400, Minneapolis, MN 55401 USA.

ISBN: 978-1-59186-901-6

Printed in China

10 9 8 7 6 5 4 3

Library of Congress Cataloging-in-Publication Data

The complete guide to bathrooms : design, update, remodel, improve, do it yourself. -- 4th edition.
    pages cm.
  At head of title: Black & Decker.
  Summary: "Detailed step-by-step photos and how-to information for all of the most common bathroom remodeling and repair projects"-- Provided by publisher.
  ISBN 978-1-59186-901-6 (paperback)
  1. Bathrooms--Remodeling--Amateurs' manuals. I. Black & Decker Corporation (Towson, Md.) II. Title: Black & Decker the complete guide to bathrooms. III. Title: Black and Decker the complete guide to bathrooms.

TH4816.3.B37C66 2015
643'.52--dc23

                    2014038225

Acquisitions Editor: Mark Johanson
Design Manager: Brad Springer
Layout: Danielle Smith-Boldt

Photography: Rau + Barber
Photo Assistance: Adam Esco, Alexandra Burniece, Natalie Williams

The Complete Guide to Bathrooms
Created by: The Editors of Cool Springs Press. in cooperation with Black+Decker.
Black+Decker and the Black+Decker logo are trademarks of The Black & Decker Corporation and are used under license. All rights reserved.

NOTICE TO READERS

Contents

The Complete Guide to
Bathrooms

Contents (Cont.)

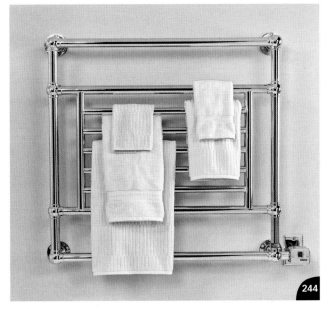

Introduction

More than any other space in the house, a bathroom represents the intersection of form and function. Every design feature in the room—no matter how good it looks—must take safety, efficiency, and comfort into account. And it's not just a matter of practicality; legal and code restrictions increasingly affect the design elements that can or must be included in a modern, up-to-date bathroom.

That represents a huge design challenge, but one that bathroom manufacturers are meeting in high style more than ever before.

It shouldn't be surprising, given that there is so much potential payoff in bathroom design. Bathroom remodeling projects remain some of the highest return-on-investment changes you can make to your home. Homeowners and prospective homeowners alike clearly understand how much impact a handsome, thoughtfully designed bathroom can have on day-to-day living.

It's almost an understatement to say that impact can be profound. And no more so than for the growing number of homeowners and residents with disease and age-related mobility issues. America's aging population and increasing awareness of the functional challenges people with disabilities face, have spurred ever-growing design and code-related changes when it comes to bathrooms. Whether grouped under the general category of *Universal Design* or filed under the more contemporary and overarching term *Aging-in-Place*, these changes are intended to make a bathroom more usable for anyone who might occupy or visit the house.

Consequently, this updated edition of *The Complete Guide to Bathrooms* includes a wealth of new information and projects addressing the issue of bathroom accessibility. It's not just a matter of accommodating those people with limited mobility; these innovations help everyone. A curbless shower may be a great improvement for someone in a wheelchair or walker, but it also means less possibility that an unencumbered homeowner stumbles as he shambles bleary eyed into the bathroom for his watery wake-up call. A hands-free faucet doesn't just serve the grandparents with arthritis, it can also be a big help to little ones who lack the fine motor skills or height to reach and use traditional faucet handles.

Of course, no matter how functional the element, there's no reason to give up style. That's why you'll find a vast range of design options to choose from in the pages that follow, whether you're looking to update your master bath with a full complement of grab bars, or simply want to introduce a new faucet and vanity top to a powder room. Want to install a cool retro clawfoot tub? You'll see how on page 107. Looking for new sink options (including chic roll-under alternatives)? Check out page 134. No matter what you're looking to add or change in your bathroom, you'll find the latest and greatest in this revised edition of *The Complete Guide to Bathrooms*.

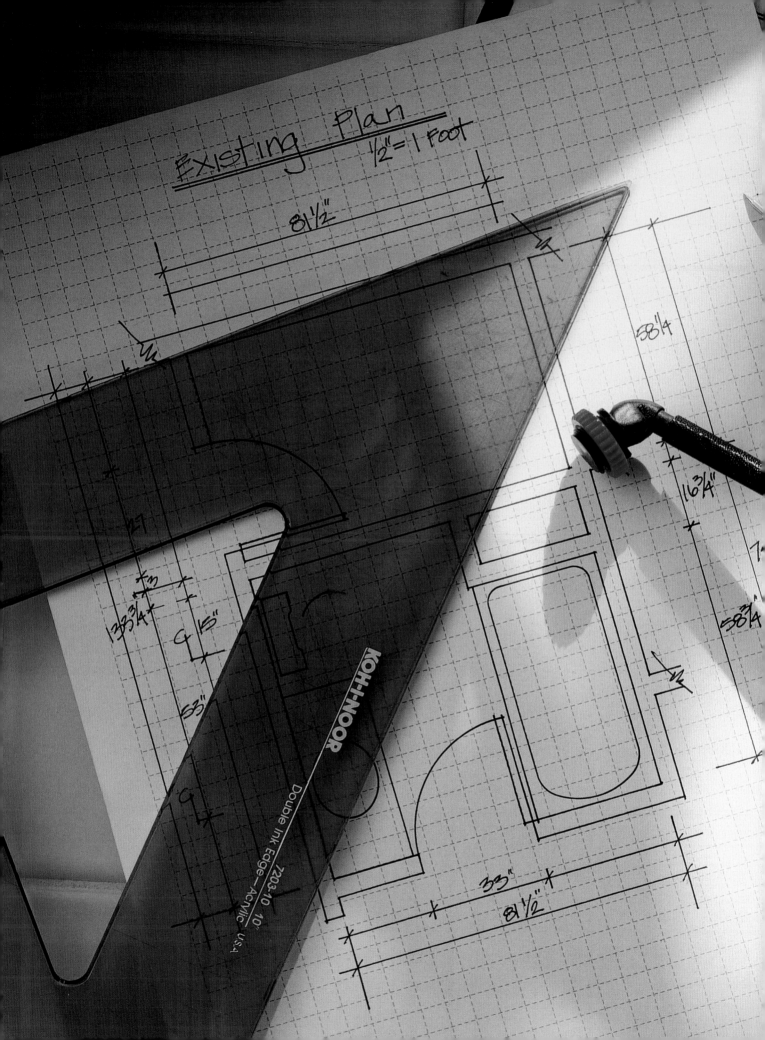

PLANNING & DESIGNING YOUR BATHROOM

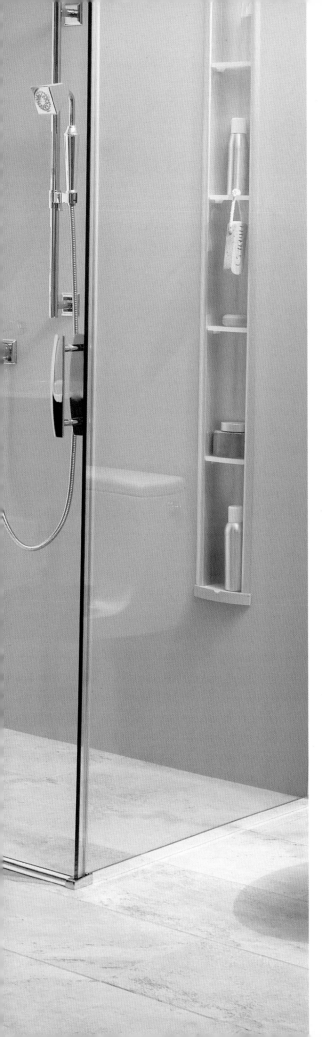

Gallery of Bathrooms

The bathroom fulfills many functions. First and foremost, it addresses the specific wishes of the homeowner—whether it's a standalone shower enclosure that's easier to walk into than a tub, or small luxuries like a towel warmer or an in-floor warming system. But the bathroom must be comfortable to use, with grab bars where necessary, vanities and cabinets that provide sensibly placed storage space, and surfaces that feel good to the touch.

The specific features of a well-designed bathroom also depend on what type of bathroom it is. A half bath for guests, or a powder room, may require only a quiet, highly efficient toilet and a focal-point vessel sink. The design of a family bath is more involved, with upgraded ventilation and multi-user features such as double sinks and a segregated toilet area. A master bathroom suite may include luxury touches such as a sunken tub or a shower with multiple heads and a sound system.

Regardless of the type of bathroom you're looking to create, you'll find a wealth of design options in the following gallery pages. Even if the specific features shown in these pages aren't exactly what you want for your own project, they will inspire and help you to discover your perfect bathroom.

The polished stone tub deck and flooring lends a feeling of luxury to this bathroom. The hard surfaces have the added benefit of water and mold resistance. The wood floor adds warmth, but is kept away from the tub and toilet areas. The large window bathes the room with natural light.

A clean European look combines functionality with style in this simple and elegant bathroom. The wood floor is easy to keep clean because of the clear space under the wall-mounted toilet and vanity. Wall mounting bathroom elements continues to grow in popularity for just this reason. The toilet can also be mounted at a custom height to better accommodate a wheelchair user.

Vessel bathroom sinks have become so popular that the range of styles and materials is very nearly limitless. This sleek fixture is formed of volcanic rock and the sophisticated color won't chip, fade, or stain.

A tray vessel sink offers style and ample space, while a freestanding soaking tub will afford an incredible bathing experience in a tub that fits into tight spaces.

If traditional is your style in the rest of the house, you can define the bathroom with the same flair. Use signature elements including framed mirrors and shower doors, wood structures like the face-frame double vanity cabinets shown here, and traditional fixtures like the dual, double-handled faucets in this restrained and appealing bathroom.

A freestanding tub is the ideal accent for a contemporary or modern bathroom. It is easier to install, pleasing to the eye, and the tubs come in a vast range of styles, sizes, and features.

The widespread bathroom faucet is mounted to the countertop and is paired with a stainless steel under-mount sink, adding to the high-tech look of the room. A striking backdrop of metal wall tiles reflects light and creates a bright atmosphere.

This wall-hung sink with its traditional two-handled faucet reflects the Art Deco style of the floor tiles. The glass-and-steel base is mostly decorative.

Gorgeous bathroom design elements deserve a proper stage, and few are as ideal for a bathroom setting as the luxurious quartz floor in this room. Durable, scratchproof, moisture resistant, and wonderful underfoot, a quartz surface is as useful as it is beautiful.

A towel warmer drawer built into a linen cabinet is a discreet yet extravagant addition to the bathroom.

Storage space is at a premium in bathrooms. Employing some kitchen-style cabinet organizing tricks helps boost efficiency.

Style and accessibility can go hand in hand, as this stunning shower illustrates. A chic trench drain ensures no water from this curbless shower makes it onto the floor outside, and a seat and hand-held shower wand on a sliding bar make showering as easy for people with mobility issues as it is for anyone else in the house.

Coordinated lighting is part of any truly stylish bathroom. The matching wall fixtures here provide abundant warm light for a true image in the mirror, safe movement in and out of the bath, and a great look on the wall.

Deep soaking luxury is combined with accessibility in this useful and stylish tub. The bather simply sits on the bench seat, swings their legs over the side and raises the tub's movable sidewall to enjoy a wonderful jetted bathtub experience in a seated position.

Bathroom Elements

The number of styles and materials used in bathroom fixtures and surfaces continues to grow. As design options multiply, manufacturers are also answering the need for usable (and often code-required) safety features, water-conserving faucets, toilets, and showers, and ADA (Americans with Disabilities Act)-compliant essentials.

You'll find choices from the plain and simple to over-the-top luxurious. In fact, the biggest chore you'll usually face in remodeling a bathroom is whittling down all those choices.

Even when you're working with a fairly tight budget, consider splurging where the money will have the biggest impact. Love a long, leisurely bath? A jetted tub, or a deep soaking unit, may be the ideal luxury. Is there a gang of kids constantly using the guest bathroom? A stylish hands-free faucet with built-in water timer might be the answer to your prayers.

Whatever feature you're shopping for, bring along measurements of the current space, a measuring tape, and a notebook and pen. You'll probably be surprised by the options you find, and you'll want to make sure anything that catches your fancy will fit where it needs to go.

In this chapter:

- Bathtubs & Jetted Tubs
- Showers
- Sinks
- Toilets & Bidets
- Cabinets & Vanities
- Lighting
- Heating & Ventilation
- Walls & Ceilings
- Flooring

Bathtubs & Jetted Tubs

Although you can find bathtubs in a wide variety of sizes and shapes, your existing bathroom floorplan usually dictates exactly what size you should buy. But if you don't mind moving some plumbing, or you are building an all-new bathroom, your options expand dramatically.

Tubs are categorized first by the method used to install them. The three basic installation styles are alcove, deck-mounted, and freestanding.

Alcove tubs are the most common. They are often enclosed on three sides, which is why they are also called "recessed tubs". One-piece tub-and-shower combination fixtures are also available to fit standard-size alcoves. Custom sizes can be made for odd-size alcoves.

Deck-mounted tubs and whirlpools, also called drop-in tubs, generally rest directly on the subfloor or in a thinset mortar base. They are surrounded by custom-built decks or platforms. Typically, these tubs have a larger capacity than attached-apron tubs. The cost of making the deck can cause these tubs to be more expensive than other types, but the design possibilities are nearly limitless.

Freestanding tubs are available in an amazing range of styles and materials. The two basic types of freestanding tub are *footed* and *pedestal*, but within those two groups are a large number of interpretations that range from the classic clawfoot tub, to ultra-modern units that are almost works of art. In any case, these are most often fabricated from enameled iron, polymer or, on the high side, marble or other stone surfaces. They are meant to hold up to abuse because they lack the protective structure of an apron or deck. The plumbing is most often exposed, and the hardware presents even more design possibilities.

Rectangular tubs are the most common shape and are often combined with showers. They come in a wide range of widths, lengths, depths, and colors in addition to the traditional 30" × 60" × 14" white version.

Square and triangular tubs are very uncommon. They fit into corners to help visually open up small bathrooms, and they are often combined with a shower.

This jetted tub features a side-mounted faucet that allows for complete reclining and an utterly relaxing, spa-like bathing experience.

A claw-foot tub is an iconic bathroom fixture. The original models made of cast iron with an enameled porcelain finish can be found through architectural salvage companies, although the supply is dwindling and the prices are climbing. Reproductions of this style are made with lighter-weight composites and polymers.

The traditional one-piece white alcove tub remains one of the most popular choices among homeowners for its low cost and durability—no customization required.

This tub bridges the line between an alcove and a drop-in model. The three-sided wood cladding is supplied by the manufacturer along with the tub, which features luxurious jets and side-mounted controls. Paired with a wall-mount faucet and shower paddle, it's easy for the bather to completely recline in the relaxing tub.

Tub Materials

Tubs are manufactured from many different materials, each with its own pros and cons.

Fiberglass is an inexpensive, lightweight material that can be finished in a variety of colors. It is easily molded, so fiberglass tubs can have seats, grab bars, soap dishes, and shampoo shelves molded into the sides. Though fiberglass has many benefits, its surface can scratch easily and its color will fade.

Acrylic, like fiberglass, can be molded into just about any size and shape. Unlike fiberglass, however, the color runs through the entire substance rather than just on the surface coat, making it less likely to show scratches or to fade.

Enameled steel tubs are pressed from sheets of steel and coated with a baked-on enamel similar to that of cast-iron tubs. The enamel layer is usually thin, though, and is susceptible to chipping. In addition, enameled steel doesn't retain heat well and tends to be noisy.

Cast iron is the most durable material available for tubs. Iron is cast into a tub shape, then coated with a baked-on enamel that is relatively thick ($\frac{1}{16}$"), resulting in a richly colored finish. The enamel is strong, durable, and resistant to chips, scratches, and stains.

Cast iron is just about indestructible, but it's also extremely heavy. In some cases, the floor framing must be reinforced to support the additional weight. Cast iron is used most commonly for claw-foot and other stand-alone bathtubs.

Polymer can be cast into just about any tub shape, and is a solid color throughout, making it impervious to scratches. The finish can be made to mimic quality surfaces such as marble or granite. Polymer also retains heat well, although the gel coat used on polymer breaks down over time.

Solid surface tubs are gaining popularity. As with solid surface countertops, the tubs can be made in one piece of resins or quartz, and formed into many different shapes—including some with built-in features such as soap dishes. The material retains heat well, comes in many surface looks, and is durable.

Specialty Tubs

Soaking tubs are deeper with higher sides than other styles. Traditional Japanese versions feature sides as high as 4 feet, but contemporary American soaking tubs usually have walls from 20 to 36 inches high. Traditional soaking tubs are tall enough that bathers may sit, rather than recline, although the shallowest modern models are soaking tubs only to the extent that they will allow an adult to be covered completely with water when reclined. The experience is luxurious and meditative.

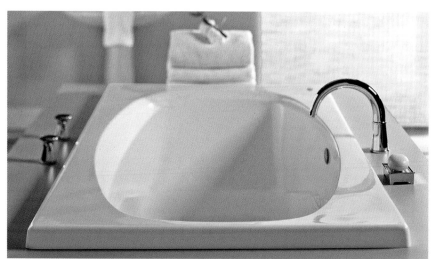

Large deck-mounted tubs offer options when it comes to locating the spout and valve handles. In many cases this means you can position the spout near the tub center so you can lean back against either end of the tub without hitting any hardware.

Jetted tubs circulate water that's mixed with air through jets mounted in the body of the tub. The pumps move as much as 50 gallons of water per minute to create a massaging effect that relieves stress and muscle pain. Better quality jets can be adjusted to alter both the stream's direction and the proportion of air and water (more air means a more vigorous massage).

Jetted tubs are almost always made of acrylic, and sizes and shapes vary tremendously. Prices also vary—whirlpools can range from $700 to $10,000 and up before installation. Price is determined by the number of jets (from four to ten or more), size of the water pump, and options such as an in-line heater.

You can find a variety of accessories for jetted tubs. A multispeed motor allows you to choose various settings from a gentle, relaxing soak to a vigorous massage. An in-line heater maintains the water temperature. Grab bars, mood lights, pillows, timers, mirrors, and touch-pad controls are all available for added convenience and comfort.

Before you invest in a jetted tub, review the maintenance requirements. Some demand extensive upkeep of pumps, timers, and controls, and many roomy models require an extra large water heater.

A jetted tub can be installed by a skilled homeowner familiar with the basic techniques of carpentry, plumbing, and tile setting. Some are small enough to fit in the alcove used for standard bathtubs, though most models require the construction of a surrounding deck or platform.

A tub platform can be tucked into a corner or even an alcove. If you add tile or another moisture-resistant wallcovering on the corner walls, you may consider adding a hand-held shower near the corner. Hand-held showers are not a good idea for island tubs.

An oversized tub can be installed in a bathroom with limited wallspace if you have sufficient floor area to accommodate an extra-wide tub like this arched-front model.

Showers

Showers can stand alone or be combined with tubs, and they come in a number of styles and materials.

A tub/shower combination is more common than a standalone shower stall. It uses space efficiently, is cheap to install, and can easily be added to an alcove tub. One-piece molded fiberglass and acrylic tub-and-shower units are available, but they are often too large to fit through doors and are better suited for new construction.

Shower stalls are ideal for small bathrooms or as a tub supplement in master or luxury bathrooms. They can be purchased prefabricated or they can be custom-built.

One-piece alcove showers are a common option for do-it-yourself installation. The seamless stall is molded from a single piece of fiberglass or acrylic, making it easy to clean and maintain. A wide range of shower stall sizes and styles are available. Some feature seats, steam bath fixtures, or other added-value functions.

Neo-angle showers are designed to fit into a corner. They are usually made of acrylic or fiberglass, and have doors that open at an angle.

Shower surround panels are used to construct simple, inexpensive shower stalls. They are built above a preformed shower base made of PVC plastic, fiberglass, acrylic, solid-surface material, quartz, or natural stone. Three individual panels are bonded to the walls of the framed alcove, and the seams are sealed.

Freestanding showers are complete units that are not attached to walls. They range from inexpensive sheet metal or fiberglass units to elaborate glass block showers. The vast majority of showers, however, fit into corners or against one wall.

Custom shower stalls can be designed to fit into odd spaces (pages 72 to 89). The walls can be finished with ceramic tile, glass block, or a solid-surface

One-piece alcove shower enclosures can be simple and modest, or incredibly upscale and detailed, such as the oversized unit shown here.

A combination bathtub-shower—with a shower curtain or sliding glass door—remains one of the most popular choices for more modest homes and bathrooms.

material. Specialized options, such as seats, steam bath fixtures, and soap dishes, can be incorporated into the design.

Curbless showers are designed for physically challenged users. The shower entrance has no curb at all, providing easy access to the shower. One-piece molded units are available, or barrier-free showers can be custom-built. Most have built-in shower seats and grab bars. See pages 78 to 89 for more information on curbless showers.

Shower doors and curtains are usually purchased separately from the shower itself. Options range from simple plastic curtains costing a few dollars to custom-made tempered glass doors.

Multiple showerheads, shower towers, and steam showers can create a more luxurious shower. Steam showers require extra plumbing, wiring, and a shower stall with doors that seal tightly.

Shower Lights ▸

An overhead light ensures safety in the shower. Make sure that any light installed in a shower area is moisture-resistant. Some shower lights include a heating element.

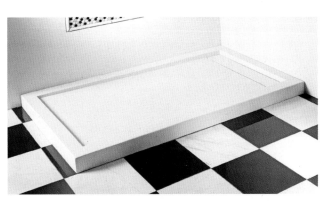

Prefab shower trays come with a variety of styles, including sleek features like the concealed trench drain in this unit.

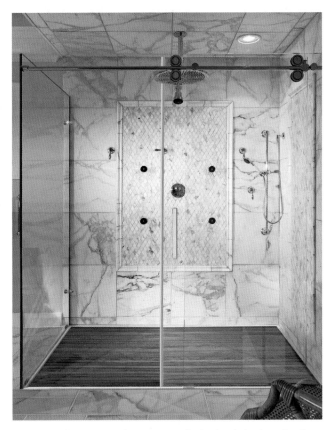

A simple shower enclosure using off-the-shelf pan, hardware, fixtures, and frameless glass panels can create a stunning centerpiece to an already stunning bathroom.

Custom shower enclosures are limited only by imagination and can include, as this one does, a wood slat floor over a curbless drain pan, marble walls, and multiple showerheads for a sumptuous experience.

Sinks

The variety of sinks available today practically guarantees that you can find a lavatory sink to match your space, budget, and taste. The most significant difference between the major sink types is the manner in which they are installed: wall mounted, pedestal or console, and countertop.

Wall-mounted sinks hang directly from the wall, taking up little space and offering easy access to plumbing hookups. Basic wall-mounted sinks are good options for utility bathrooms or half baths, where exposed plumbing and lack of storage space are not serious drawbacks. Designer wall-mounted styles feature attached aprons that hide plumbing. These are also accessibility features, allowing people in wheelchairs to roll under the sink for easy use.

Pedestal sinks and **console sinks** are wall-mounted styles that rest on a pedestal or legs that may or may not provide actual support to the sink bowl. A decorative pedestal may conceal plumbing and can be a smart choice for a small guest bathroom or powder room where floorspace is particularly scarce. Console sinks have legs supporting the front two corners and often feature an apron to mask plumbing connections. The advantage of a console sink over a pedestal model is that small baskets or a modest, simple shelving unit can be placed underneath for additional storage.

Self-rimming sinks drop into a cutout in the countertop, with its rim overlapping the cutout's edges.

Integral sinks, usually made of solid-surface material or cultured marble, are molded into countertops and are easy to install and maintain.

Undermounted sinks are attached with clips beneath a cutout in a solid-surface, stone, or concrete countertop.

Vessel sinks sit on top of a countertop, with only a small cutout for the drain.

Sinks can be made of a number of materials. **Cultured marble** is an inexpensive material often used to create integral sink-and-countertop combinations to fit standard vanity sizes.

A pedestal sink has visual appeal and an efficient footprint, but lacks any storage function.

A solid-surface sink and countertop is the perfect match for a modern single-handle faucet and chic wall-mounted vanity.

Porcelain (vitreous china) may be used for self-rimming sinks. It has a durable glossy surface that is nonporous and easy to clean. Porcelain sinks are readily available in white and almond, and you can special order other colors. For a truly unique addition to your bathroom decor, consider a hand-painted porcelain sink in a floral or other one-of-a-kind design.

Solid-surface material is long lasting and easy to clean; scratches can be buffed or sanded out. It is one of the more expensive choices for bathroom sinks, but its durability and ease of care help justify the price. Solid-surface sinks are available in self-rimming, undermounted, and integral models, with a variety of colors and patterns to choose from.

Stainless steel brings a high-tech look and durability to bathroom sinks. It is available in either a satin or mirror finish. Price varies according to thickness, or gauge—the lower the gauge number, the thicker the steel. Look for 18-gauge material with a noise-reducing undercoating. Because they are lightweight, stainless steel sinks are often used for undermounting.

Composite and acrylic sinks are less common because they aren't ideal in high-traffic areas. However, where the sinks won't see a lot of use, these can be low-cost, attractive alternatives to more durable materials.

Tempered glass is used to create stylish vessel sinks for bathrooms. Undermounted styles can be lit from underneath to create a mood-setting glow. Art glass sinks continue to grow in popularity and, if crafted properly, a cast or fused glass sink can be every bit as durable and safe as tempered glass—with a nearly infinite number of possible designs and colors.

Other materials such as concrete, copper, carved stone, and wood can be used to create more stylized bathrooms. Enameled cast iron is extremely durable, but available in limited shapes and colors, which is why it is used less often than other options. Volcanic rock is a relatively new material, but one that comes in a range of bold and subtle colors and appearances, and is amazingly durable. Before you select a sink made of an unusual material, consider the shipping time, installation procedures, maintenance, and cost.

Self-rimming sinks (also called drop-ins) fit into a cutout in a countertop and usually are secured with mounting clips from below.

Undermount sinks have a very contemporary appearance and offer some clean-up advantages, but they can only be installed in countertops that have a contiguous waterproof composition (such as solid surface or poured concrete).

These stunning, artistic sinks are crafted from volcanic rock, as is the counter they rest on. The material offers a unique and incredibly durable surface.

Toilets & Bidets

Toilets and bidets are increasingly becoming more distinctive design elements rather than merely function-first fixtures. This is understandable given the trend toward including bidets in bathroom design. A popular and ubiquitous feature in European homes, the bidet has not yet developed a majority following in North America. But that may be changing, as more and more homeowners discover the usefulness of bidets. Most large manufacturers offer suites including coordinated bidets and toilets.

Toilets alone, however, continue to dominate in the modern American bathroom. Designs and technology continue to evolve, and water conservation remains at the forefront of that evolution. Where the standard residential toilet thirty years ago used an average of 6 gallons per flush, the most streamlined models on the market today boast a usage that is slightly more than half a gallon per flush. Dual flush models have become common, featuring two handles—one for a lighter flush and a second that provides a more energetic flush to remove solids.

Technology and efficiency notwithstanding, toilet style continues to be refined. A walk through the plumbing section of any large home center will reveal toilet designs from the staid and traditional, to ultra-modern streamlined units that are just short of artworks.

That variety of styles is no less apparent in the latest trend toward wall-mounted units. These are a space-saving addition to any bathroom but, more importantly, they are increasingly answering the call for bathroom accessibility and Age-in-Place features. That's because a wall-mount toilet can be adjusted to any height, to suit the intended users. You can find more information on wall-mounted units—as well as installation instructions—on page 164.

The toilet can be hidden in an alcove and kept as simple as can be, or it can exhibit a bit of design flourish. If you really want your toilet to make a design statement, combine it with a matching bidet for the ultimate in European-style luxury.

Fixture Types

Two-piece toilets have a separate tank and bowl, and they account for the vast majority of toilets in homes today. Their main advantage is low cost.

Wall-mounted toilets are space-saving options that offer other advantages as well.

Flushing mechanisms are changing rapidly to keep pace with the demand for greater water economy. One new technology is the dual-flush design, which has a light flush option for liquid waste only that can save 20% on water usage over standard 1.6 gallon models.

Bidets are essentially wash basins with a very specific function.

Cabinets & Vanities

The typical bathroom lacks storage space. In fact, creating better storage is one of the most common reasons people remodel their bathrooms. As you design your new bathroom, keep in mind three basic types of storage: cabinetry, open shelving, and linen closets.

Wall cabinets, because they are shallow, are versatile storage units for small spaces like bathrooms. They can be installed on any available wall space—the most popular spot is over the toilet. Some are freestanding units with legs that straddle the toilet tank. Wall cabinets can even be mounted low and topped with a counter. Or, they can be installed in banks.

Vanity cabinets hide plumbing, provide storage, and support the countertop and sink. A vanity is often a bathroom's visual focal point and can set the decorative tone for the whole room.

Wall-mounted storage, like the contemporary vanity and matching cabinet here, can be a space-saving solution—one that allows for cleaning underneath while still supplying handy, accessible storage space.

Medicine cabinets offer quick access to toiletries and keep storage items beyond the reach of young children. Most are designed with a mirror on the door or doors and are installed above a sink. They can be either surface-mounted or recessed into walls between studs to exploit otherwise unused space. Many incorporate lighting.

Linen cabinets are tall and narrow, taking advantage of floor-to-ceiling space. They can add significant towel and bedding storage without taking much floor space.

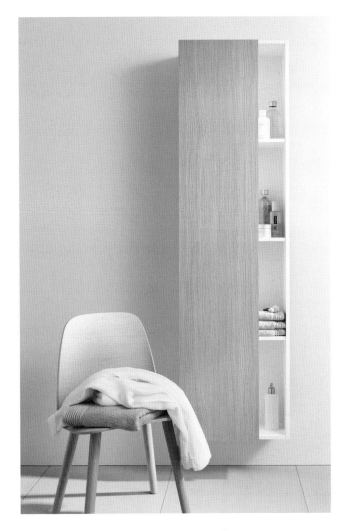

Tall, thin cabinets are often excellent choices for additional storage in a bathroom. The shape takes up a modest amount of space and provides abundant storage. Combining open shelving with enclosed cabinetry in a unit such as this ensures that just about anything you might need to store in the room has a proper place to go.

Vanities with legs lend an open and airy feeling to the bathroom, and provide an option for useful shelving underneath. The hardware on this vanity was selected to match the brushed finish of the chic faucet and shower fixtures, creating a very unified look.

(continued)

Whatever type of cabinet you're considering, you'll have the choice of stock or custom-made designs:

Stock cabinets are mass-produced in standard sizes and warehoused for quick delivery. They are less expensive than custom-made cabinets of comparable wood species, but a wide range of prices can be had within both categories.

Custom cabinets are built to order by a cabinetmaker or cabinet shop, so you get exactly the combination of size, style, material, and finish that you want. Start shopping for custom cabinets early and plan on at least six to eight weeks and probably longer from design to delivery.

Other storage options for bathrooms include shelves and closets:

Shelves are a useful addition to bathrooms that don't have room for elaborate cabinetry. They can be recessed or surface-mounted and are often combined with baskets and storage bins.

Linen closets are recessed in the wall and extend from floor to ceiling. Adding or relocating a closet requires significant structural modifications to your walls.

Medicine chest designs have evolved right along with the look and function of most other bathroom features. This sleek unit represents a significant departure from the traditional swing-out door medicine chest. The mirror slides up to allow access to the shelving inside, eliminating the door swing arc that can be an awkward nuisance in the ever-space-challenged bathroom. Notice that in keeping with the sophisticated technology, the mirror is frameless, offering an appealingly streamlined and modern look.

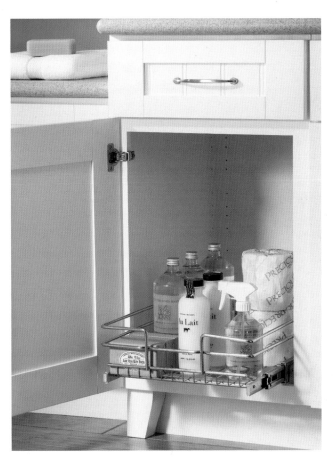

A linen cabinet is a freestanding furnishing, but it can take on a built-in appearance if you integrate it with other cabinets and wall trim. Linen cabinets and linen closets can be made more efficient by customizing with features such as door-back shelves and pull-out laundry bins.

Slide-out storage racks are especially useful in base cabinets. Functioning basically as drawers, slide-out racks can be included at the time of purchase or added later.

A full-length single door cabinet makes efficient use of space and can be matched stylistically to your medicine cabinet for extra impact.

Lighting

Lighting can set the mood of any room. Dim lights and lit candles are perfect for a leisurely soak in the tub. When it comes to shaving or applying makeup, though, bright lights are best.

As with the rest of the house, the bathroom is best served by a combination of general, task, and accent lighting, to ensure personal safety, provide ambience, and permit various uses of the space.

General lighting usually involves an overhead fixture or fixtures that illuminate the whole room. Natural lighting is considered part of your general lighting.

Task lighting provides directed light for specific activities, such as applying makeup or shaving.

Accent lighting can be used to highlight decorative points of interest, such as architectural details or artwork.

Surface-mounted fixtures are easy to install and available in a variety of styles. Just be sure that all fixtures you choose are moisture-proof and meant for use in a bathroom environment.

Recessed ceiling fixtures are set into canisters and have trim kits that are mounted flush with the surface of the ceiling and some include adjustable heads that allow you to direct the light one way or another. This improves headroom in a small bath.

Never lose sight of the fact that the right bathroom lighting not only supplies illumination, it can also be a decorative accent.

Wall-mount fixtures are common in bathrooms, and provide ideal lighting for personal grooming, especially when placed on both sides of a mirror, as well as above.

Ceiling mount fixtures are excellent overall light sources in the small spaces of most bathrooms.

This opulent bathroom features just about every type of bathroom lighting you might need, including pendants for specific task areas, overhead ambient fixtures, accent lighting behind the mirror and under the wall-mounted vanities, and shelf lighting. It's a handsome, safe, and easy space to navigate.

Heating & Ventilation

Consider room size, the number of windows, and the type of heat in the rest of the house when making decisions about your bathroom heating system. Consult a professional before making final decisions. If your primary heat system is inadequate, you have three basic choices for auxiliary heat in bathrooms:

Electric heaters are mounted either by themselves or as part of light/vent/heating units.

Heat lamps use infrared lightbulbs to provide radiant heat.

Radiant floor-heating systems are installed beneath the flooring and circulate either hot water or electricity.

Good ventilation protects surfaces from moisture damage, deters mold and mildew, and keeps air fresh. Vents with electric fans (pages 188 to 191) are required by code in any bathroom without windows. The vent must exhaust moist air directly outdoors, not into attics or wall cavities.

Purchase a vent fan that's rated at least 5 cfm higher than the square footage of your bathroom. Local building codes may have specific requirements, so check with your building inspector or HVAC contractor before selecting a ventilation unit.

DIY radiant heat floor systems are electric mats installed beneath floor coverings to warm your feet and heat your room.

Vent and light combinations serve the dual purpose of lighting the room and reducing moisture and odors. Some contain an infrared heating element for a third function (inset).

Walls & Ceilings

If you add, move, replace, or resurface walls in your bathroom, use the best materials for the job. Options include:

Drywall is adequate for most bathrooms, except for the area around tubs and showers.

Greenboard is a drywall with waterproof facing. It has fallen out of usage in recent years.

Cementboard is used primarily as an underlayment for ceramic tile.

Glass block is a decorative building block that has great visual appeal, but can't bear loads.

You'll want the wall and ceiling finishes to be easy to maintain. Wall finishes for tub and shower surrounds, and behind sinks and toilets, should be waterproof.

Solid-surface panels, such as this black quartz accent surface that matches the tub deck, can make ideal waterproof bathroom wall surfaces.

Paint finishes range from flat to glossy (enamel). Glossy finishes are best for areas that will be cleaned often. Latex (water-based) paints are more environmentally friendly than oil-based paints.

Wallpaper should be treated to withstand moisture. Choose smooth-textured, solid vinyl, or vinyl-coated wallpaper in a bathroom.

Wall tiles are durable, easy to clean, and available in hundreds of styles, colors, and materials, including stone, ceramic, glass, and—if you want a really unusual look—metals.

Solid-surface material is often used to fashion walls in tub and shower surrounds.

Bathroom ceilings need moisture-resistant finishes. Avoid textured ceilings, which peel in humid conditions and are difficult to clean, repair, or paint.

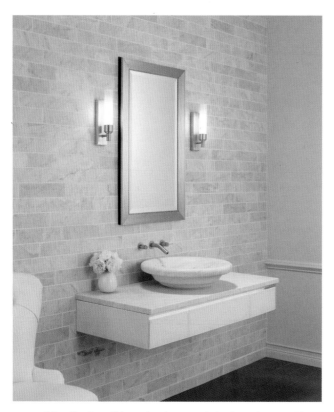

A marble-tiled wall is a classic upscale look and a matching marble counter and vessel sink on top of a wall-hung vanity is a space-saving update to that look.

Flooring

Bathroom floors should stand up to daily use, frequent cleaning, and moisture.

Resilient sheet flooring is inexpensive but is seldom the first choice of professional designers. It is simple to install, easy to clean, seamless, and available in a vast number of colors, patterns, and styles. Resilient sheet products include linoleum, which is incredibly eco-friendly, and vinyl, which is far less so.

Resilient tile and planks made of vinyl are easy to install. The latest versions are made to stand up to even the most demanding bathroom conditions. These products are easier to install than ever, and include marmoleum, a very green option.

Ceramic tile is available in three main types: glazed ceramic tile, quarry tile, and water-resistant porcelain tile. Although cleaning issues are created by the grout lines, mosaic sheets of ceramic tile are highly popular.

Natural stone tile is a premium flooring material. Granite, marble, and slate are the most common stone products for bathroom floors.

Hardwood floors are difficult to totally waterproof so they should be limited to half baths, where moisture will not be a big problem.

A **faux-wood laminate floor** provides an ideal durable stage. The star on that stage is a dramatic and luxurious jetted tub tucked in an alcove with a view.

A **dramatic black marble tile floor** helps a simple and elegant deep freestanding tub pop in this chic bathroom.

Larger ceramic tiles are ideal for more modest bathrooms. Choose a subtle color to complement other surfaces, like the sharp and refined quartz countertops and bathtub half wall here.

Laminates offer an easy-to-install flooring option that is water-resistant, durable, and available in an amazing selection of surface appearances from stone tiles to wide wood planks.

The condition of your floor structure may affect the cost of installing new flooring. If the subfloor must be replaced or repaired, more time and money will be required. Consult a professional to assess the state of your subfloor.

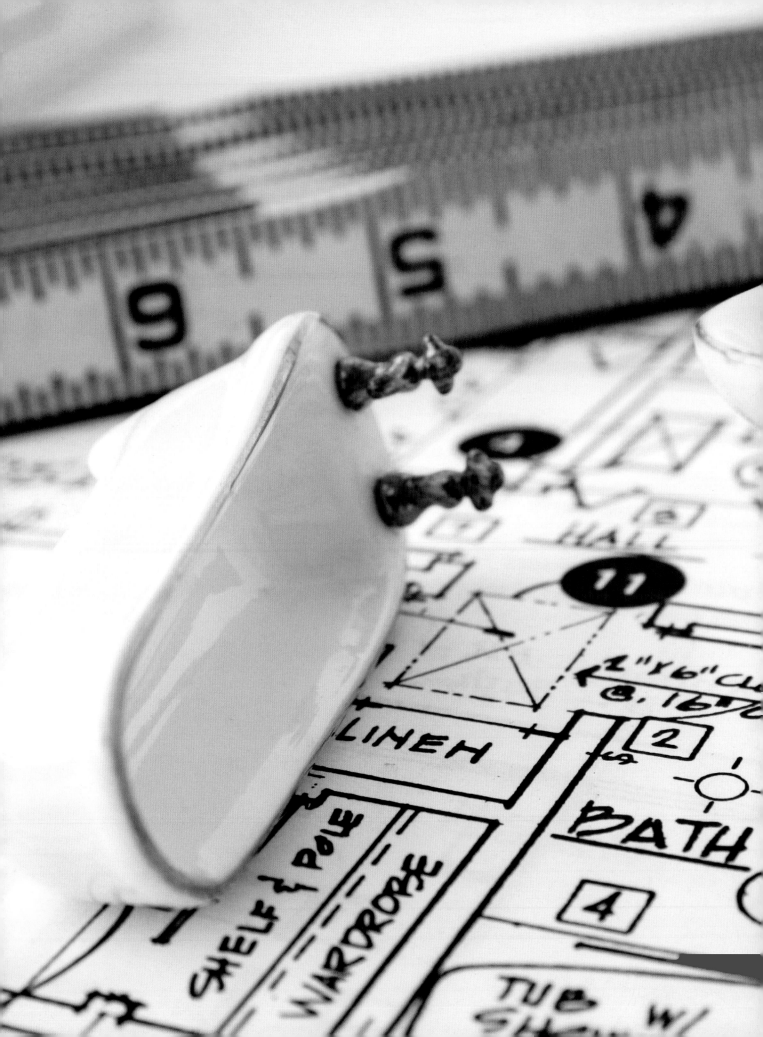

Getting Started

A great bathroom provides a comfortable, attractive, and convenient setting. It is a private retreat, where you can tend to your needs in a relaxed and pleasant fashion.

When designing a new bathroom or renovating an existing one, style can be as big a consideration as function. From the choice of materials to the layout of fixtures, the space should reflect your individual sense of style through the use of particular colors, textures, and patterns.

And yet, a bathroom does have to be functional. Without a strong foundation on which to express your style, you may spend money and time creating your new bath, yet it may not turn out as you'd hoped. So the first step is to determine your needs and budget, and draw up some plans.

In this chapter:

- Determining Your Needs
- Designing for Accessibility
- Design Standards
- Drawing Plans
- Removal & Demolition: Toilets
- Removal & Demolition: Sinks & Cabinets
- Removal & Demolition: Showers & Tubs

Determining Your Needs

A typical bathroom is divided into three activity areas: the toilet, the sink, and the shower/tub. To create a successful bath design, you need to consider the relationship of these areas, allowing for accessibility and safety. This relationship varies depending on the type of bathroom being renovated: half bath, family bath, or master bath.

Half baths, also called powder rooms or guest baths, are small rooms near common areas of the home. They are designed largely for visitors to use. They can be as small as 20 square feet and are often located near entrances or entertainment areas of a home. It's best to have their doors open into hallways.

Half baths typically feature a toilet and a vanity or pedestal sink finished with smaller fixtures and finer materials. When designed as a guest bath that includes a shower, these rooms require more space and are called three-quarter baths.

The family bath is usually located near the sleeping areas in a home. It is used by more than one family member, and it should provide storage for toiletries, towels, laundry, and cleaning supplies. It features at least one sink, one toilet, and a shower and tub or tub/shower combination.

The typical family bath can fit in a 5 × 7-foot area. A larger bathroom allows space for extra features, such as double sinks or separate shower and tub areas. A small family bath may conserve space by combining the tub and shower, incorporating recessed shelving, and featuring space-efficient fixtures and storage cabinets. Finishes and fixtures should be low-maintenance and highly durable, such as ceramic tile and enameled fixtures.

Bathrooms for children must be safe for them to use unsupervised and should be easy to adapt as the children grow. Features that make daily hygiene easier and safer for children include single-handle faucets with antiscald guards, adjustable showerheads, safety plugs in receptacles, grab bars, smaller toilets, lowered sinks, and vanities with built-in step stools.

The master bath is usually connected to the master bedroom and is a sanctuary for the owners of the house. It is typically quite large and may have separate activity centers containing features such as a jetted tub, shower, toilet partition, and multiple sinks and vanities. It may even feature a sauna or steam room. The fixtures and finishing materials generally feature ceramic, stone, or marble tiles; custom cabinets; and upscale accessories.

The half-bath, sometimes called a powder room, consists of a toilet and sink, but no shower or tub. It is usually found near entertainment areas for guest convenience.

There's no rule that says a modest family bath needs to be less than opulent. You can fit a lot into a small space, like this skylight-lit, simple and elegant, deep drop-in tub.

A master bathroom is the place to splurge, especially when modern is your style. The floors and walls in this room are beautiful and waterproof quartz composite; every feature in the room combines luxurious comfort and astounding sculptural beauty.

Designing for Accessibility

Accessibility has become a key issue not only in the codes that regulate residential bathroom construction, but with almost every feature designed for bathrooms. From toilets to faucets to lighting and beyond, manufacturers are responding to an aging population and the need to accommodate all potential users of a home's bathroom.

Designing bathrooms to accommodate the needs of any individual—including those with mobility limitations and even the severely disabled—is at the heart of what is known as "Universal Design." The term was coined by disabled architect Ronald Mace. The goal? In Mace's words, "The design of products and environments to be usable by all people to the greatest extent possible, without the need for adaptation or specialized design." In practice, that translates to turnkey fixtures that work for able-bodied individuals and those who use a wheelchair or walker alike.

More recently, a focus has been placed on accommodating the 78 million baby boomers who are rapidly aging into a incredibly large elderly population. Studies show that these people want to stay in their homes and remain independent as long as possible. The Aging-in-Place movement has sprung up to facilitate that, and to set guidelines for bathroom design specifically to suit elderly users. But in reality, Aging-in-Place is a subset of Universal Design and it is a difference largely without a distinction. If you take the steps outlined here, and select fixtures and features designed for maximum accessibility, your bathroom will be welcoming and user-friendly now and as you age, and for anyone who might need to use it.

Aging-in-Place bathroom design often deals with remodeling existing spaces to better suit users with age-related mobility issues. Those who can't stand for the span of a shower can take one while sitting in this specially adapted stool. They can use the ergonomic hand-held showerhead with a handle that clips onto a nearby grab bar. Even the toilet paper holder has been replaced with one that has a grab bar built in.

Universal Design Standards

Bathroom elements that meet the mandates of Universal Design are continually being refined by manufacturers as they respond to legislation such as the ADA (Americans with Disabilities Act) and the needs of an aging population. Design style is inevitably a part of the process. Utilitarian features such as grab bars are increasingly crafted with stunning looks and finishes that make them easy to integrate into even the most sophisticated bathroom style.

Grab bars. The new rule for grab bars is "dual-purpose." Towel racks, toilet paper holders, and bathroom shelving are all being crafted with integrated grab bars. Not only does this mean buying and installing one fixture in place of two, it means the grab bars are a blended part of the overall look of the bathroom. Even the grab bars used in bathtubs and showers are seeing style upgrades, with molded finger grips and the same selection of surface finishes that you'll find in other fixtures, such as showerheads and faucets.

Toilets. The key to making this essential fixture comfortable for every potential user lies in seat height. Manufacturers have come up with a multitude of solutions, including power-lift toilet seats, height adapters, higher-than-normal traditional toilets and those that can be adjusted, and wall-mounted toilets that can installed at any height. Grab bars are essential to assist movement on and off any toilet, so it's fortunate that you can find attractive toilet paper holder–grab bar combinations.

Faucets. The first step in making faucets accessible was the use of paddle handles and single-handle faucets that could easily be manipulated by those lacking dexterity, hand strength, or motor skills. Nowadays, technology is aiding people with coordination and hand-strength difficulties in the form of motion-activated and touch-activated faucets. These make using the faucet as easy as moving a hand. They are also a breeze to install (see page 146).

Bathtubs. The standard bathtub-shower combination can be retrofitted to accommodate limited mobility users with the addition of special stools and hand-held showerheads with ergonomic grips. Better yet, consider replacing an existing tub with a walk-in model equipped with a door. These tubs typically have seats at chair height to make the transition into the tub easier. Many also feature jets and heaters to create a luxurious experience. When shopping for a walk-in tub, pay close attention to the contours of the seat and back support. These will be key to how comfortable and supportive the tub is over the course of a nice long soak. Choose a door style that best accommodates the user's preference; available styles open in or out, up or down. The lower the threshold, the better, and the door handle should be easy for the intended user to operate.

Other types of tubs can be made easier to use by locating the controls on the outside edge of the tub or tub deck. This allows the user to fill the tub without leaning over and possibly losing balance.

Understanding Aging in Place ▸

The Aging-in-Place movement shares much with the general Universal Design trend, the key difference being the focus on the needs of the elderly. As we age, we lose strength in our hands, arms, and legs, and often have to deal with nagging chronic injuries associated with aging—arthritis and limited flexibility and mobility chief among those complaints. Many Aging-in-Place changes are focused on accommodating those conditions and preventing any injury that could short-circuit independence.

Lighting. Older people often deal with diminished vision, so effective lighting is key to making Aging-in-Place bathrooms more user-friendly and safer.

This entails a combination of undercabinet and undercounter lighting, baseboard or cove lighting, special shower lights and more powerful ambient lights on the wall and ceiling to dispel any visually confusing shadows.

Non-slip surfaces. Falls are the number-one cause of elderly immobilization and can have serious health ramifications. It's essential that tubs, floors, and shower stalls have truly non-slip surfaces that maintain traction even when wet. This means a slip resistant glaze or texture on any bathroom flooring, and decals or slip-preventing strips in bathtub-shower combinations.

Showers. The two areas of continuing development in terms of Universal Design showers are the shower pan and the fixtures. Low-threshold, walk-in showers were the ideal a few years ago (often equipped with ramps for wheelchairs), allowing anyone with strength and balance issues to easily step into a shower stall. That idea has evolved into true curbless showers that are on the same level as the surrounding floor. Although installing a curbless shower was once a major custom construction project, you can now buy a kit with a relatively streamlined and simple installation process (see page 78). Grab bars remain an essential addition to any shower enclosure, and the increasing variety of designs and finishes virtually guarantees you can match grab bar finish to that of the shower controls and showerhead.

Showerheads themselves have been made more accessible by mounting hand-held styles on slide bars so that the height can be adjusted to suit any user, and the showerhead itself can be removed as needed. Non-slip ergonomic grips are making hand-held showerheads even easier to use for people with motor skill and grip limitations.

Most modern shower enclosures—whether one-piece prefab units or those built from the shower pan up—include some sort of seat. Fold-down seats are easy to retrofit into an existing shower, but many showers now include built-in or molded shower seats. Either way, the seat should be 18 inches high and at least 15 inches deep. Shower anti-scald devices are also a wise addition to any shower, to protect all users from burns.

Sinks and vanities. More and more wall-mounted sinks and vanities are being offered at retail. These ensure that wheelchair-bound bathroom users can roll under the sink to wash their hands or brush their teeth. Many wall-mounted sinks come with attractive aprons to conceal plumbing. Roll-out vanity cabinets can be used as storage accents, replacing the under-sink space in traditional vanities.

Doors and doorways. Bathroom doorways should be 32 to 36 inches wide to allow passage of a wheelchair. Shower doors should open out, or both ways, to ensure user safety.

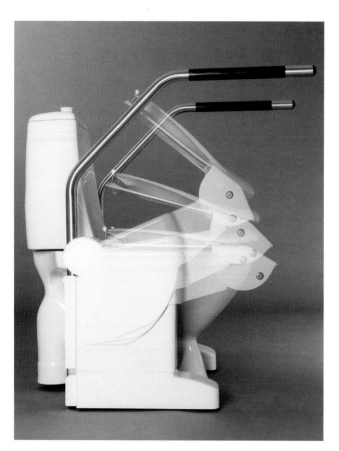

Power-lifts make toilet use easier for people with limited leg or joint strength.

A side-mounted faucet is easier to reach on this wheelchair-accessible, roll-under, wall-mounted sink.

A motion-sensing faucet is not only easier for the elderly and children to use, it helps stop the spread of disease.

This bathroom sacrifices nothing to style but is completely accessible, with a roll-in curbless shower, roll-under sink with handy side ledges, and sturdy grab bars everywhere they might be needed.

A simple soap dish becomes a useful tub side grab bar featuring an elegant circular shape.

This innovative grab bar uses suction to hold to just about any bathroom surface, and it can be released and repositioned as needed with a click of the gray release tabs on either end.

This alcove tub features a chair-height seat and a slide-down front wall. To take a bath, the user simply sits on the seat, swings their legs over, and pulls the wall up. The tub offers many amenities, including simple-to-use controls, a heater, and jets.

Recommended Clearances ▸

A bathroom should be planned with enough approach space and clearance room to allow a wheelchair or walker user to enter and turn around easily. The guidelines for approach spaces (patterned areas) and clearances shown here include some ADA guidelines and recommendations from Universal Design specialists.

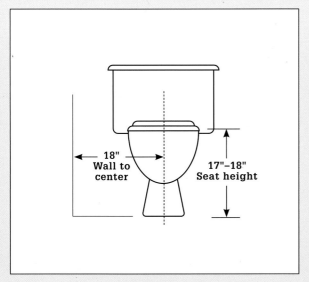

Toilet

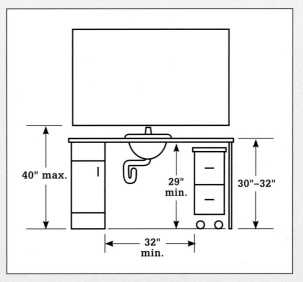

Sink & Vanity

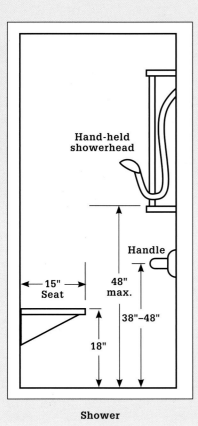

Shower

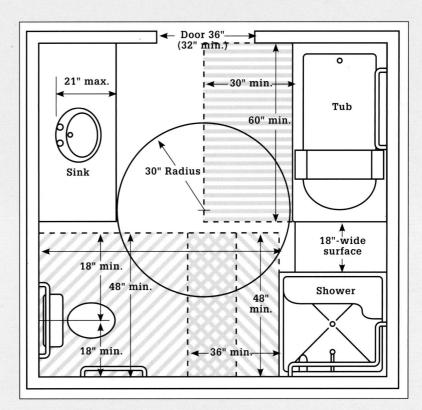

Floor Plan

Design Standards

Once you've drawn up your plan and created a materials list, you'll need to have them reviewed by your local building department. Getting approval early in the process can save you time and expense later. To help ensure success, here are some design standards for you to follow.

The National Kitchen and Bath (NKBA) publishes a list of bathroom design standards to help people plan rooms that are safe and accessible to all users (see Resources, page 251).

Your bathroom probably won't conform to all of the recommended standards, but they can help guide your overall plan. What your plan must include is everything prescribed by the local building codes, including plumbing and wiring codes (see pages 246 to 250).

Bathroom Design Standards ▸

Codes and permits are necessary to ensure safety in any remodel. They're not the most fun to focus on—not like choosing just the right floor covering or deciding between granite or marble countertops—but they are important.

- Plan doorways with a clear floor space equal to the door's width on the push side and greater than the door's width on the pull side. *Note: Clear floor spaces within the bathroom can overlap.*
- Design toilet enclosures with at least 36" × 66" of space; include a pocket door or a door that swings out toward the rest of the bathroom.
- Install toilet-paper holders approximately 26" above the floor, toward the front of the toilet bowl if possible.
- Place fixtures so faucets are accessible from outside the tub or shower. Add antiscald devices to tub and sink faucets (they are required for shower faucets).
- Avoid steps around showers and tubs, if possible.
- Fit showers and tubs with safety rails and grab bars.
- Install shower doors so they swing open into the bathroom, not the shower.
- Use tempered glass or another type of safety glass for all glass doors and partitions.
- Include storage for soap, towels, and other items near the shower, located within 15 to 48" above the floor. These should be accessible to a person in the shower or tub.
- Provide natural light openings equal to at least 10% of the floor area in the room.
- Illuminate all activity centers in the bathroom with task and ambient lighting.
- Provide a minimum clearance of 15" from the centerline of sinks to any sidewalls. Double-bowl sinks should have 30" clearance between bowls from centerline to centerline.
- Provide access panels for all electrical, plumbing, and HVAC systems connections.
- Include a ventilation fan that exchanges air at a rate of 8 air changes per hour.
- Choose countertops and other surfaces with edges that are smoothed, clipped, or radiused.

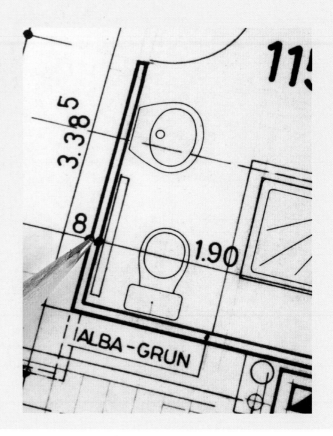

Building Codes for Bathrooms ▸

The following are some of the most common building codes for bathrooms. Contact your local building department for a list of all codes enforced in your area.

- The minimum ceiling height in bathrooms is 7 ft. (Minimum floor area is determined by clearances around fixtures.)
- Sinks must be at least 4" from side walls and have 21" of clearance in front.
- Sinks must be spaced 4" away from neighboring sinks and toilets, and 2" away from bathtubs.
- Toilets must be centered 15" from side walls and tubs, with 21" clearance in front.
- New and replacement toilets must be low-flow models (no more than 1.6 gal./flush).
- Shower stalls must be at least 30" × 30", with 24" of clearance in front of shower openings.
- Faucets for showers and combination tub/showers must be equipped with antiscald devices.
- Supply lines that are ½" in diameter can supply a single fixture, or one sink and one toilet.
- A ¾"-diameter supply line must be used to supply two or more fixtures.
- Waste and drain lines must slope ¼" per foot toward the main DWV stack to aid flow and prevent blockage.

- Each bathroom must be wired with at least one 20-amp circuit for GFCI-protected receptacles, and one 15-amp (minimum) circuit for light fixtures and vent fans without heating elements.
- All receptacles must be GFCI-protected.
- There must be at least one permanent light fixture controlled by a wall switch.
- Wall switches must be at least 60" away from bathtubs and showers.
- Toilet, shower, vanity, or other bathroom compartments must have adequate lighting.
- Light fixtures over bathtubs and showers must be vaporproof, with a UL rating for wet areas.
- Vanity light fixtures with built-in electrical receptacles are prohibited.
- Whirlpool motors must be powered by dedicated GFCI-protected circuits.
- Bathroom vent ducts must terminate no less than 10 ft. horizontally or 3 ft. vertically above skylights.

Note: Codes for accessible bathrooms may differ.

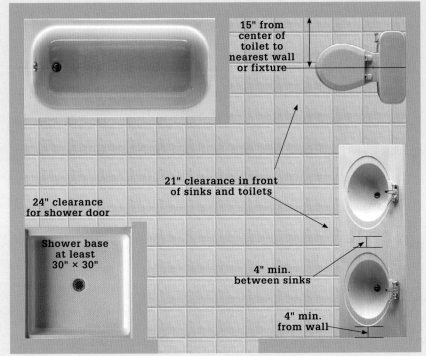

15" from center of toilet to nearest wall or fixture

21" clearance in front of sinks and toilets

24" clearance for shower door

Shower base at least 30" × 30"

4" min. between sinks

4" min. from wall

Follow minimum clearance and size guidelines when planning locations of bathroom fixtures. Easy access to fixtures is fundamental to creating a bathroom that is comfortable, safe, and easy to use.

Drawing Plans

If your new bathroom involves a layout change or expansion, you'll find it helpful to create floor plans and elevation drawings. A floor plan illustrates an overhead view, while an elevation drawing illustrates a face-on view. Your drawings will be the basis for obtaining permits, negotiating contracts with tradespeople, and ordering products.

To begin, make a rough sketch of the existing floor plan. Measure and record the size and location of all existing fixtures and mechanicals from a fixed point. Sketch an elevation of each wall.

Use these rough sketches to draft a precise scale drawing of your existing floor plan. You can now sketch variations of your new bathroom using the scale drawing of the floor plan as a guide.

Use the overall dimensions of your new floor plan to sketch elevation options. In the end, the elevations and floor plans must agree.

A scale drawing shows everything in accurate proportion. After measuring the dimensions of your existing bathroom, draft a floor plan, including any adjoining space that could be used for expansion of the layout (such as the storage closet shown on next page). The normal scale for bathroom plans is ½" = 1 ft.

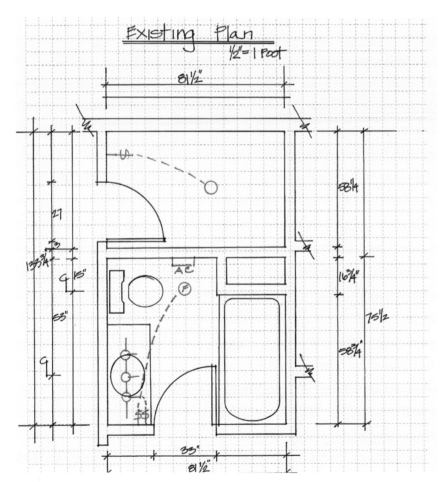

The existing floor plan draft should contain dimension lines noting the accurate measurements of the space, including the location of all existing fixtures. This draft also shows the location of electrical circuits. It is the starting point for your remodeled bathroom plan.

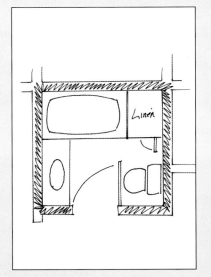

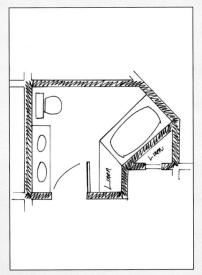

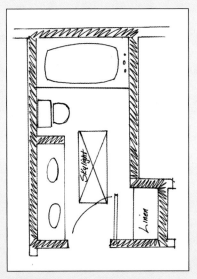

Option A: This floor plan option of the draft on the opposite page shows a layout change within the existing space. The sink and vanity stay in the same place, but the tub and toilet have been switched. There is room to add a linen cabinet, but the space is still very cramped.

Option B: This option explores expanding the room and experimenting with some interesting angles. There is now plenty of floor space for two people, plus room for a double vanity and a large linen cabinet for increased storage.

Option C: The existing room is expanded by annexing the adjacent closet. There's plenty of floor space, a double vanity, and a built-in linen cabinet. This plan has the practical benefits of Option B, but is less expensive to build.

Bathroom Elevation Options ▸

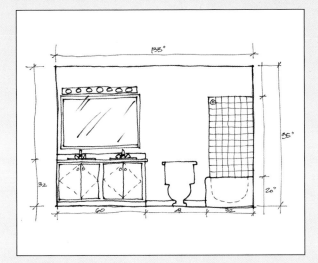

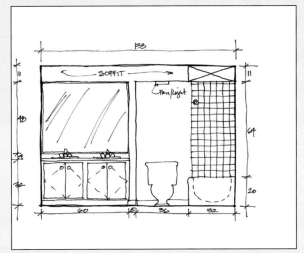

Option A: This elevation shows a simple arrangement with a standard mirror and light fixture. It also shows ceramic tile in the shower area, ending just above the shower curtain.

Option B: This variation shows a custom mirror framed in by a partition wall, and a soffit that runs above the vanity, toilet, and tub. Lights are recessed in the soffit.

Removal & Demolition: Toilets

The toilet is the first fixture to be removed in most remodeling projects. Loosening corroded or rusted nuts and bolts is the most difficult part of the process.

Old toilets that will not be reinstalled may be broken up into small, easily managed pieces, using a sledgehammer. Disconnect the toilet and cover it with a heavy blanket before breaking it. Wear eye protection, long sleeves, and heavy gloves during the demolition.

Tools & Materials ▸

Adjustable wrench
Ratchet wrench and
  sockets
Screwdriver
Putty knife

Basin wrench
Sponge
Rag
Bucket
Drop cloth

Most toilets are fragile and should be removed during full remodeling projects, even if you do not plan to replace them. Always use care when handling any fixture made of china or porcelain.

Tips for Removing Toilets ▸

Protect your floor with a drop cloth when removing the toilet, if you plan to keep the original floor covering. Residue from the wax ring seal between the bottom of the toilet and the toilet flange is very difficult to remove from floor coverings.

Disconnect any pipes between a wall-mounted toilet tank and the bowl, after turning off the water supply and emptying the tank. Older toilets often have a metal elbow that connects the tank to the bowl. Set 2 × 4 braces below the tank before detaching it from the wall.

How to Remove a Toilet & Wax Ring

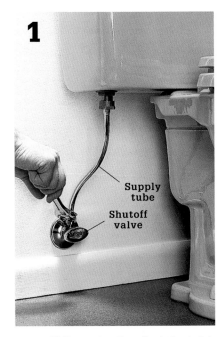

1

Turn off the water, then flush the toilet to empty the tank. Use a sponge to remove the remaining water in the tank and bowl. Disconnect the supply tube with an adjustable wrench.

Supply tube

Shutoff valve

2

Remove the nuts from the tank bolts with a ratchet wrench. Carefully remove the tank and set it aside.

Tank bolt

3

Pry off the floor bolt trim caps at the base of the toilet, then remove the floor nuts with an adjustable wrench.

4

Straddle the toilet and rock the bowl from side to side until the seal breaks. Carefully lift the toilet off the floor bolts and set it on its side. A small amount of water may spill from the toilet trap.

Floor bolts

Wax ring

5

Remove the old wax from the toilet flange in the floor. Plug the drain opening with a damp rag to prevent sewer gases from rising into the house.

Toilet flange

6

If the old toilet will be reused, clean the old wax and putty from the horn and the base of the toilet.

Base

Horn

Removal & Demolition: Sinks & Cabinets

Replacing bathroom sinks, countertops, and cabinets is a quick and relatively inexpensive way to give your bathroom a fresh, new look.

First, disconnect the plumbing, then remove the sink basin or integral sink/countertop unit. Next, take out any remaining countertops. Finally, remove the cabinets and vanities.

Tools & Materials ▸

Bucket	Hacksaw
Channel-type pliers	or pipe cutter
Adjustable wrench	Screwdriver
Basin wrench	Utility knife
Reciprocating saw	Flat pry bar

Cut apart cabinets and vanities to simplify their removal and disposal. A reciprocating saw or jigsaw works well for this job. Wear eye protection.

How to Disconnect Sink Plumbing

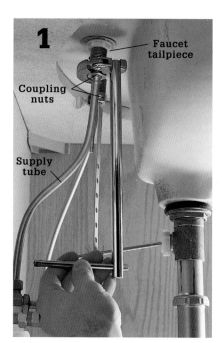

Turn off the shutoff valves, then remove the coupling nuts that connect the supply tube to the faucet tailpieces using a basin wrench. If the supply tubes are soldered, cut them above the shutoff valves.

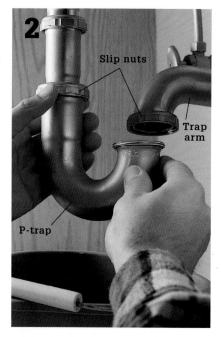

With a bucket beneath, remove the P-trap by loosening the slip nuts at both ends. If the nuts will not turn, cut out the drain trap with a hacksaw. When prying or cutting, take care to avoid damaging the trap arm that runs into the wall.

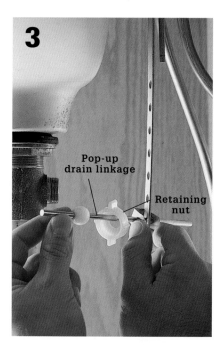

Disconnect the pop-up drain linkage from the tailpiece of the sink drain by unscrewing the retaining nut.

Tips for Removing Sinks ▸

Self-rimming sink: Disconnect the plumbing, then slice through any caulking or sealant between the sink rim and the countertop using a utility knife. Lift the sink off the countertop.

Shown in cross-section for clarity

Mounting clips

Under-mount sink: Disconnect the plumbing, including the drain tailpiece. To support the sink, tie wire around a piece of scrap wood and set the wood across the sink opening. Thread the wire down through the drain hole and attach it to another scrap of wood. Twist the wire until taut, then detach the mounting clips. Slice through any caulking, slowly loosen the wire, then remove the sink.

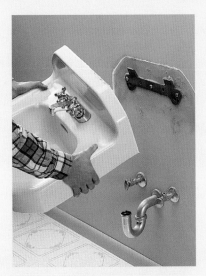

Wall-mounted sink: Disconnect the plumbing, slice through any caulk or sealant, then lift the sink off the wall brackets. For models attached with lag screws, wedge 2 × 4s between the sink and floor to support it while the screws are removed.

Pedestal sink: Disconnect the plumbing. If the sink and pedestal are bolted together, disconnect them. Remove the pedestal first, supporting the sink from below with 2 × 4s. Lift the sink off the wall brackets (photo, left).

Integral sink/countertop: Disconnect the plumbing, then detach the mounting hardware underneath the countertop. Slice through any caulk or sealant between the countertop and wall, and between the countertop and vanity. Lift the sink/countertop unit off the vanity.

Removal & Demolition: Showers & Tubs

Bathtubs and showers are heavy and bulky fixtures, so they pose special problems for removal. Unless the tub or shower has unique salvage value, cut or break the unit into pieces for easy removal and disposal. This technique allows one person to handle most of the disposal chores. Always wear eye protection and heavy gloves when cutting or breaking apart fixtures.

For most tubs and showers, you need to remove at least 6" of wall surface around the tub or shower pan to gain access to fasteners holding it to the wall studs. Maneuvering a tub out of an alcove is also easier when the wall surfaces are removed. If you are replacing the entire wall surface, do all the demolition work before removing the tub.

Tools & Materials ▸

Reciprocating saw	Hammer
Channel-type pliers	Masonry chisel
Screwdriver	Wire cutter
Hacksaw	Eye protection
Adjustable wrench	Utility knife
Flat pry bar	2 × 4 or 1 × 4 lumber
Wrecking bar	Rag

Disconnect the faucet through the access panel, usually located on the wall surface behind or next to the tub faucet and drain. (If the tub does not have an access panel, add one.) Turn off the shutoff valves, then cut the shower pipe above the faucet body. Disconnect or cut off the supply pipes above the shutoff valves.

How to Remove Handles & Spouts

1 **Shut off the water supply,** then remove the faucet handles by prying off the covers and unscrewing the mounting screws.

2 **Remove the tub spout** by inserting a screwdriver into the spout and twisting counterclockwise until it unscrews from the stub-out that extends from the wall plumbing.

3 **Unscrew the collar nut** to remove the showerhead. Loosen the escutcheon, then twist the shower arm counterclockwise to unscrew it from the wall plumbing.

How to Disconnect Drain Plumbing

1

Drain plug linkage

Drain crosspiece

Remove the drain plug. Most bathtub plugs are connected to drain plug linkage that is lifted out along with the plug.

Spring-mounted drain plugs: Remove the plug by unscrewing it from the drain crosspiece.

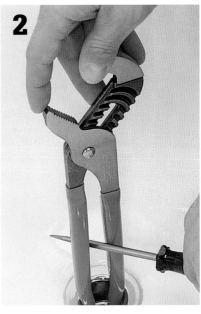

2

Disconnect the drain assembly from the tub by inserting a pair of pliers into the drain opening and turning the crosspiece counterclockwise. Insert a long screwdriver between the handles and use it to twist the pliers.

3

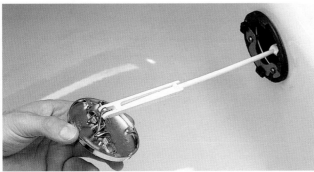

Remove the screws in the overflow coverplate (top photo). Remove the coverplate along with any attached drain plug (bottom photo).

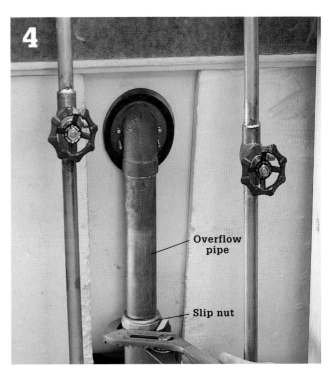

4

Overflow pipe

Slip nut

Remove the overflow pipe by unscrewing the slip nut that holds it to the rest of the drain assembly, then lift out the pipe. Stuff a rag into the waste pipe after the overflow pipe is removed to keep debris from entering the trap.

How to Remove a Shower Stall

After disconnecting the faucet handles, spout, and showerhead, remove the shower curtain rod or shower door, molding or trim, and any other accessories.

Slice the caulking around each shower panel using a utility knife. Remove any screws holding the panels together.

Pry shower panels away from the wall using a flat pry bar. If the panels are still intact, cut them into small pieces for easier disposal using a jigsaw or a sharp utility knife.

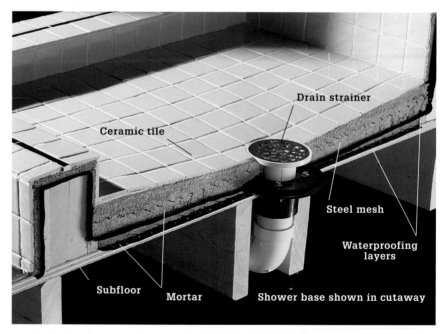

Ceramic tile

Drain strainer

Steel mesh

Waterproofing layers

Subfloor   Mortar   Shower base shown in cutaway

Fabricated shower bases (fiberglass or plastic): Slice the caulking between the base and the floor, then unscrew any fasteners holding the base to the wall studs. Pry the base from the floor with a wrecking bar.

Ceramic-tile shower base: Remove the drain strainer, and then stuff a rag into the drain opening. Wearing protective equipment, break apart a section of tile with a hammer and masonry chisel. Cut through any steel mesh reinforcement using a wire cutter. Continue knocking tile and mortar loose until the waterproofing layers are exposed, then scrape off the layers with a long-handled floor scraper.

How to Remove a Bathtub

Use a reciprocating saw to cut away at least 6" of the wall surface above the tub on all sides. Before cutting into a wall, be sure faucet handles, spouts, and drains are all disconnected.

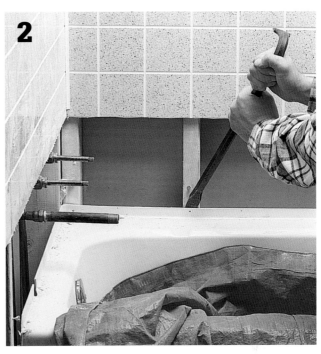

Remove the fasteners that hold the tub flanges to the wall studs, then use a wrecking bar or a piece of 2 × 4 to pry the bathtub loose.

Lift the edge of the bathtub and slip a pair of 1 × 4 runners beneath the tub apron. Pull the tub away from the wall using the runners as skids. Have helpers when removing steel and cast-iron tubs.

Cut or break the bathtub into small pieces for easy disposal. Fiberglass, reinforced polymer, or pressed steel tubs can be cut with a reciprocating saw. Cast-iron and steel tubs should be carried out.

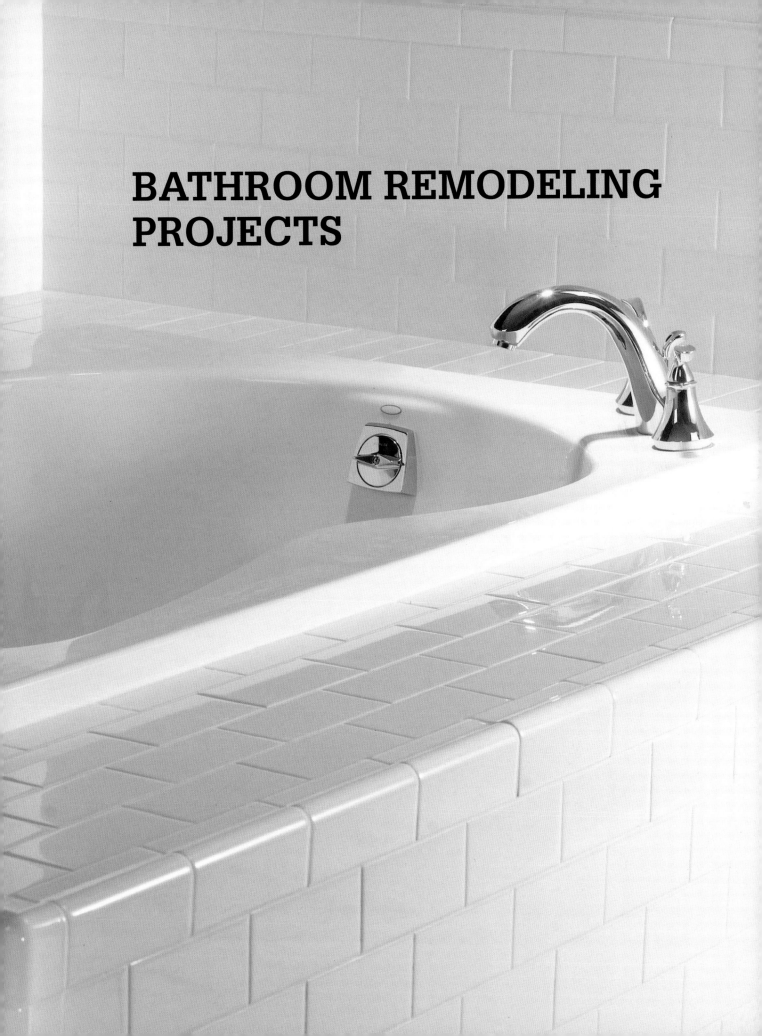

BATHROOM REMODELING PROJECTS

Showers, Tubs & Whirlpools

Installing and hooking up plumbing for bathtubs and showers is a fairly simple job. Jetted tubs are more complicated because they require electrical hookups, as well as structural frames.

The most difficult task you'll face when installing tubs, showers, and spas may be moving the bulky fixtures and materials up stairways and through narrow doorways. With a two-wheel dolly and a little help, the job is much easier. Be sure to measure doorways and hallways.

If you do not plan to remove and replace your wall surfaces, you should still cut away at least six inches of wall surface above a tub or whirlpool to allow easier access during installation (unless, of course, you're installing a freestanding tub).

In this chapter:

- Installing Showers
- Shower Enclosure Kits
- Custom Shower Bases
- Wet Rooms & Curbless Showers
- Alcove Bathtubs
- 3-Piece Tub Surrounds
- Soaking Tubs
- Freestanding Tubs
- Sliding Tub Doors
- Air-Jet Tubs
- Tub & Shower Fittings
- Adding a Shower to a Bathtub

Installing Showers

Showers can be built in a number of ways, from a number of materials, as discussed on pages 24 to 26. One of the easiest ways to build a shower is to frame an alcove and line it with prefabricated panels. Though water-resistant drywall is the standard backer for prefab panels, always check the manufacturer's recommendations. Some building codes also require a waterproof membrane between the studs and the backer material.

The type of shower pan you use will affect the installation sequence. Some bases are made to be installed after the backer; others should be installed first. If your base is going in after the wall surface, be sure to account for the thickness of the surface material when framing the alcove.

Tools & Materials ▸

Circular saw	2 × 4 and 1 × 4 lumber
Drill	16d and 8d nails
Plumbing tools	Plumbing supplies
Hacksaw	Shower base
Channel-type pliers	Rag
Trowel	Dry-set mortar (optional)
Level	Soap

Ceramic tile for custom showers is installed the same way as in other applications. Ceramic shower accessories, such as a soap dish, are mortared in place during the tile installation.

Antiscald Valves

Antiscald valves are safety devices that protect against sudden water temperature changes. They are required by most building codes for faucets in showers and combination tub/showers. Once installed, faucets with antiscald valves look like standard faucets.

Anatomy of a Shower

Shower stalls are available in many different sizes and styles, but the basic elements are the same. Most shower stalls have a shower alcove, a supply system, and a drain system.

Shower alcove: The alcove is the frame for the stall, with 2 × 4 walls built to fit around a shower pan and blocking to secure the plumbing. The pan—in most cases—sets into a mortar bed for support, and water-resistant drywall or cementboard covers the alcove walls.

The supply system: The shower arm extends from the wall, where an elbow fitting connects it to the shower pipe. The pipe runs up from the faucet, which is fed by the hot and cold water supplies.

The drain system: The drain cover attaches to the drain tailpiece. A rubber gasket on the tailpiece slips over the drainpipe, leading to the P-trap and the branch drain.

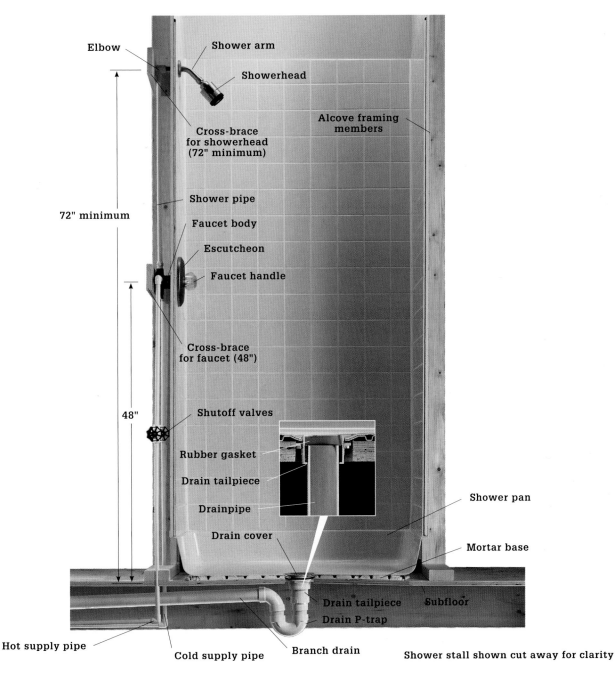

Elbow

Shower arm

Showerhead

Alcove framing members

Cross-brace for showerhead (72" minimum)

Shower pipe

Faucet body

Escutcheon

Faucet handle

72" minimum

Cross-brace for faucet (48")

48"

Shutoff valves

Rubber gasket

Drain tailpiece

Drainpipe

Drain cover

Shower pan

Mortar base

Drain tailpiece

Subfloor

Drain P-trap

Hot supply pipe

Cold supply pipe

Branch drain

Shower stall shown cut away for clarity

Shower Enclosure Kits

The fastest and easiest way to create a new shower in your bathroom is to frame in the stall area with lumber and wallboard and then install a shower enclosure kit. Typically consisting of three fiberglass or plastic walls, these enclosure kits snap together at the corners and nestle inside the flanges of the shower pan to create nearly foolproof mechanical seals. Often the walls are formed with shelves, soap holders, and other conveniences.

If you are on a tight budget, you can find extremely inexpensive enclosure kits to keep costs down. You can even create your own custom enclosure using waterproof beadboard panels and snap-together connectors. Or, you can invest in a higher-grade kit made from thicker material that will last much longer. Some kits are sold with the receptor (and perhaps even the door) included. The kit shown here is designed to be attached directly to wall studs, but others require a backer wall for support. The panels are attached to the backer with high-tack panel adhesive.

Tools & Materials ▸

Tape measure
Pencil
Hammer
Carpenter's square
Screwdrivers
Pipe wrench
Level
Strap wrench
Adjustable wrench
Pliers
Drill/driver
Center punch
File
Utility knife
Hacksaw
Masking tape

Slicone caulk
  and caulk gun
Shower enclosure kit
Shower door
Showerhead
Faucet
Plumbing supplies

A paneled shower surround is inexpensive and easy to install. Designed for alcove installations, they often are sold with matching shower pans (called receptors). Some include molded-in accessories such as shelves or soap dishes.

How to Install a Shower Enclosure

Mark out the location of the shower, including any new walls, on the floor and walls. Most kits can be installed over wallboard, but you can usually achieve a more professional looking wall finish if you remove the wall covering and floor covering in the installation area. Dispose of the materials immediately and thoroughly clean the area.

If you are adding a wall to create the alcove, lay out the locations for the studs and plumbing on the new wood sill plate. Also lay out the stud locations on the cap plate that will be attached to the ceiling. Refer to the enclosure kit instructions for exact locations and dimensions of studs. Attach the sill plate to the floor with deck screws and panel adhesive, making sure it is square to the back wall and the correct distance from the side wall.

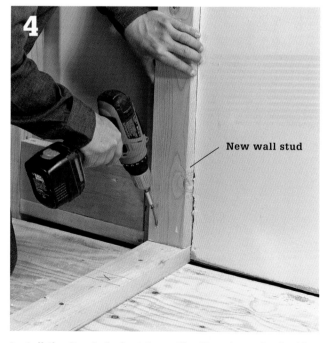

Sill plate

New wall stud

Align a straight 2 × 4 right next to the sill plate and make a mark on the ceiling. Use a level to extend that line directly above the sill plate. Attach the cap plate at that point.

Install the 2 × 4 studs at the outlined locations. Check with a level to make sure each stud is plumb and then attach them by driving deck screws toenail style into the sill plate and cap plate.

(continued)

Cut an access hole in the floor for the drain, according to the installation manual instructions. Drill openings in the sill plate of the wet wall (the new wall in this project) for the supply pipes, also according to the instructions.

Install a drain pipe and branch line and then trim the drain pipe flush with the floor. If you are not experienced with plumbing, hire a plumber to install the new drain line.

Faucet body

Cross brace

Ball valves

Supply riser

Install new supply risers as directed in the instruction manual (again, have a plumber do this if necessary). Also install cross braces between the studs in the wet wall for mounting the faucet body and shower arm. *NOTE: Some local codes require that you use gate valve shutoffs, not ball valves.*

If the supply plumbing is located in a wall (old or new) that is accessible from the non-shower side, install framing for a removable access panel.

9

Attach the drain tailpiece that came with your shower pan to the underside of the unit, following the manufacturer's instructions precisely. Here, an adjustable spud wrench is being used to tighten the tailpiece.

Option: To stabilize the pan, especially if the floor is uneven, pour or trowel a layer of thinset mortar into the installation area, taking care to keep the mortar out of the drain access hole. Do not apply mortar in areas where the pan has feet that are intended to make full contact with the floor.

10

Set the pan in place, check to make sure it is level, and shim it if necessary. Secure the pan with large-head roofing nails driven into the wall stud so the heads pin the flange against the stud. Do not overdrive the nails.

11

Lay out the locations for the valve hole or holes in the end wall panel that will be installed on the wet wall. Check your installation instructions. Some kits come with a template marked on the packaging carton. Cut the access hole with a hole saw and drill or with a jigsaw and fine-tooth blade. If using a jigsaw, orient the panel so the good surface is facing down.

(continued)

Position the back wall so there is a slight gap (about 1/32") between the bottom of the panel and the rim of the pan—set a few small spacers on the rim if need be. Tack a pair of roofing nails above the top of the back panel to hold it in place (or use duct tape). Position both end walls and test the fits. Make clip connections between panels (inset) if your kit uses them.

Remove the end walls so you can prepare the installation area for them. If your kit recommends panel adhesive, apply it to the wall or studs. In the kit shown here, only a small bead of silicone sealant on the pan flange is required.

Reinstall the end panels, permanently clipping them to the back panel according to the kit manufacturer's instructions. Make sure the front edges of the end panels are flush with the front of the pan.

Once the panels are positioned correctly and snapped together, fasten them to the wall studs. If the panels have predrilled nail holes, drive roofing nails through them at each stud at the panel tops and every 4 to 6" along vertical surfaces.

16

Install wallcovering material above the enclosure panels and anywhere else it is needed. Use moisture-resistant materials, and maintain a gap of ¼" between the shoulders of the top panel flanges and the wallcovering.

17

Finish the walls and then caulk between the enclosure panels and the wallcoverings with silicone caulk.

18

Install the faucet handles and escutcheon and caulk around the escutcheon plate. Install the shower arm escutcheon and showerhead. Add a shower door.

19

Access panel

Make an access panel and attach it at the framed opening created in step 8. A piece of ¼" plywood framed with mitered case molding and painted to match the wall is one idea for access panel covers.

Custom Shower Bases

Building a custom-tiled shower base lets you choose the shape and size of your shower rather than having its dimensions dictated by available products. Building the base is quite simple, though it does require time and some knowledge of basic masonry techniques because the base is formed primarily using mortar. What you get for your time and trouble can be spectacular.

Before designing a shower base, contact your local building department regarding code restrictions and to secure the necessary permits. Most codes require water controls to be accessible from outside the shower and describe acceptable door positions and operation. Requirements like these influence the size and position of the base.

Choosing the tile before finalizing the design lets you size the base to require mostly or only full tiles. Consider using small tile and create a color graduation from top to bottom or in a sweep across the walls. Or, use trim tile and listellos on the walls to create an interesting focal point.

Whatever tile you choose, remember to seal the grout in your new shower and to maintain it carefully over the years. Water-resistant grout protects the structure of the shower and prolongs its useful life.

Tools & Materials ▶

Tape measure
Circular saw
Hammer
Utility knife
Stapler
2-ft. level
Mortar mixing box
Trowel
Wood float
Felt-tip marker
Ratchet wrench
Expandable stopper
Drill
Tin snips
Torpedo level
Tools & materials for installing tile
2 × 4 and 2 × 10 framing lumber

16d galvanized common nails
15# building paper
3-piece shower drain
PVC primer & cement
Galvanized finish nails
Galvanized metal lath
Thick-bed floor mortar
Latex mortar additive
CPE waterproof membrane & preformed dam corners
CPE membrane solvent glue
CPE membrane sealant
Cementboard & materials

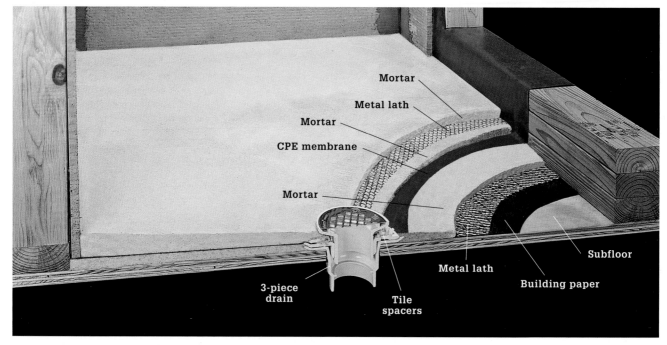

A custom shower base is built in three layers to ensure proper drainage: the underlayment, the shower pan, and the shower floor.

How to Build a Custom-Tiled Shower Base

Remove building materials to expose subfloor and stud walls. Cut three 2 × 4s for the curb and fasten them to the floor joists and the studs at the shower threshold with 16d galvanized common nails. Also cut 2 × 10 lumber to size and install in the stud bays around the perimeter of the shower base. Install (or have installed) drain and supply plumbing.

Staple 15-pound building paper to the subfloor of the shower base. Disassemble the 3-piece shower drain and glue the bottom piece to the drain pipe with PVC cement. Partially screw the drain bolts into the drain piece, and stuff a rag into the drain pipe to prevent mortar from falling into the drain.

Mark the height of the bottom drain piece on the wall farthest from the center of the drain. Measure from the center of the drain straight across to that wall, then raise the height mark ¼" for every 12" of shower floor to slope the pre pan toward the drain. Trace a reference line at the height mark around the perimeter of the entire alcove, using a level.

Staple galvanized metal lath over the building paper; cut a hole in the lath ½" from the drain. Mix thinset mortar to a fairly dry consistency, using a latex additive for strength; mortar should hold its shape when squeezed (inset). Trowel the mortar onto the subfloor, building the pre pan from the flange of the drain piece to the height line on the perimeter of the walls.

(continued)

5

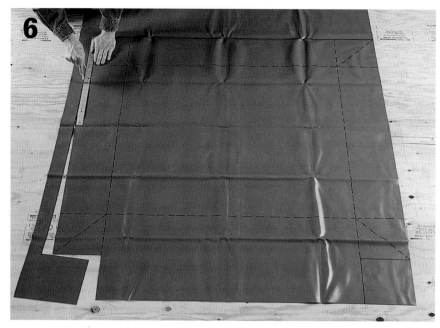

6

Continue using the trowel to form the pre pan, checking the slope using a level and filling any low spots with mortar. Finish the surface of the pre pan with a wood float until it is even and smooth. Allow the mortar to cure overnight.

Measure the dimensions of the shower floor, and mark it out on a sheet of CPE waterproof membrane, using a felt-tipped marker. From the floor outline, measure out and mark an additional 8" for each wall and 16" for the curb end. Cut the membrane to size, using a utility knife and straightedge. Be careful to cut on a clean, smooth surface to prevent puncturing the membrane. Lay the membrane onto the shower pan.

7

8

Measure to find the exact location of the drain and mark it on the membrane, outlining the outer diameter of the drain flange. Cut a circular piece of CPE membrane roughly 2" larger than the drain flange, then use CPE membrane solvent glue to weld it into place and reinforce the seal at the drain.

Apply CPE sealant around the drain. Fold the membrane along the floor outline. Set the membrane over the pre pan so the reinforced drain seal is centered over the drain bolts. Working from the drain to the walls, carefully tuck the membrane tight into each corner, folding the extra material into triangular flaps.

9

Apply CPE solvent glue to one side, press the flap flat, then staple it in place. Staple only the top edge of the membrane to the blocking; do not staple below the top of the curb, or on the curb itself.

10

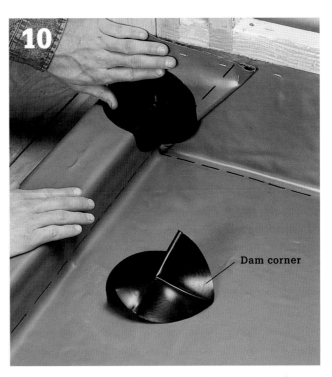

Dam corner

At the shower curb, cut the membrane along the studs so it can be folded over the curb. Solvent glue a dam corner at each inside corner of the curb. Do not fasten the dam corners with staples.

11

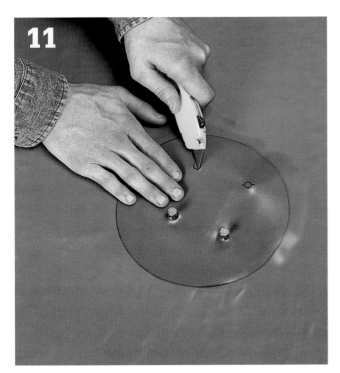

At the reinforced drain seal on the membrane, locate and mark the drain bolts. Press the membrane down around the bolts, then use a utility knife to carefully cut a slit just large enough for the bolts to poke through. Push the membrane down over the bolts.

12

Use a utility knife to carefully cut away only enough of the membrane to expose the drain and allow the middle drain piece to fit in place. Remove the drain bolts, then position the middle drain piece over the bolt holes. Reinstall the bolts, tightening them evenly and firmly to create a watertight seal.

(continued)

Test the shower pan for leaks overnight. Fill the shower pan with water, to 1" below the top of the curb. Mark the water level and let the water sit overnight. If the water level remains the same, the pan holds water. If the level is lower, locate and fix leaks in the pan using patches of membrane and CPE solvent.

Install cementboard on the alcove walls, using ¼" wood shims to lift the bottom edge off the CPE membrane. To prevent puncturing the membrane, do not use fasteners in the lower 8" of the cementboard. Cut a piece of metal lath to fit around the three sides of the curb. Bend the lath so it tightly conforms to the curb. Pressing the lath against the top of the curb, staple it to the outside face of the curb. Mix enough mortar for the two sides of the curb.

Overhang the front edge of the curb with a straight 1× board so it is flush with the outer wall material. Apply mortar to the mesh with a trowel, building to the edge of the board. Clear away excess mortar; then use a torpedo level to check for plumb, making adjustments as needed. Repeat for the inside face of the curb. *Note: The top of the curb will be finished after tile is installed (Step 19). Allow the mortar to cure overnight.*

Attach the drain strainer piece to the drain, adjusting it to a minimum of 1½" above the shower pan. On one wall, mark 1½" up from the shower pan, then use a level to draw a reference line around the perimeter of the shower base. Because the pre pan establishes the ¼" per foot slope, this measurement will maintain that slope.

17

Spread tile spacers over the weep holes of the drain to prevent mortar from plugging the holes. Mix the floor mortar, then build up the shower floor to roughly half the planned thickness of this layer. Cut metal lath to cover the mortar bed, keeping it ½" from the drain (see photo in Step 18).

18

Continue to add mortar, building the floor to the reference line on the walls. Use a level to check the slope, and pack mortar into low spots with a trowel. Leave space around the drain flange for the thickness of the tile. Float the surface using a wood float until it is smooth and slopes evenly to the drain. When finished, allow the mortar to cure overnight before installing the tiles.

19

Install the tile. At the curb, cut the tiles for the inside to protrude ½" above the unfinished top of the curb, and the tiles for the outside to protrude ⅝" above the top, establishing a ⅛" slope so water drains back into the shower. Use a level to check the tops of the tiles for level as you work.

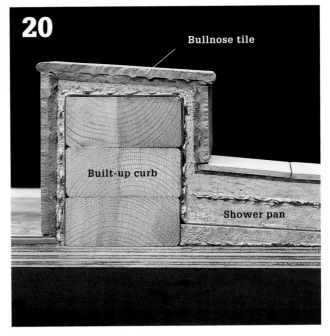

20

Bullnose tile

Built-up curb

Shower pan

Mix enough mortar to cover the unfinished top of the curb, then pack it in place between the tiles, using a trowel. Screed off the excess mortar flush with the tops of the side tiles. Allow the mortar to cure, then install bullnose cap tile. Install the wall tile, then grout, clean, and seal all the tile. After the grout has cured fully, run a bead of silicone caulk around all inside corners to create control joints.

Wet Rooms & Curbless Showers

Wet rooms—a bathroom in which all surfaces are waterproof—have long been a popular choice for upscale remodeling projects and new construction in the UK. But now, thanks to the increasing focus on Universal Design and an ongoing desire for sophisticated bathroom looks, wet rooms are becoming a popular option for American homeowners.

The idea behind a wet room is that moisture doesn't need to be contained in any single area of the room because the whole room is as waterproof as a shower stall. This alleviates the need for divider walls and enclosures, freeing up space and giving a wet room a seamless, streamlined look. Because of the space-saving aspects, wet rooms are particularly well suited for smaller bathrooms.

Installing a wet room involves laying down layers that work together to provide an impermeable barrier to water, in a process called "tanking." That process is made easy with the use of special rubberized waterproof tape and waterproofing compound that is simply rolled onto wall and floor surfaces. Some companies even provide complete wet room kits (see Resources, page 251). The finished surface can be traditional tile (the most common choice), solid panels like the quartz composite surfaces used in contemporary vanity countertops, or sheet flooring, such as vinyl or linoleum.

In practice, the preliminary work is a lot like taping and skim coating a newly drywalled room. The more challenging aspects of wet room installation are making sure all the openings—from drains to water-supply inlets—are properly sealed with special membranes, and correctly sloping the floor to a central drain. Normally, a wet room floor is sloped from all four corners for this purpose, but you can opt for a sleeker look with the use of a concealed linear "trench" drain along one edge of the room. This type of drain requires that the floor be sloped in one direction only.

Regardless of the drain used, wet rooms normally include a curbless shower, because there is no need to contain runoff water. Curbless showers present a sleek and sophisticated look, which is why homeowners are choosing to include them in many different bathrooms—including those that are not true wet rooms. Properly installed within an enclosure, a curbless shower can serve a traditional bathroom every bit as well as a raised-pan shower would.

Installing a curbless shower has become a feasible project for even modestly skilled home DIYers thanks to well-thought-out kits that include all the materials you'll need (see page 80). Wet rooms, on the other hand, usually require professional installation to ensure the leaks never become a problem and that all applicable building codes are met.

A curbless shower is a natural part of a wet room. A single wall surface material is commonly used on all walls for ease of installation and to unify the look.

Typical Wet Room Construction ▸

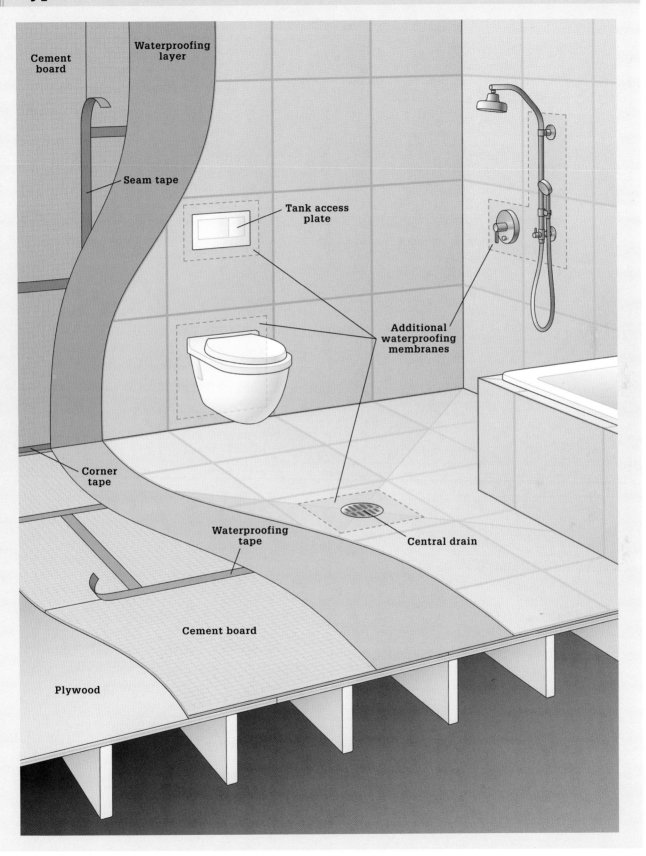

Cement board

Waterproofing layer

Seam tape

Tank access plate

Additional waterproofing membranes

Corner tape

Waterproofing tape

Central drain

Cement board

Plywood

Installing a Curbless Shower

Whether it's part of a complete "wet room," or installed as a standalone feature, a curbless shower combines easy access for those with limited mobility, convenience for other users, and a look that is trendy, sophisticated, and attractive. The trick to installing one of these water features is to ensure the moisture stays inside the shower.

Once upon a time, creating a reliably waterproof enclosure for a curbless shower was no small chore. It meant putting a lot of work into creating a custom shower pan. This kind of project was usually above the skill level or desire of the weekend DIYer, and it generally meant hiring a contractor.

Now you can buy curbless shower pan kits that make installation a breeze. The manufacturers have thought through all the issues that can arise and have developed the kits and shower pans to be as foolproof as possible, while also meeting prevailing codes and best standards and practices. Installing a curbless shower using one of these kits is a realistic project for any home handyperson with even moderate DIY skills and a weekend to spare.

These pans come with preconfigured slopes to ensure optimal drainage away from the shower's edges. The product we used for this project, the Tuff Form kit from Access Reliability Center (See Resources, page 251), includes an offset drain hole that offers the option of rotating the pan in the event of a joist or mechanicals that are in the way. This product is offered in nine different sizes and can be cut with a circular saw to just about any shape—including more unusual, curvy shapes for a truly custom look.

Curbless shower pan manufacturers also sell pans with trench drains for an even sleeker look. The pan we used for this project is typical of the prefab curbless pan construction; it can support 1,100 pounds even though the pan itself weighs less than 70 pounds. It sits right on floor joists, with the addition of blocking to support the area around the drain, and to provide nailing surfaces around the edges.

Kits like these offer advantages beyond the ease of installation and a thoughtful configuration of parts. Usually, the plumbing can be completely adjusted and connected from above, so you won't need to work in the basement or a crawl space, or open up a first-floor ceiling to install a second-floor shower. The kits themselves generally include almost everything you'll need for the installation.

Tools & Materials ▸

Circular saw	Putty knife
Caulking gun	Palm sander and
Torpedo level	120-grit pad
Cordless drill and bits	Scissors
PVC cement	Rubber gloves
and brush	Synthetic paintbrush
Screwdriver	Roller and
Speed square	roller handle

A curbless shower kit includes almost everything you need. All you have to supply are some basic tools, the tile, and a little elbow grease.

Wet Rooms and Universal Design ▸

Because a wet room allows the bathroom to be designed with fewer barriers and a single-level floor surface, these rooms are natural partners to a Universal Design approach. If you're thinking about converting a bathroom to a wet room, it's worthwhile to consider a little extra effort to make the space as accessible as possible for the maximum number of users.

Walls. Where codes allow it, consider using thick plywood rather than cementboard for the wall subsurfaces. Plywood allows for direct installation of grab bars without the need for blocking or locating studs. If you're set on using cementboard, plan out locations for grab bars near toilets, behind and alongside bathtubs, and

in showers. Most codes specify that grab bars must be able to support up to 200 pounds—which usually means adding blocking in the walls behind the grab bars.

Shower stall. One of the benefits to adding a curbless shower is easy wheelchair (or walker) access. For maximum accessibility, the shower area should be at least 60 inches wide by at least 36 inches deep (60 inches by 60 inches is preferable). This allows a wheelchair-bound user to occupy the stall with a helper. And, although the idea is a wide-open shower space, it's always a good idea to add a fold down seat. This allows for transfer from a wheelchair, or a place for someone with limited leg strength and endurance to sit.

How to Install a Waterproof Subbase for a Curbless Shower

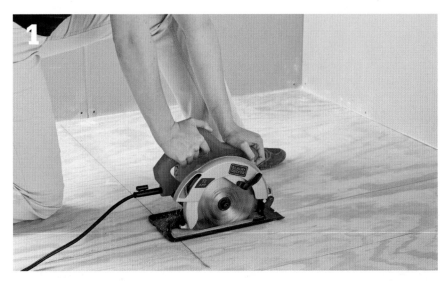

Remove the existing flooring material in the area of the shower pan (if you're remodeling an existing bathroom). Use a circular saw to cut out and remove the subfloor in the exact dimensions of the shower pan. Finish the cuts with a jigsaw or handsaw.

Reinforce the floor with blocking between joists as necessary. Toenail bridge blocking in on either side of the drain waste pipe location, and between joists anywhere you'll need a nailing surface along the edges of the shower pan. If trusses or joists are spaced more than 16" O.C., add bridge blocking to adequately support the pan.

(continued)

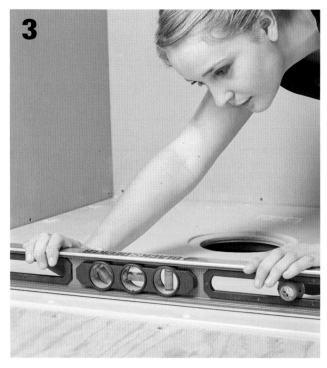

3

Set the pan in the opening to make sure it fits and is level. If it is not level, screw shims to the tops of any low joists and check again: repeat if necessary until the pan is perfectly level in all directions.

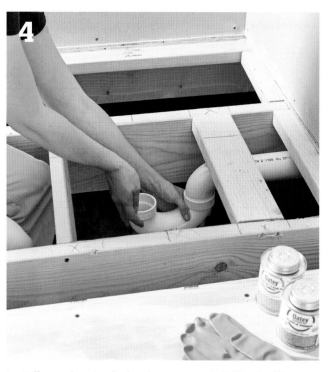

4

Install or relocate drain pipes as needed. Check with your local building department: if the drain and trap are not accessible from below you may need to have an on-site inspection before you cover up the plumbing.

5

Check the height of the drainpipe—its top should be exactly 2⅜" from the bottom of the pan—measure down from the top of the joist. If the drainpipe is too high, remove it and trim with a tubing cutter. If it is too low, replace the assembly with a new assembly that has a longer tailpiece.

6

Lay a thick bead of construction adhesive along the contact areas on all joists, nailing surfaces, and blocking.

7

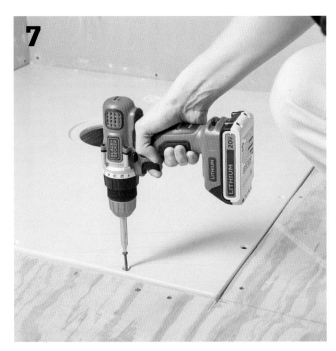

Set the pan in place and screw it down, using at least 2 screws along each side. Do not overtighten the screws. If you've cut off the screwing flange on one or more sides to accommodate an unusual shape, drill ⅛" pilot holes in the cut edges at joist or blocking locations, and drive the screws through the holes.

8

Disassemble the supplied drain assembly. Be careful not to lose any of the screws. Place the drain tailpiece on the waste pipe under where the pan's drainhole will be located, and measure to check that it sits at the correct level. Solvent-glue the tailpiece to the end of the waste pipe.

9

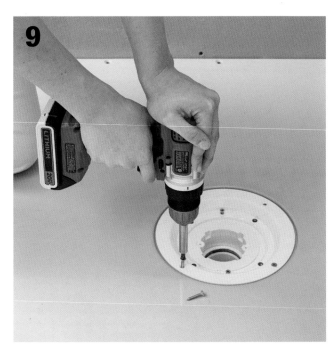

Position the supplied gaskets on top of the tailpiece (check the manufacturer's instructions; the gaskets usually need to be layered in the correct order). Set the drain flange piece on top of the tail, and into the drain hole in the pan. Drill ⅛" pilot holes through the flange and into the pan. Screw the flange to the pan.

10

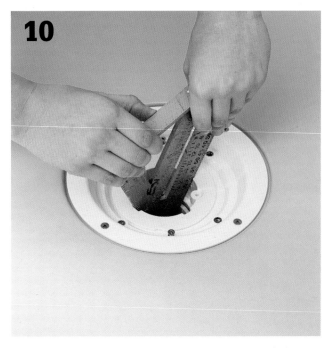

Thread the tail top piece into the tail through the drain flange. Use a speed square or other lever, such as spread channel lock pliers, to snugly tighten the tail top piece in place.

(continued)

11

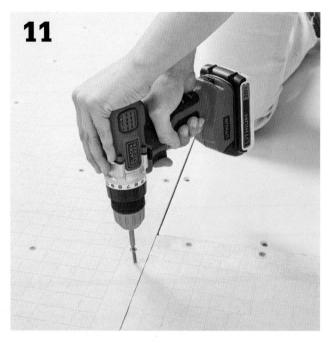

Install tile underlayment for the rest of the project area. If the underlayment is higher than the top of the pan once it is installed, you'll have to sand it to level, gradually tapering away from the pan.

12

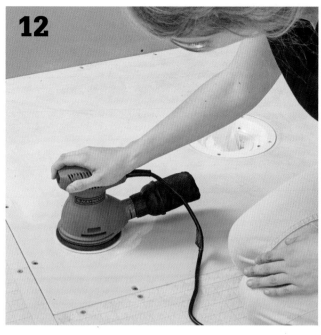

Scrape any stickers or other blemishes off the pan with a putty knife. Lightly sand the entire surface of the pan using 120-grit sandpaper to help the sealant adhere. After you're done sanding, wipe down the sanded pan with a damp sponge. Make sure the entire area is clean.

13

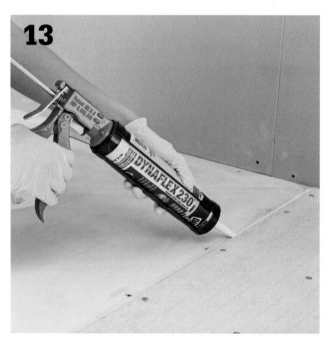

Seal the edge seams at the wall and between the pan and subfloor with waterproof latex sealant. Caulk any pan screw holes that were not used.

14

Cut strips of waterproofing tape to cover all seams in the tile underlayment (both walls and floor). Also cut strips for the joints where walls and floor meet. Open the pail of liquid waterproofing membrane and mix the liquid thoroughly. Beginning at the top and working down, brush a bed of waterproofing liquid over the seams. Before it dries, set the tape firmly into the waterproofing. Press and smooth the tape. Then brush a layer of waterproofing compound over the tape.

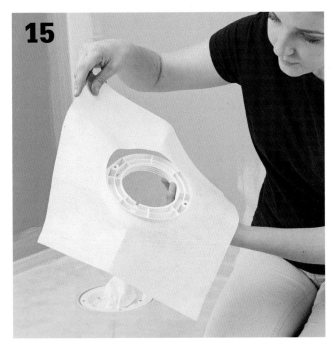

15

Trace a hole in the center of the waterproof drain gasket, using the bottom of the drain clamping donut. Cut the hole out using scissors. Be careful cutting the gasket because it is a crucial part of the drain waterproofing. Check the fit with the gasket against the underside of the clamping donut top flange.

16

Apply a thin coat of the waterproofing compound around the drain hole and to the back of the drain gasket. Don't apply too much; if the waterproofing is too thick under the gasket, it may not dry correctly.

17

Put the gasket in place and brush a coat of the waterproofing over the gasket. Screw the clamping donut in place on the top of the drain and over the membrane. Hand-tighten the bolts and then cover the clamping donut with the waterproofing compound (avoid covering the slide lock for the drain grate).

18

Use a roller to roll waterproofing compound across the walls and over the entire pan surface. The ideal is 4mm thick (about the thickness of a credit card). Allow this first coat to dry for 2 hours, then cover with a second coat. This should conclude the waterproofing phase of the project and you're ready to begin laying tile once the waterproofing compound has dried thoroughly.

How to Install Tile for a Curbless Shower

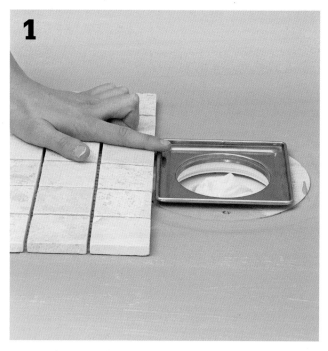

1

Set the floor tile first. Begin by placing a sample of the floor tile directly next to the drain so you can set the drain grate height to match. The adjustable mounting plate for the grate should be flush with the tops of the tile.

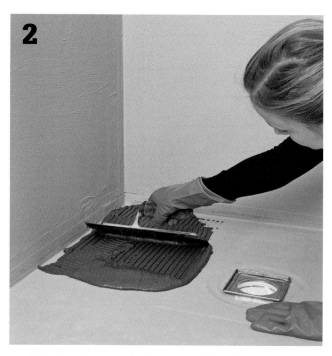

2

Begin laying floor tile in the corner of the shower. Lay a bed of thinset tile adhesive, using a notched trowel. The thinset container should specify the notch size (⅜" square notch is common).

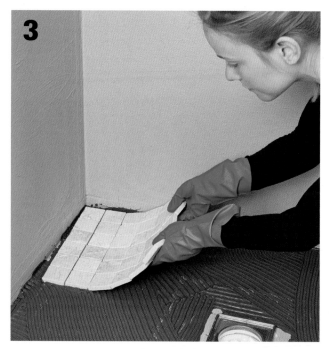

3

Place the corner tile into the bed of thinset and press it to set it. Don't press down too hard or you will displace too much of the material. Continue laying tile, fanning out from the corner toward the drain opening. Leave space around the drain opening as it is likely you'll need to cut tiles to fit.

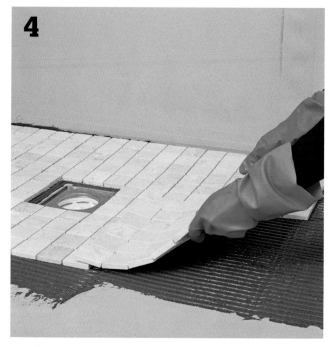

4

Install tile so a small square of untiled area is left around the drain opening (which, in the system seen here, is square, making for an easier cutting job).

5

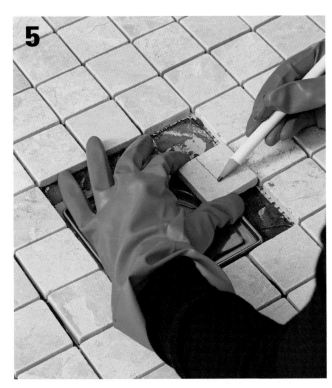

Mark the tiles that surround the drain opening for cutting. Leave a small gap between the tiles next to the drain grate mounting plate.

6

Cut the tiles along the trim lines using a tile saw. If you are not comfortable using a tile saw, score the tiles and cut them with tile nippers.

7

Apply thinset onto the shower pan, taking care not to get any on the drain grate mounting plate. You may need to use a small trowel or a putty knife to get into small gaps.

8

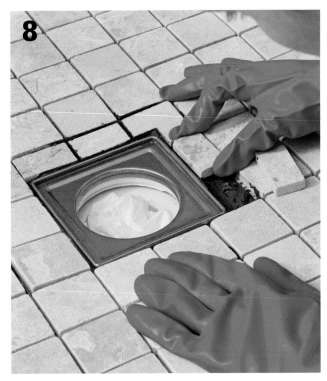

Set the cut tiles around the drain opening, doing your best to maintain even gaps that match the gaps in the rest of the floor. Once you've finished tiling around the drain, complete setting floor tile in the rest of the project area.

(continued)

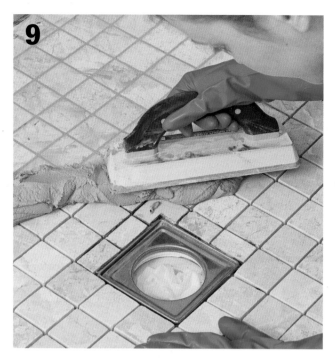

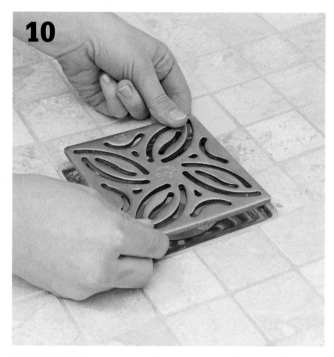

Let the floor tile set overnight and then apply grout. Using a grout sponge, wipe the grout over the gaps so all gaps are filled evenly. After the grout dries, buff the floor with a towel to wipe up excess residue.

Snap the grate cover into the cover mounting plate (if you've stuffed a rag into the drain opening to keep debris out, be sure to remove it first). The grate cover seen here locks in with a small key that should be saved in case you need to remove the grate cover.

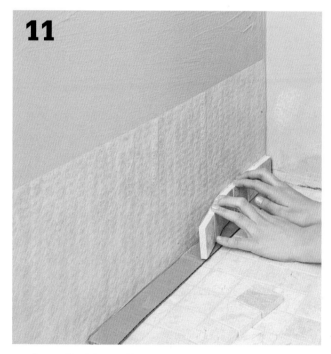

Begin setting the wall tile. Generally, it's easiest if you start at the bottom and work upward. Instead of thinset adhesive, an adhesive mat is being used here. This relatively new product is designed for walls and is rated for waterproof applications. It is a good idea to use a spacer (¼" thick or so) to get an even border at the bottoms of the first tiles.

In the design used here, a border of the same mosaic tile used in the floor is installed all around the shower area to make the first course. Dark brown accent tiles are installed in a single vertical column running upward, centered on the line formed by the shower faucet and showerhead. This vertical column is installed after the bottom border.

13

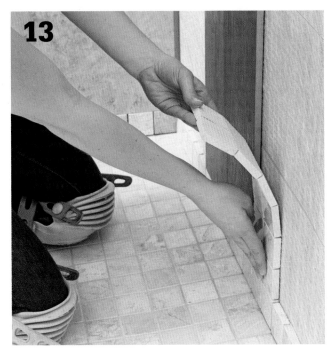

Next, another vertical column of accent tiles is installed on each side of the large, dark tiles. These columns are also laid using the floor tile, which connects the walls and floor visually in an effective way.

14

Finally, larger field tiles that match the floor tile used outside the shower area are installed up to the corner and outward from the shower area. Starting at the bottom, set a thin spacer on top of the border tiles to ensure even gaps.

15

Grout the gaps in the wall tiles. It's usually a good idea to protect any fittings, such as the shower faucet handle escutcheon, with painters tape prior to grouting. If you wish, a clear surround may be installed to visually define the shower area, as in the photo to the right, but because the shower pan is pitched toward the drain it really is not necessary.

Alcove Bathtubs

Most of our homes are equipped with an alcove tub that includes a tub surround and shower. By combining the tub and the shower in one fixture, you conserve precious bathroom floor space and simplify the initial installation. Plus, you only have one bathing fixture that needs cleaning.

But because tub/showers are so efficient, they do get a lot of use and tend to have fairly limited lifespans. The fact that the most inexpensive tubs on the market are designed for alcove use also reduces the average tub/shower lifespan. Pressed steel tubs have enamel finishes that crack and craze; plastic and fiberglass tubs get grimy and stained; even acrylic and composite tubs show wear eventually (and as with other fixtures, styles and colors change too).

Plumbing an alcove tub is a relatively difficult job because getting access to the drain lines attached to the tub and into the floor is often very awkward. Although an access panel is required by most codes, the truth is that many tubs were installed without them or with panels that are too small or hard to reach to be of much use. If you are contemplating replacing your tub, the first step in the decision process should be to find the access panel and determine if it is sufficient. If it is not (or there is no panel at all), consider how you might enlarge it. Often, this means cutting a hole in the wall on the adjoining room and also in the ceiling below. This creates more work, of course, but compared to the damage caused by a leaky drain from a subpar installation, making an access opening is little inconvenience.

Tools & Materials ▶

Channel-type pliers	Galvanized deck screws
Hacksaw	Drain-waste-
Carpenter's level	overflow kit
Pencil	1 × 3, 1 × 4,
Tape measure	2 × 4 lumber
Saw	Galvanized roofing nails
Screwdriver	Galvanized roof
Drill	flashing
Adjustable wrench	Thinset mortar
Trowel	Tub & tile caulk
Shims	Propane torch

A tub alcove is sized to accept a standard bathtub, usually 5 ft. long in most of North America. A tub with an apron is typical, but you can build out the front instead if you choose.

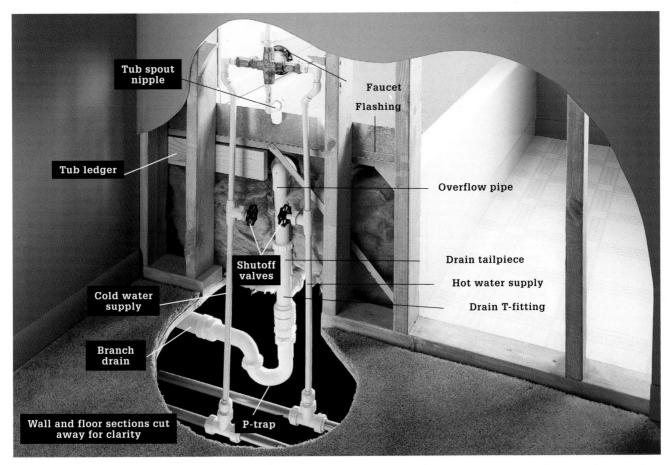

Tub spout nipple

Faucet
Flashing

Tub ledger

Overflow pipe

Shutoff valves

Cold water supply

Drain tailpiece
Hot water supply
Drain T-fitting

Branch drain

Wall and floor sections cut away for clarity

P-trap

The plumbing for a bathtub includes hot and cold supply pipes, shutoff valves, faucet, and a spout. Supply connections can be made before or after the tub is installed. The drain-waste-overflow system for a bathtub includes the overflow pipe, drain T-fitting, P-trap, and branch drain. The overflow pipe assembly is attached to the tub before installation.

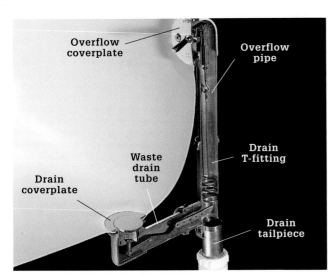

Overflow coverplate

Overflow pipe

Drain T-fitting

Waste drain tube

Drain coverplate

Drain tailpiece

A drain-waste-overflow kit with a stopper mechanism must be attached to the tub before it is installed. Available in both brass and plastic types, most kits include an overflow coverplate, a height-adjustable overflow pipe, a drain T-fitting and tailpiece, a waste drain tube, and a drain coverplate that screws into the drain tube.

Add fiberglass insulation around the body of a steel bathtub to reduce noise and conserve heat. Before setting the tub in position, wrap unfaced batting around the tub, and secure it with string or twine. For showers, deck-mounted whirlpools, and saunas, insulate between the framing members.

How to Install a New Alcove Tub

Prepare for the new tub. Inspect and remove old or deteriorated wall surfaces or framing members in the tub area. With today's mold-resistant wallboard products, it makes extra sense to go ahead and strip off the old alcove wallcoverings and ceiling down to the studs so you can replace them. This also allows you to inspect for hidden damage in the wall and ceiling cavities.

Check the subfloor for level—if it is not level, use pour-on floor leveler compound to correct it (ask at your local flooring store). Make sure the supply and drain pipes and the shutoff valves are in good repair and correct any problems you encounter. If you have no bath fan in the alcove, now is the perfect time to add one.

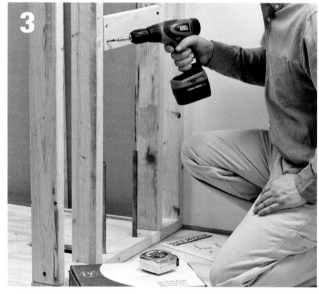

Check the height of the crossbraces for the faucet body and the showerhead. If your family members needed to stoop to use the old shower, consider raising the brace for the showerhead. Read the instructions for your new faucet/diverter and check to see that the brace for the faucet body will conform to the requirements (this includes distance from the surround wall as well as height). Adjust the brace locations as needed.

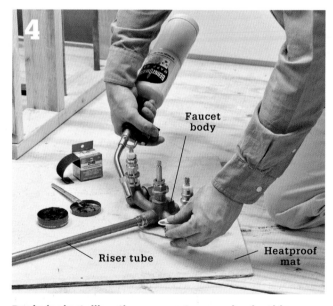

Faucet body

Riser tube

Heatproof mat

Begin by installing the new water supply plumbing. Measure to determine the required height of your shower riser tube and cut it to length. Attach the bottom of the riser to the faucet body and the top to the shower elbow.

5

Attach the faucet body to the cross brace with pipe hanger straps. Then, attach supply tubing from the stop valves to the faucet body, making sure to attach the hot water to the left port and cold to the right port. Also secure the shower elbow to its cross brace with a pipe strap. Do not attach the shower arm yet.

6

Slide the bathtub into the alcove. Make sure the tub is flat on the floor and pressed flush against the back wall. If your tub did not come with a tub protector, cut a piece of cardboard to line the tub bottom, and tape pieces of cardboard around the rim to protect the finish from damage.

7

Mark locations for ledger boards. To do this, trace the height of the top of the tub's nailing flange onto the wall studs in the alcove. Then remove the tub and measure the height of the nailing flange. Measure down this same amount from your flange lines and mark new ledger board locations.

8

Install 1 × 4 ledger boards. Drive two or three 3"-galvanized deck screws through the ledger board at each stud. All three walls should receive a ledger. Leave an open space in the wet wall to allow clearance for the drain-waste-overflow (DWO) kit.

(continued)

9

Install the drain-waste-overflow (DWO) pipes before you install the tub. Make sure to get a good seal on the slip nuts at the pipe joints. Follow the manufacturer's instructions to make sure the pop-up drain linkage is connected properly. Make sure rubber gaskets are positioned correctly at the openings on the outside of the tub.

10

Drain strainer

Thread the male-threaded drain strainer into the female-threaded drain waste elbow. Wrap a coil of plumber's putty around the drain outlet underneath the plug rim first. Hand tighten only.

11

Attach the overflow coverplate, making sure the pop-up drain controls are in the correct position. Tighten the mounting screws that connect to the mounting plate to sandwich the rubber gasket snugly between the overflow pipe flange and the tub wall. Then, finish tightening the drain strainer against the waste elbow by inserting the handle of a pair of pliers into the strainer body and turning.

12

Place the tub back into the alcove, taking care not to bump the DWO assembly and disturb the connections. You definitely will want a helper for this job. If the drain outlet of the DWO assembly is not directly over the drain pipe when the tub is in position, you'll need to remove it and adjust the drain line location.

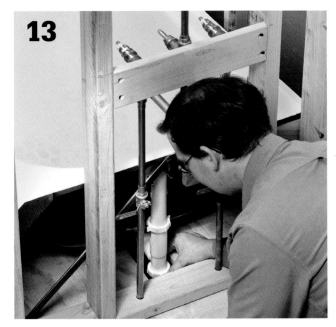

13

Attach the drain outlet from the DWO assembly to the drain P-trap. If your alcove walls are covered, you will appreciate that you spent the time to create a roomy access panel for the tub plumbing. Test the drain and overflow to make sure they don't leak. Also test the water supply plumbing, temporarily attaching the handles, spout, and shower arm so you can operate the faucet and the diverter.

14

Drive a 1½" galvanized roofing nail at each stud location, just over the top of the tub's nailing flange (inset). The nail head should pin the flange to the stud. For extra protection against moisture penetration, nail strips of metal flashing to the studs so they cover the tub flange.

15

Install the wallcoverings and tub surround (see pages 97 to 99 for a 3-piece surround installation). You can also make a custom surround from tileboard or cementboard and tile.

16

Install fittings. First, thread the shower arm into the shower elbow and attach the spout nipple to the valve assembly. Also attach the shower head and escutcheon, the faucet handle/ diverter with escutcheon, and the tub spout. Use thread lubricant on all parts.

3-Piece Tub Surrounds

Tools & Materials ▸

Jigsaw	Adhesive
Hole saw	Screwdriver
Drill	Adjustable wrench
Measuring tape	Pry bar
Level	Hammer
Caulking gun	3-piece tub surround

No one wants bathroom fixtures that are aging or yellowed from years of use. A shiny new tub surround can add sparkle and freshness to your dream bath.

Tub surrounds come in many different styles, materials, and price ranges. Choose the features you want and measure your existing bathtub surround for sizing. Surrounds typically come in three or five pieces. A three-panel surround is being installed here, but the process is similar for five-panel systems.

Surface preparation is important for good glue adhesion. Plastic tiles and wallpaper must be removed and textured plaster must be sanded smooth. Surrounds can be installed over ceramic tile that is well attached and in good condition, but it must be sanded and primed. All surfaces must be primed with a water-based primer.

Three-piece tub surrounds are inexpensive and come in many colors and styles. The typical unit has two end panels and a back panel that overlap in the corners to form a watertight seal. They are formed from fiberglass, PVC, acrylic, or proprietary resin-based polymers. Five-piece versions are also available and typically have more features such as integral soap shelves and even cabinets.

How to Install a 3-Piece Tub Surround

1

Remove the old plumbing fixtures and wallcoverings in the tub area. In some cases you can attach surround panels to old tileboard or even tile, but it is generally best to remove the wallcoverings down to the studs if you can, so you may inspect for leaks or damage.

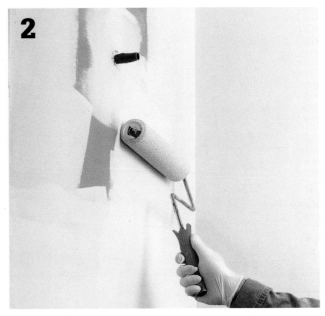

2

Replace the wallcoverings with appropriate materials, such as water and mold resistant wallboard or cementboard (for ceramic tile installations). Make sure the new wall surfaces are smooth and flat. Some surround kit manufacturers recommend that you apply a coat of primer to sheet goods such as greenboard to create a better bonding surface for the panel adhesive.

3

Test-fit the panels before you start; the tub may have settled unevenly or the walls may be out of plumb. Check the manufacturer's directions for distinguishing right and left panels. Place a panel in position on the tub ledge. Use a level across the top of the panel to determine if it is level. Create a vertical reference line to mark the edge of the panel on the plumbing end.

Test-fitting ▶

Ensure a perfect fit by taping the surround panels to the walls in the tub area. Make sure the tops are level when the overlap seams are aligned and that you have a consistent gap between the panel bottoms and the tub flange. Mark the panels for cutting if necessary and, once the panels have been removed, make any adjustments to the walls that are needed.

(continued)

4

After performing the testfit, check the fitting instructions to see if you need to trim any of the pieces. Follow the manufacturer's instructions for cutting. Here, we had to cut the corner panels because the instructions advise not to overlap the back or side panel over the corner panels by more than 3". Cut panels using a jigsaw and a fine-tooth blade that is appropriate for cutting fiberglass or acrylic tileboard.

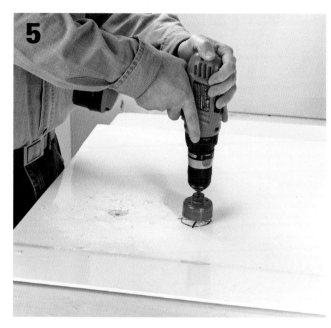

5

Lay out the locations of the faucets, spout, and shower arm. Measure in from the vertical reference line (made in Step 3) and up from the top of the tub ledge. Re-measure for accuracy, as any cuts to the surround are final. Place the panel face-up on a sheet of plywood. Mark the location of the holes. Cut the holes ½" larger than the pipe diameter. If your faucet has a recessed trim plate, cut the hole to fit the recess. Using a hole saw or a jigsaw, cut out the plumbing access holes.

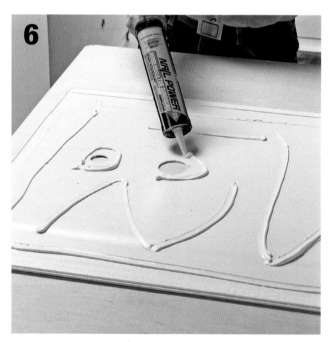

6

Apply the panel adhesive to the back of an end plumbing panel. Circle the plumbing outlet holes 1" from the edge. Follow the manufacturer's application pattern. Do not apply adhesive closer than 1" to the double-sided tape or the bottom edge of the panel.

7

Remove the protective backing from the tape. Carefully lift the panel by the edges and place against the corner and top of the tub ledge. Press firmly from top to bottom in the corner, then throughout the panel.

8

Test-fit the opposite end panel and make any necessary adjustments. Apply the adhesive, remove the protective backing from the tape, and put in place. Apply pressure to the corner first from top to bottom, and then apply pressure throughout.

9

Apply adhesive to the back panel following the manufacturer's instructions. Maintain a 1" space between adhesive tape and the bottom of the panel. Remove protective backing from the tape. Lift the panel by the edges and carefully center between the two end panels. When positioned, firmly press in place from top to bottom.

10

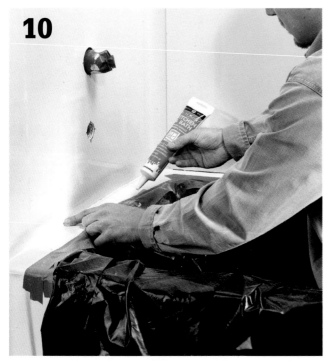

Apply caulk to the bottom and top edges of the panels and at panel joints. Dip your fingertip in water and use it to smooth the caulk to a uniform bead.

11

Apply silicone caulk to escutcheons or trim plates and reinstall them. Allow a minimum of 24 hours for caulk and adhesive to cure thoroughly before using the shower or tub.

Soaking Tubs

Long a favorite in the Japanese culture, soaking tubs continue to gain fans in America. Although you can soak in any tub, an actual soaking tub is designed so that the bather sits—rather than reclines—immersed in water up to the chin. It usually only takes one long soak for a person to become a devotee of the soaking tub's relaxing benefits.

Traditional soaking tubs are manufactured with sides that can rise 36" high or higher; but today's soaking tubs for home use are available in a range of sizes, many with sides around 24" deep. (It's crucial for proper soaking that the overflow drain is positioned 20" or more from the bottom to allow the tub to be almost completely filled.)

Getting in and out of these types of tubs can be a challenge, which is why they are often installed into a platform built especially for the tub. The platform allows you to sit and then ease into the tub. A wide platform such as the one discussed here leaves plenty of space for candles, bath salts, plants, or other decor- and mood-enhancing additions.

The platform described in the instructions that follow is 22" high with a 14" wide ledge—comfortably accommodating seating around the tub. The tub itself is 24" high, with a 2" lip. You can build a platform so that the tub rim fits flush, but a lip is a good idea to keep towels and other items from accidentally sliding off the platform and into the bathwater.

As with other types of tubs, soaking tubs come in a range of styles, shapes, and colors.

A soaking tub needs to be deep, but not necessarily wide. That makes them ideal for long narrow spaces such as this under-window area. Here, a soaking tub with a modest ledge adds big luxury in a small footprint.

Tools & Materials ▸

Plumbing tools & supplies	Cementboard
Tape measure	Hacksaw
Drill	Circular saw
Hammer	Torpedo level
4-ft. level	Thin-set mortar
Utility knife	Silicone caulk
2 × 4 lumber	Deck-mount faucet set
2" screws	Soaking tub
1¼" cementboard screws	Tile mortar
Notched trowel	Tile grout
Grout sponge	Grout float
CDX plywood	Ceramic tile (field and bullnose)

Access Panels ▸

Making the supply and drain hook-ups on a bathtub usually requires access from below or behind the installation area. When installing a drop-in tub in a framed deck platform, you can gain access through the platform apron area, too. If you are hooking up the drain with a slip connection, the Universal Plumbing Code requires that you install a permanent access panel (see page 246) in the wall behind the tub or in the floor and ceiling below. But regardless of codes, you should make a point of creating permanent access to the plumbing hook-ups whenever possible. In the tub installation seen here, a removable access panel on the opposite side of the wet wall provides access to both the drain and supply hookups. This allows the platform deck and apron to be tiled in a contiguous manner. Because the faucet plumbing is readily accessible, each supply tube is connected to a shutoff valve next to the fixture and supply risers are used to bring water to the faucet valve.

How to Install a Soaking Tub with Platform

Place the tub in position on the subfloor. The tub should be 14½" from the two corner walls, measured from the underside of the tub lip—where the inside edge of the platform deck will run—to wall studs. This allows for ½"-thick wall surface. Shim as necessary to level the tub both ways, or adjust self-leveling feet if tub has them. Hang a plumb bob from the underside of the lip at each corner of tub and mark the subfloor. Check that marks on adjacent corners are the same distance from the wall.

Measure from under the lip edge to the subfloor. This will be the height of the platform wall framing, minus the CDX plywood decking, ½" cementboard, and tile.

Remove the tub and hammer a nail in at each corner point. Snap chalk lines to represent the inside lines of the inner platform wall. Measure, cut, and align the 2 × 4 sole plates with the chalk lines. Screw all four sole plates for the inside platform wall into position. Check diagonal measurements or use a framing square to ensure the sole plates are square.

Measure and mark 13½" from the inside edge of the open side sole plates, at several points along the plates. These marks will serve as guide points for placing the sole plates of the outside platform walls. Line up the outside edge of the two outer wall sole plates and screw them in place to the subfloor. Measure again to ensure the sole plates are positioned correctly.

Measure and cut studs to create the proper platform height. Install studs for both inside and outside platform walls, spacing them every 16". Use L configurations at corners so that the top plates intersect opposite the sole plates. Cut cross braces and screw them in place, staggering with the stud placement.

Route supply lines from the wet wall to the location of the deck-mount faucet. The connections will depend on what type of deck-mount faucet you've chosen. Follow the manufacturer's instructions for securing the hot and cold connections for the faucet. If you're unsure of how to plumb the faucet, hire a plumber.

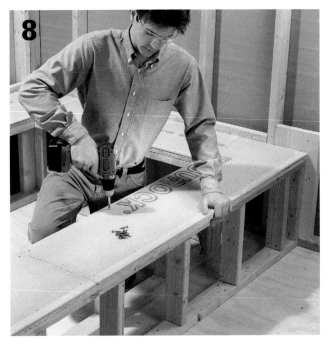

Measure and cut CDX plywood for the platform deck (the deck for the two open sides should overhang the outside wall edge by ½" to cover the cementboard that will be used on the walls). Screw the decking into position. If you will be mounting the faucet on the deck, cut holes for the valve handles and spout before screwing down that portion of the deck.

Measure and cut the deck cementboard to cover the plywood. Cut to the same overhang as the plywood and drill holes for the faucet if it will be deck-mounted (the one seen here is mounted to the tub deck). Screw cementboard to the plywood deck over top rail and cross braces. Also attach cementboard to the platform aprons.

(continued)

9

10

Attach wallcoverings in the installation area. Here, six courses of wall tile will be installed on the walls above the tub deck. A strip of cementboard the same width as the total tile height is attached to the wall as a backer for the tile. Then, water-resistant drywall is installed to span from the cementboard to the ceiling to create a smooth, paintable wall surface.

Lay tile over the deck surface and the platform aprons using bullnose tile around the two outside edges. Tile on the inside edge of the platform does not need to be finished—it will be covered by the tub lip. Also install wall tiles.

11

Grout the platform and walls with sanded grout. Buff off excess grout with a coarse rag. Apply a grout sealing product after the grout has dried for several days (this may be done after the tub is installed if you do not want to wait).

12

Install the tub. Attach the drain-waste-overflow connection to the tub. Trowel a ½" bed of mortar on the subfloor where the tub bottom will sit (unless manufacturer's directions state otherwise). Set the tub in place in the platform opening, press down into the mortar, and check for level. There should be a very slight gap between tub lip bottom edge and top of tile.

13

Let the mortar bed dry and, working through the open walls and under the platform deck, connect the drain tailpiece to the trap. A large access panel lets you get at both the supply and drain hook ups.

14

Apply a bead of tub-and-tile caulk in the seam between the tub lip and the tiled deck surface. Wet your finger and smooth the bead for a finished look.

Freestanding Tubs

Freestanding tubs offer maximum versatility in bathroom design because, theoretically, they can be placed anywhere in the bathroom. They can even be installed in an alcove, in place of an alcove tub. However, because they are attractive from all sides, and one of the key benefits is total access, most homeowners install freestanding tubs with some measure of floor space all around the tub.

Another selling point is the amazing variety among freestanding tubs. Options include the vast array of clawfoot tubs and pedestal tubs in styles from modern to classical. Roll-top freestanding tubs feature a rolled top lip that makes getting into and out of the tub easy. These are often egg-shaped and deep, offering a comfortable soak after a long day. Slipper tubs offer a more dramatic shape, like Cinderella's ball slipper, with a high, sloped back that allows the bather to recline in ultimate comfort.

Clawfoot tubs are a category all their own. Although cast iron is the traditional material for clawfoots, manufacturers also offer easier-to-move acrylic and polymer options. You can pick from many different foot styles, including ball feet, ornamental feet, and, of course, the traditional claw feet. You can also outfit a clawfoot tub with a shower extension on the faucet body, a direct spray "rainwater" head, and a shower ring from which a shower curtain can be hung (see pages 110 to 111).

The clawfoot tub seen here is a salvaged, cast-iron rolltop tub. Although the supply of vintage tubs is dwindling, they are still not hard to find and in many cases you can get one for the price of hauling it away (no easy task). Often, the porcelain enamel finish needs refurbishing, which is a job best done by a tub reglazing specialist. The installation process is a fairly simple one. The hardest part is usually running new drain and supply lines under the floor, so if you can place the tub over existing lines, you greatly simplify the installation process.

Regardless of the tub you choose, check with your local building inspector to help you determine whether your floor has adequate structural strength to safely support a freestanding tub. The inspector may suggest (or require) that you have the potential location evaluated by a qualified structural engineer.

Tools & Materials ▶

Adjustable wrench	Teflon tape	Carpenter's level
Plumber's putty or silicone plumber's grease	Cordless drill and bits	Hole saw

Prepping for a Clawfoot Tub ▶

The actual installation of a clawfoot tub is fairly basic. Success, though, relies on proper preparation so that the tub is positioned just where you want it, and the supply and drain lines are correctly aligned with the tub. Place the tub roughly where you want it and use a stud finder or other method to isolate the floor joists. Determine the location for connections under the floor (new tubs usually come with a template) and mark them by drilling pilot holes all the way through the subflooring. Install new drain and supply plumbing—this is a good time to call in a professional plumber. Finally, lay the finish flooring, if it is not already in place, before installing the tub. Make sure the floor is as level as possible.

How to Install a Clawfoot Tub

Position the tub exactly where you'd like it to rest, ideally over existing supply and drain lines. Install the feet first if they were not preattached (inset photo).

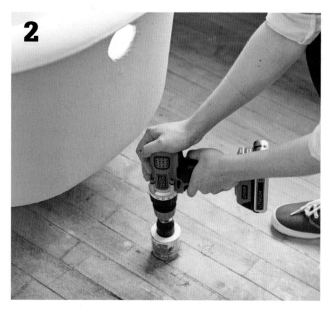

Mark locations for supply risers and drain tailpipe on the floor. Drill starter holes and doublecheck below the floor to make sure floor joists will not be directly under the access holes. Use a hole saw slightly wider than each pipe to drill access holes. Install supply lines and drainline.

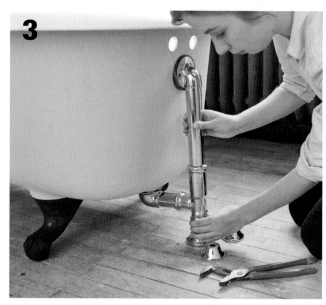

Install the drain-waste-overflow assembly according to the manufacturer's instructions. With a freestanding tub, it is often easiest to join the assembly parts working upward from the drainpipe connection in the floor. Install the drain flange in the tub, fastening it from the top into the drain shoe. Make the connection to the drain pipe in the floor—if the kit comes with a floor escutcheon that covers the drain connection, make sure it is in place before you attach the tailpipe to the T.

Fasten the overflow cover to the overflow receiver with the bolt or bolts that are provided. Be sure to position the rubber gasket that came with the drain kit so it fits neatly against the tub wall. Do not overtighten the fasteners.

Assemble the faucet according to the manufacturer's instructions. Most older clawfoot tubs have a two-valve faucet with a gooseneck spigot that mounts directly to the wall of the tub at the foot end. Many newer freestanding tubs utilize a wall-mounted faucet.

Mount the faucet body to the tub wall with the retainer nuts that thread onto the faucet valve stems.

Attach the supply risers to the valve inlets for the faucet. Put the supply pipe base escutcheons in place on the floor over the supply line connections. Secure the risers into the supply connections below the floor. Turn on the water supply and test to make sure there are no leaks in any of the pipes or fitting connections, including the drain and overflow.

Feet First ▸

Despite their great weight, it is always a good idea to anchor cast-iron tubs—even a small shift in position can cause the drain or supply connections to fail. Older tubs often have screwholes in the bottoms of the feet so they may be fastened to the floor once the hookups are made. Newer lighter weight tubs generally use floor pins to stabilize the tub. Some manufacturers recommend using rubber pads and epoxy under each foot, in conjunction with dowels or mounting studs. Some tubs have self-leveling feet, with integral adjustment posts—check and follow the manufacturer's installation instructions.

Adding a Shower to a Freestanding Tub

Complete kits for converting a freestanding tub to a shower are widely available through plumbing supply retailers. A quick online search will give you an idea of what's out there (use key phrases such as "clawfoot tub to shower", "clawfoot tub shower set", or "shower enclosure"). Kits include a special faucet with a built-in diverter, a riser pipe (extending from the faucet to the showerhead), and a rectangular shower curtain frame that mounts to the ceiling and wall. Prices range from less than $100 to more than $500, depending on the style of the faucet and showerhead and the quality of the materials.

Examine your faucet and its water hookups carefully before ordering a kit. Measure the distance between the faucet tailpieces and the length and offset of the water supply risers. The new faucet must fit into the existing holes in your tub. You may need to buy new supply risers to connect to the faucet.

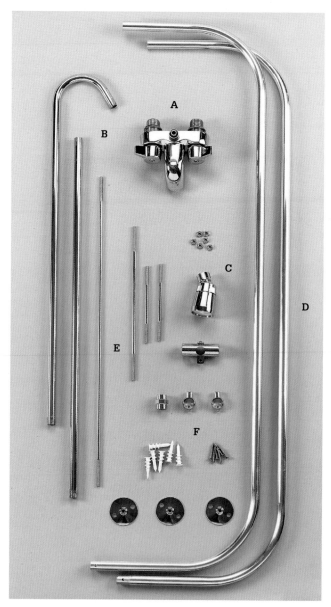

A packaged kit for adding a shower to your tub features a faucet with diverter (A), shower riser plumbing (B), showerhead (C), a frame for the shower curtain (D) that mounts on the wall and ceiling with threaded rods (E), and fasteners and fittings (F).

A spout with a diverter, some metal supply tubing, and a shower curtain frame can add showering capacity to a standalone tub.

Tools & Materials ›

Adjustable wrench
Plumber's putty or silicone plumber's grease
Teflon tape
Cordless drill and bits

How to Install a Shower Conversion Kit

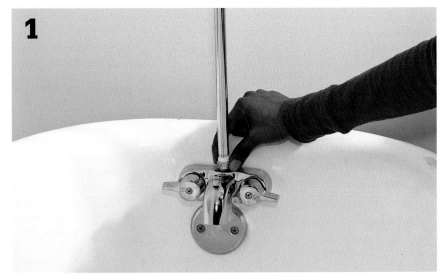

Remove the old tub faucet and replace it with the new diverter-type faucet from the kit. Fit the assembled shower riser into the top of the faucet and hand-tighten. Apply Teflon tape to the threads before making the connection. This assembly includes one straight and one curved section, joined by a coupling. The top, curved pipe includes a connector to a wall brace. Shorten the straight section using a tubing cutter, to lower the showerhead height, if desired. Slip the compression nut and washer onto the bottom end of the shower riser, and attach the riser to the top of the faucet, hand-tightening for the time being.

With a helper, assemble the curtain frame, securing it with setscrews. Hold the frame level and measure to the ceiling to determine the ceiling brace pipe length. Cut the pipe and complete the ceiling brace assembly. Set the shower riser to the desired height and connect the brace to the wall (ensure strong connections by driving the mounting screws into a wall stud and ceiling joist, if possible).

After the curtain frame is completely assembled and secured, tighten the faucet connection with a wrench. Full-size shower kits require one shower curtain on each side of the curtain frame. The hooks seen here feature roller bearings on the tops so they can be operated very smoothly with minimal resistance.

Sliding Tub Doors

Curtains on your bathtub shower are a hassle. If you forget to tuck them inside the tub, water flows freely onto your bathroom floor. If you forget to slide them closed, mildew sets up shop in the folds. And every time you brush against them they stick to your skin. Shower curtains certainly don't add much elegance or charm to a dream bath. Neither does a deteriorated door. Clean up the look of your bathroom, and even give it an extra touch of elegance, with a new sliding tub door.

When shopping for a sliding tub door, you have a choice of framed or frameless. A framed door is edged in metal. The metal framing is typically aluminum but is available in many finishes, including those that resemble gold, brass, or chrome. Glass options are also plentiful. You can choose between frosted or pebbled glass, clear, mirrored, tinted, or patterned glass. Doors can be installed on ceramic tile walls or through a fiberglass tub surround.

Tools & Materials ▸

Measuring tape	Masonry bit
Pencil & marker	for tile wall
Hacksaw	Phillips screwdriver
Miter box	Caulk gun
Level	Masking tape
Drill	Silicone sealant
Center punch	Tub door kit

A sliding tub door in a metal frame gives the room a sleek, clean look and is just one of the available options.

How to Install Sliding Tub Doors

1   **Remove the existing door** and inspect the walls. Use a razor blade to cut sealant from tile and metal surfaces. Do not use a razor blade on fiberglass surfaces. Remove remaining sealant by scraping or pulling. Use a silicone sealant remover to remove all residue. Remove shower curtain rods, if present. Check the walls and tub ledge for plumb and level.

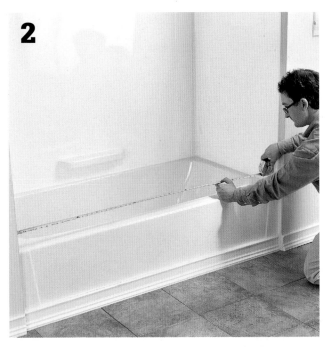

2   **Measure the distance** between the finished walls along the top of the tub ledge. Refer to the manufacturer's instructions for figuring the track dimensions. For the product seen here, 3/16" is subtracted from the measurement to calculate the track dimensions.

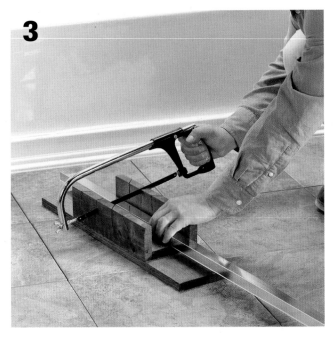

3   **Using a hacksaw and a miter box,** carefully cut into the track to the proper dimension. Center the track on the bathtub ledge with the taller side out and so the gaps are even at each end. Tape into position with masking tape.

4   **Place a wall channel against the wall** with the longer side out and slide into place over the track so they overlap. Use a level to check the channel for plumb, and then mark the locations of the mounting holes on the wall with a marker. Repeat for the other wall channel. Remove the track.

(continued)

5

Drill mounting holes for the wall channel at the marked locations. In ceramic tile, nick the surface of the tile with a center punch, use a ¼" masonry bit to drill the hole, and then insert the included wall anchors. For fiberglass surrounds, use a ⅛" drill bit; wall anchors are not necessary.

6

Apply a bead of silicone sealant along the joint between the tub and the wall at the ends of the track. Apply a minimum ¼" bead of sealant along the outside leg of the track underside.

7

Position the track on the tub ledge and against the wall. Attach the wall channels using the provided screws. Do not use caulk on the wall channels at this time.

8

At a location above the tops of the wall channels, measure the distance between the walls. Refer to the manufacturer's instructions for calculating the header dimensions. For the doors seen here, the header dimension is the distance between the walls minus ¹⁄₁₆". Measure the header and carefully cut it to length using a hacksaw and a miter box. Slide the header down on top of the wall channels until seated.

9

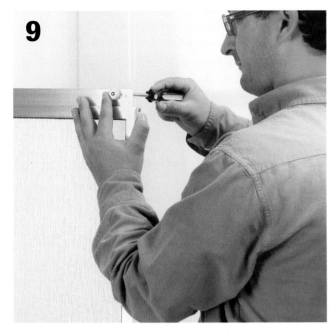

Mount the rollers in the roller mounting holes. To begin, use the second from the top roller mounting holes. Follow the manufacturer's instructions for spacer or washer placement and direction.

10

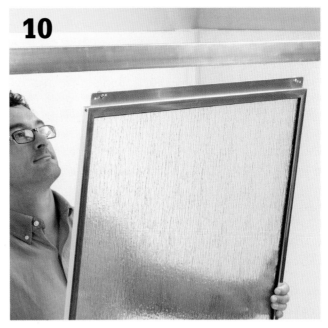

Carefully lift the inner panel by the sides and place the rollers on the inner roller track. Roll the door toward the shower end of the tub. The edge of the panel should touch both rubber bumpers. If it doesn't, remove the door and move the rollers to different holes. Drive the screws by hand to prevent overtightening.

11

Lift the outer panel by the sides with the towel bar facing out from the tub. Place the outer rollers over the outer roller track. Slide the door to the end opposite the shower end of the tub. If the door does not contact both bumpers, remove the door and move the rollers to different mounting holes.

12

Apply a bead of silicone sealant to the inside seam of the wall and wall channel at both ends and to the U-shaped joint of the track and wall channels. Smooth the sealant with a fingertip dipped in water.

Air-Jet Tubs

A jetted tub is basically a bathtub that recirculates water, air, or a combination of the two to create an effect known as hydromassage. Hydromassage increases blood flow, relieves pressure on joints and muscles, and relieves tension. Indoor hydromassage tubs usually have a water pump that blows a mixture of air and water through jets located in the tub body. Many include an integral water heater.

The product you'll see installed on these pages is a bit different. It is an air-jet tub: a relatively new entry in the jetted spa market that circulates only warm air, not water. This technology makes it safe to use bath oils, bubble bath, and bath salts in the spa. A model with no heater requires only a single 120-volt dedicated circuit. Models with heaters normally require either multiple dedicated 120-volt circuits or a 240-volt circuit.

Like normal bathtubs, jetted tubs can be installed in a variety of ways. Here, we install a drop-in tub (no

nailing flange) in a 3-wall alcove. This may require the construction of a new stub wall, like the short wall we plumbed as the wet wall for this installation. Unless you have a lot of wiring and plumbing experience, consider hiring professionals for all or parts of the project.

Plumbing tools & supplies	Drain-waste-overflow assembly
Utility knife	Shims
4-foot level	1 × 4 lumber
Square-edge trowel	Deck screws
Drill or power driver	Roofing nails
Channel-type pliers	Plumber's putty
Hacksaw	Dry-set mortar
Level	Trowel
Circular saw	Silicone caulk
Screwdriver	Jetted tub
Adjustable wrench	Faucet set

Air-jet tubs create massaging action, stirring the water with warm air. Air-jets eliminate concerns about stagnant water and bacteria that can remain in the pipes of whirlpool tubs.

Whirlpools ▸

Installing a whirlpool is very similar to installing a bathtub, once the rough-in is completed. Completing a rough-in for a whirlpool requires that you install a separate GFCI-protected electrical circuit for the pump motor. Some building codes specify that a licensed electrician be hired to wire whirlpools; check with your local building inspector.

Select your whirlpool before you do rough-in work, because exact requirements will differ from model to model.

Select your faucet to match the trim kit that comes with your whirlpool. When selecting a faucet, make sure the spout is large enough to reach over the tub rim. Most whirlpools use "widespread" faucets because the handles and spout are separate, and can be positioned however you like, even on opposite sides of the tub. Most building centers carry flex tube in a variety of lengths for connecting the faucet handles and spout.

A whirlpool circulates aerated water through jets mounted in the body of the tub. Whirlpool pumps move as much as 50 gallons of water per minute to create a relaxing hydromassage effect. The pump, pipes, jets, and most of the controls are installed at the factory, making the actual hookup in your home quite simple.

How to Install a Jetted Tub

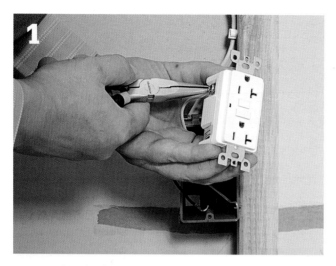

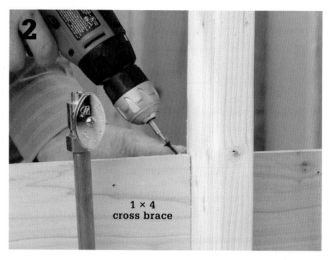

Prepare the site for the installation. Remove wall coverings in the installation area to expose bare studs. Provide a dedicated electrical circuit or circuits to the tub area according to the specifications in your installation manual (hire an electrician if you are not comfortable with wiring). This model plugs into a GFCI-protected receptacle on a dedicated 120-volt, 20-amp circuit.

Make framing improvements such as adding 1 × 4 bracing at supply risers and faucet body locations. For drop-in tubs that do not have nailing flanges, you may need to add short stub walls to provide a stable resting point. Here, a short stub wall was installed at one end to serve as the tub wet wall.

Requirements for Making Electrical Hookups ▸

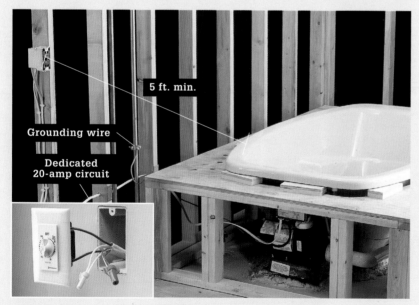

The electrical service for a whirlpool should be a dedicated 115- to 120-volt, 20-amp circuit. The pump motor should be grounded separately, normally to a metal cold water supply pipe. Most whirlpool motors are wired with 12/2 NM cable, but some local codes require the use of conduit. Remote timer switches (inset), located at least 5 ft. from the tub, are required by some codes, even for a tub with a built-in timer.

A GFCI circuit breaker at the main service panel is required with whirlpool installations. Hire an electrician to connect new circuits at your service panel if you are uncomfortable installing circuit cables on your own.

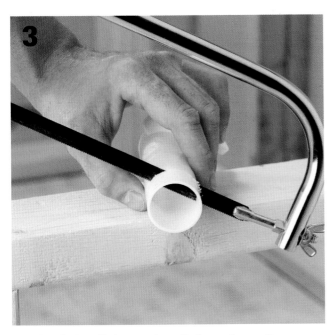

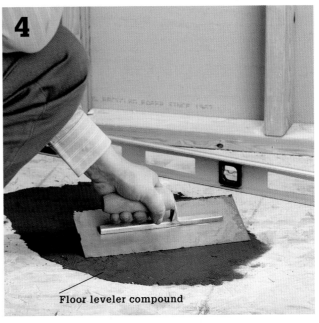

Cut the drain tailpiece to length depending on the distance you'll need to span to the trap. Use a hacksaw or tubing cutter to make the cut.

Prepare the floor or subfloor. Check with a level and fill any dips with floor leveling compound or mortar. If there is a joint in the subfloor in the installation area, make sure the sides are level. (The floor has to be level in order to support the weight of the tub, the water, and bathers.) Also make sure there is no rot or weakness in the structural elements.

Floor leveler compound

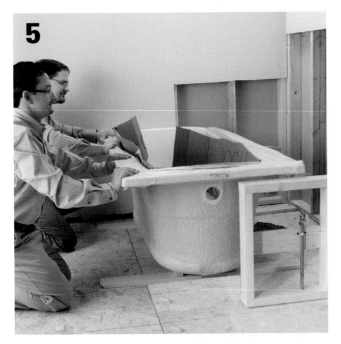

Test the tub fit. First, cut a piece of the shipping carton to fit inside the tub and protect its surface. Have someone help you slide the tub into the installation area, flush against the wall studs, so you can check the fit. *Tip: Lay a pair of 1 × 4s perpendicular to the tub opening and use them as skids to make it easier to slide the tub in. Remove the skids and lower the tub on the floor.*

Set a 4-ft. level across the rim of the tub and check it for level. If it is not level, place shims under the tub until it is.

(continued)

7

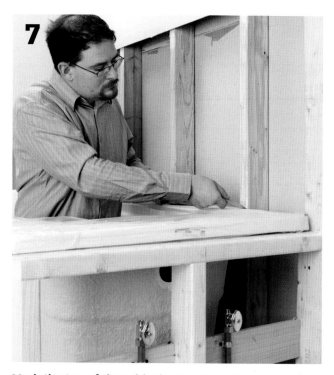

Mark the top of the tub's rim or nailing flange at each stud as a reference for installing additional supports or ledgers. Remove the tub from the alcove.

8

Add support frames or ledgers as directed by the manufacturer and secure them in the installation area so the top of the tub or nailing flange will be at the height you scribed in Step 7.

9

Assemble the drain-waste-overflow kit to fit the drain and overflow openings, following the tub manufacturer's directions. Install the DWO kit (it is virtually impossible to attach it once the tub is in place).

10

Fasten the threaded parts of the drain assembly. A ring of plumber's putty between the drain coverplate and the tub will help create a good seal. If you will be installing a pop-up drain, install it now as well.

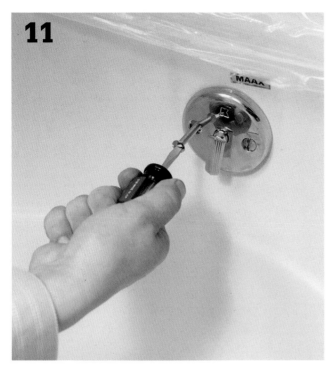

11

Attach the overflow coverplate so it conceals the overflow opening. Adjust the pop-up drain plug linkage as directed by the manufacturer.

12

Begin the actual installation. For some tubs, it is recommended that you trowel a layer of thinset mortar in the installation area. But read your instructions carefully. Many tubs feature integral feet that are meant to rest directly on the floor.

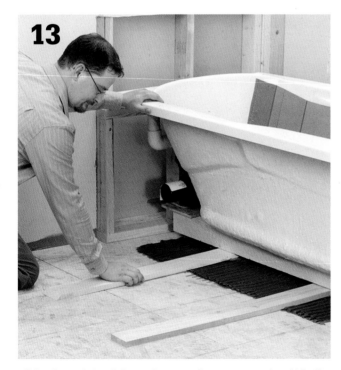

13

Slide the tub back into the opening. Remove the skids, if you are using them. Press down evenly on the tub rims until they make solid contact with the ledgers or frames.

14

Provide support for the tub on the open side if it does not have a structural skirt. Here, a 2 × 4 stub wall is built to the exact height of the underside of the rim and then attached in place. Screw it to both end walls and to the floor.

(continued)

Drain Hookups ▶

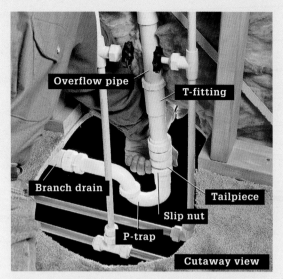

Overflow pipe
T-fitting
Branch drain
Tailpiece
Slip nut
P-trap
Cutaway view

Make the plumbing drain connections before you proceed further. To connect the drain tailpiece to the trap, you will need access either from below or from an access panel. The photo above shows a typical tub drain configuration seen cutaway through the floor.

15

Cover the gaps in the wallcoverings around the tub. Here, cementboard is installed in preparation for a tile backsplash. If your tub has nailing flanges, attach strips of metal flashing to the wall so they extend down to within about ¼" of the tub rim. If your tub has a removable apron, install it.

16

Make wiring connections according to the tub manufacturer's instructions. The requirements vary greatly among jetted spas. Some municipalities may require that a licensed professional do this work. Here, the airflow regulator is being wired. Note that most codes have a safety requirement that the on/off switch must be located so it cannot be reached by a bather in the tub.

17

Test the operation of the jetted spa before you finish the walls or deck in case there is a hidden problem. Fill it with a hose if you have not installed the faucet (the faucet normally is installed after the wall surfaces, unless you are deck-mounting the faucet on the tub rim). Run the spa. If it works, go ahead and drain the water.

18

Finish the wall surfaces. Here, a tile surround and backsplash are being installed over the cementboard backer. The wallcovering at the front of the wet wall is installed so it is easy to remove for plumbing access.

19

Hook up the faucet to the water supply plumbing according to the manufacturer's directions (or have your plumber do the job). Remove the aerator from the tip of the spout and run water through it to clear out any debris. Attach the aerator, fill the tub, and have yourself a nice, relaxing soak.

Optional Accessories ▸

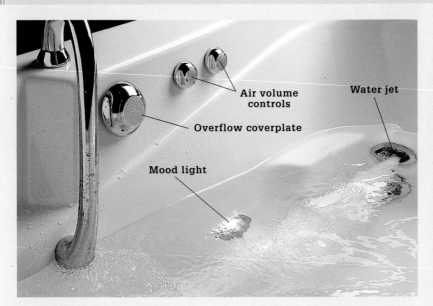

Air volume controls

Water jet

Overflow coverplate

Mood light

Mood lights are sold as factory-installed accessories by many manufacturers. Most are available with several filters to let you adjust the color to suit your mood. Mood lights are low-voltage fixtures wired through 12-volt transformers. Do not wire mood lights or other accessories into the electrical circuit that supplies the pump motor.

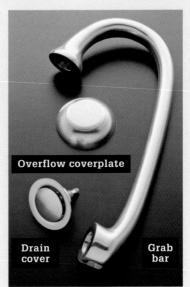

Overflow coverplate

Drain cover

Grab bar

Trim kits for whirlpools are ordered at the time of purchase. Available in a variety of finishes, all of the trim pieces except the grab bar and overflow coverplate are normally installed at the factory.

Tub & Shower Fittings

In many situations, replacing a bathtub spout can be almost as easy as hooking up a garden hose to an outdoor spigot. There are some situations where it is a bit more difficult, but still pretty simple. The only time it's a real problem is when the spout is attached to a plain copper supply nipple, rather than a threaded nipple. You'll know this is the case if the spout has a setscrew on the underside where it meets the wall. Many bathtub spouts are sold in kits with a matching showerhead and handle or handles. But for a simple one-for-one replacement, spouts are sold separately. You just need to make sure the new spout is compatible with the existing nipple (see page 128).

Tub spouts can be relatively complicated plumbing fittings, often performing three or four important functions. The spout itself is simple enough, since its only function is to deliver bathwater to the tub. But the diverter network and pop-up drain contain multiple moving parts that require precise adjustment and occasional repair or replacement (see photo, next page). The diverter is basically a stop valve that's activated by a lever or knob to block flow of water from the spout, forcing it up to a showerhead or out through a handheld showerhead, as seen here.

Diverter lever

Gate diverter

In many bathtub/shower plumbing systems, the spout has the important job of housing the diverter—a gate inside the spout that is operated by a lever with a knob. An open gate allows water to come out of the spout when the faucet is turned on. When the diverter is pulled shut, the water is redirected up a riser pipe and to the showerhead. Failure of the diverter is one of the most common reasons for replacing a spout.

Tub & Shower Combination Faucets

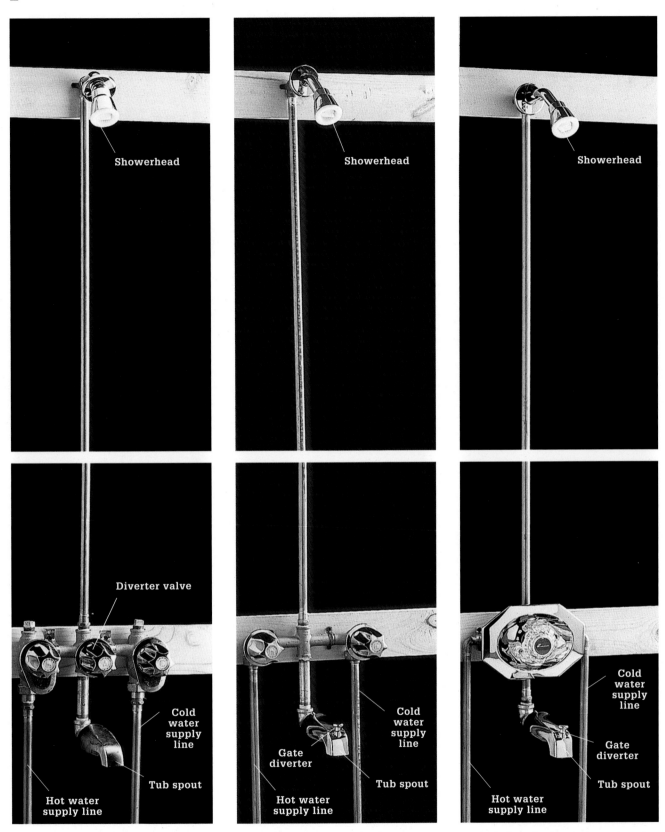

Showerhead

Showerhead

Showerhead

Diverter valve

Cold water supply line

Hot water supply line

Tub spout

Gate diverter

Cold water supply line

Hot water supply line

Tub spout

Cold water supply line

Gate diverter

Hot water supply line

Tub spout

A three-handle faucet has valves that are either compression or cartridge design.

A two-handle faucet has valves that are either compression or cartridge design.

A single-handle faucet has valves that are cartridge, ball-type, or disc design.

How to Install a Slip-Fit Spout

1

Slip fitting: Check underneath the tub spout to look for an access slot or cutout, which indicates the spout is a slip-fit style that is held in place with a setscrew and mounted on a copper supply nipple. Loosen the screw with a hex (Allen) wrench. Pull off the spout.

2

Clean the copper nipple with steel wool. If you find any sharp edges where the nipple was cut, smooth them out with emery paper. Then, insert the O-ring that comes with the spout onto the nipple (see the manufacturer's instructions) and slide the spout body over the nipple in an upside-down position.

3

With the spout upside down for ease of access, tighten the setscrews on the clamp, working through the access slot or cutout, until you feel resistance.

4

Spin the spout so it's right-side-up, then tighten the setscrew from below, making sure the wall end of the spout is flush against the wall. Do not overtighten the setscrew.

How to Install a Threaded Spout

1

If you see no setscrew or slot on the underside of the spout, it is attached to a threaded nipple. Unscrew the tub spout by inserting a heavy-duty flat screwdriver into the spout opening and spinning it counterclockwise.

Option: Grip the spout with a padded pipe wrench or channel-type pliers. Buy a compatible replacement spout at a home center or hardware store.

2

Copper nipple with threaded adapter

Wrap several courses of Teflon tape clockwise onto the pipe threads of the nipple. Using extra Teflon tape on the threads creates resistance if the spout tip points past six o'clock when tight.

3

Twist the new spout onto the nipple until it is flush against the wall and the spout is oriented properly. If the spout falls short of six o'clock, you may protect the finish of the spout with tape and twist it a little beyond hand tight with your channel-type pliers—but don't overdo it; the fitting can crack.

Adding a Shower to a Bathtub

Your dream bath remodel may include adding a shower to your old built-in bathtub—finally you will be able to enjoy the ease of waking up and hopping into a steamy shower. All you need to do is remove the spout and replace it with one equipped with an adapter hose outlet to which you can screw a flexible shower hose. Then you need to install a mounting bracket so you can hang the showerhead and free your hands. Add a telescoping shower curtain rod and a shower curtain and your new shower stall is ready for duty.

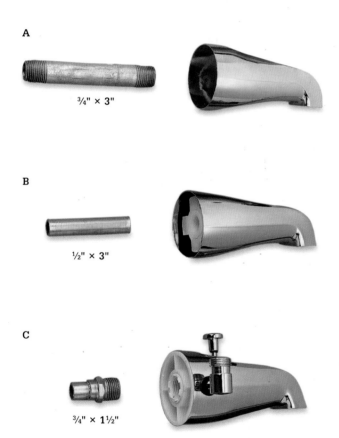

A

¾" × 3"

B

½" × 3"

C

¾" × 1½"

The appearance of the spout gives good clues as to which kind of nipple it is connected to. A) A spout with no diverter is probably connected to a 3"-long threaded nipple. To install a diverter spout you'll need to replace the 3" threaded nipple with a shorter threaded nipple that sticks out no more than ½" from the wall—not too big of a job. B) If the spout has a small setscrew in a slot on the underside, it is probably attached with a slip fitting to a ½" copper supply nipple. Unless you are able to solder a new transition fitting onto the old pipe after cutting it, call a plumber to install the new spout here. C) Spouts with outlets for shower adapters require a short threaded nipple (or comparable union) that sticks out from the wall no more than ¾".

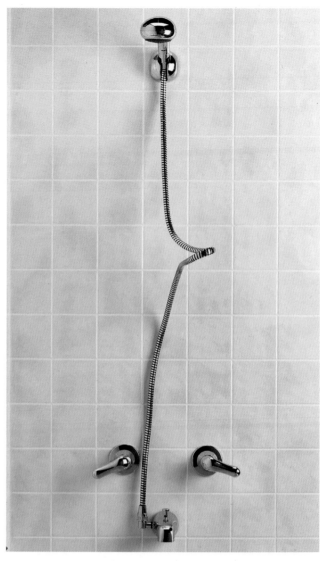

Converting a plain bathtub into a tub/shower is a relatively easy task when you use a flexible shower adapter that fits onto a special replacement tub spout.

Tools & Materials ▸

Pipe wrench	Brass nipple
Drill	Spout with diverter
Glass and tile	outlet
drill bit	Hand-held
Measuring tape	mountable
Screwdriver	showerhead
Marker	with flexible hose
Teflon tape	Mounting hardware

1

Make sure the old spout is not held in place with a setscrew (see previous page) and then remove it by wrapping it with a cloth and turning the spout with channel-type pliers or a pipe wrench.

2

If you have a long iron or brass nipple like this, you need to replace it with a short one. Threaded nipples have threads at each end, so you can usually unscrew the old ones. Mark the nipple at the face of the wall and write "front" on your side. Unscrew it counterclockwise with a pipe wrench. Get a threaded brass nipple of the same diameter that is about ½" longer than the distance from the back of your old nipple to your line.

3

Wrap six layers of Teflon tape clockwise on the nipple and thread into the wall. Thread the reducing bushing onto the nipple. Thread the adapter spout on. Tighten farther with a screwdriver or dowel to orient the spout correctly.

4

Attach a flexible shower hose to the adapter hose outlet. Tighten with an adjustable wrench.

5

Determine the location of the showerhead bracket. Use the hose length as a guide, and make sure the showerhead can be lifted off the bracket with ease.

6

Mark hole locations. Use a glass-and-tile drill bit for your electric drill in the size recommended by the shower bracket manufacturer. Put on eye protection and drill holes in the ceramic tile on your marks. Insert anchors into the holes and tap in place with a wooden or rubber mallet. Fasten the showerhead holder to the wall using a Phillips screwdriver and the mounting screws.

Sinks & Vanities

Sinks and vanities provide focal points for any bathroom, and are a chance to make a big splash in the room's design with a modest investment in time, money, or effort. You can choose from many different materials and styles, but your decision will most likely be driven first and foremost by issues of practicality.

If storage is a key requirement, pedestal, console, and most wall-mounted sinks will be crossed off the list before you begin shopping. That doesn't mean you'll lack for options; vanities come in designs and finishes to match any bathroom décor. You can select a traditional natural wood unit with abundant undersink storage, or go for a more contemporary look with a wall-hung unit featuring a drawer.

Sinks involve even more decision-making. Vessel sinks are a unique look, while more traditional under-mount or drop-in sinks are simpler to install and provide a more traditional appearance. The counter under (or around, or part of) the sink is yet another choice you'll make—one that should work with the vanity and other fixtures in the room.

These days, though, the conversation about sinks and vanities inevitably turns to Aging-in-Place and Universal Design options. That's why we've included a wall-mounted sink project (see page 156) and a hands-free faucet installation (page 152), both of which provide convenience and are ADA compliant.

In this chapter:

- Pedestal & Console Sinks
- Vessel Sinks
- Traditional Vanity
- Lavatory Faucets
- Wall-Mount Faucets
- Lavatory Drains

Pedestal & Console Sinks

Pedestal and console sinks move in and out of popularity more frequently than other types, but even during the times that they aren't particularly trendy they still find a place in many remodels because of their classic and adaptable styling. You'll find them most frequently in small half baths or powder rooms, where their modest footprints make them space-efficient options. Designers are also increasingly using these styles as his-and-her sinks for bathrooms in which the sinks are meant to visually dominate the design.

The primary drawback to pedestal sinks is that they don't offer any storage. Their chief practical benefit is that they conceal plumbing some homeowners would prefer to keep out of sight. Console sinks, with their two front legs and modest apron, offer some space underneath for rolling shelf units or a towel basket.

Pedestal sinks are mounted in one of two ways. Most inexpensive models are hung in much the same way as wall-mounted sinks. The pedestal is actually installed after the sink is hung and its purpose is purely decorative. But other, higher-end pedestal sinks have structural pedestals that bear the weight of the sink. All console sinks are mounted to the wall, although the front legs offer additional support and resistance to users leaning on the front of the sink.

Tools & Materials ▸

Pedestal sink	Basin wrench
2 × 4 lumber	Silicone caulk
Water-resistant drywall	Lag screws
Ratchet wrench	Studfinder

A console bathroom sink is a wall-mounted lavatory with two front legs that provide back-up support. Many have a narrow apron to conceal the drain trap.

A pedestal sink typically is hung on the wall. The primary function of the pedestal is to conceal plumbing and provide visual appeal.

How to Install a Pedestal Sink

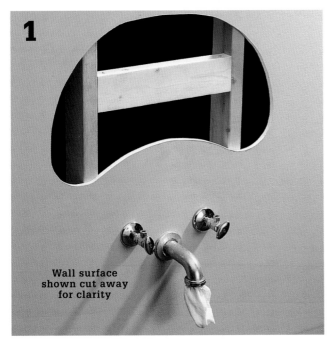

Install 2 × 4 blocking between the wall studs, behind the planned sink location. Cover the wall with water-resistant drywall.

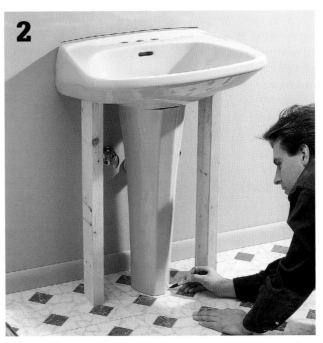

Set the basin and pedestal in position and brace it with 2 × 4s. Outline the top of the basin on the wall, and mark the base of the pedestal on the floor. Mark reference points on the wall and floor through the mounting holes found on the back of the sink and the bottom of the pedestal.

Set aside the basin and pedestal. Drill pilot holes in the wall and floor at the reference points, then reposition the pedestal. Anchor the pedestal to the floor with lag screws.

Attach the faucet, then set the sink on the pedestal. Align the holes in the back of the sink with the pilot holes drilled in the wall, then drive lag screws and washers into the wall brace using a ratchet wrench. Do not overtighten the screws.

Hook up the drain and supply fittings. Caulk between the back of the sink and the wall when installation is finished.

Wall-Mounted Sinks

There are many benefits to a wall-mounted sink that, depending on your situation and needs, will offset the inherent lack of storage space. In contrast to the footprint of a traditional vanity-mounted sink, wall-mounted units can save space on the sides and in front of the fixture. More importantly, they are an essential addition to a Universal Design bathroom where wheelchair accessibility is a key consideration. It's why these particular fixtures are sometimes called "roll-under" sinks.

All that practicality aside, early models at the lower end of the price spectrum were somewhat unattractive because their designs simply left the drain tailpiece, trap, and supply shut-off valves in plain sight. But there's no need for you to settle for a less-than-handsome wall-mounted sink. Manufacturers have developed two solutions to the problem of exposed plumbing. Some are designed with a bowl that conceals supply line shut-offs, replacing the trap with sleekly designed tailpieces and squared off trap bends. The other solution, and one more widely available, is a wall-mounted pedestal that covers the plumbing. Sinks with this feature are sometimes called "semi-pedestal."

We've opted to illustrate the installation of just such a sink in the instructions that follow. Keep in mind that different manufacturers sometimes use very different mounting procedures. In any case, the idea remains the same: strongly secure the sink to studs or blocking, so that it is completely stable and will not fall.

The most involved part of the installation process is usually rerouting water supply and drain lines as necessary. You should hire a licensed plumber for this if you're not comfortable with the work. Once the plumbing is in place, the installation is quick and easy.

Tools & Materials ▸

Carpenter's level	Phillips screwdriver
Adjustable wrenches	Standard screwdriver
Pipe wrench	Jigsaw
Channel-type pliers	Basin wrench
Cordless power drill	Tape measure
and bits	Hacksaw
Tubing cutting	2 × 8 lumber

Although a wall-mounted sink offers many benefits—accessibility to wheelchair users among them—there's no need to sacrifice chic style for that functionality. Photo courtesy of American Standard. (See resources, page 251)

How to Install a Wall-Mounted Sink

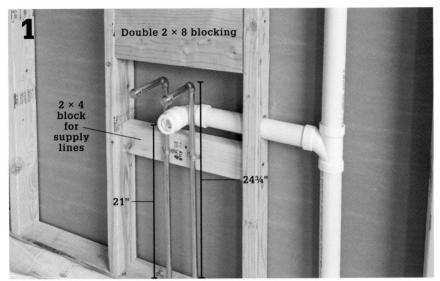

1

Double 2 × 8 blocking

2 × 4 block for supply lines

24¾"

21"

Remove the existing sink if any.
Remove wall coverings as necessary to install blocking for mounting the sink. Reroute water supply and drain lines as necessary, according to the sink manufacturer's directions. The sink in this project required the centerpoints of the waste pipe be 21", and the supply lines 24¾" up from the finished floor. If unsure of your plumbing skills or code requirements, hire a professional plumber for this part of the project. Install blocking between the studs for attaching the mounting bracket for the sink. A doubled 2 × 8 is installed here. Have your plumbing inspected, if required by your municipality, before you install the drywall and finished wall surface.

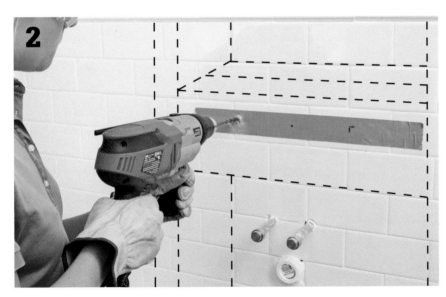

2

Drill guide holes for the mounting bolts if your sink is a direct-mount model, as this one is. Some wall-hung sinks are hung from a mounting bracket. The bolts used to hang this sink are threaded like lag screws on one end, with a bolt end that projects from the wall. The guide holes should be spaced exactly as the manufacturer specifies so they align with the mounting holes in the back mounting flange on the sink. *Tip: Protect tile surfaces with masking tape in the drilling areas to avoid chip-out.*

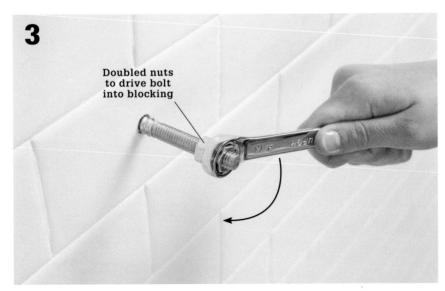

3

Doubled nuts to drive bolt into blocking

Drive the threaded mounting bolts (screw end first) into the guide holes. There should be pilot holes (smaller than the guide holes) driven into the blocking. To drive this hardware, spin a pair of nuts onto the bolt end and turn the bolt closest to you with a wrench. Drive the mounting bolt until the end is projecting out from the wall by a little more than 1½". Remove the nuts. Install the pop-up drain in the sink , and then slide the sink over the ends of the mounting bolts so the mounting flange is flush against the wall. You'll want help for this. Thread the washers and nuts onto the ends of the mounting bolts and hand-tighten. Check to make sure the sink is level and then tighten the nuts with a socket or wrench, reaching up into the void between the basin and the flange. Don't overtighten—you could crack the sink flange.

(continued)

4

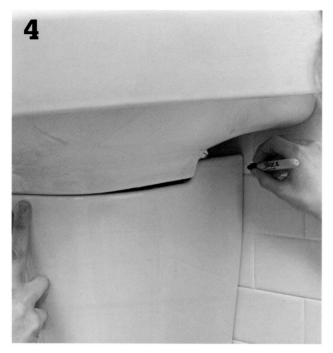

Have a helper hold the sink pedestal (in this model, a half-pedestal) in position against the underside of the sink. Mark the edges of the pedestal on the wall covering as reference for installing the pedestal-mounting hardware. Remove the pedestal.

5

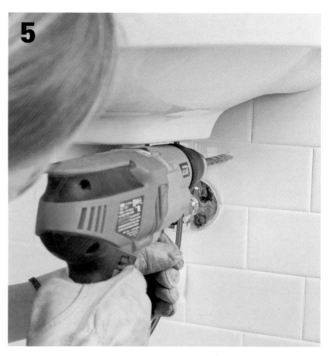

Remove the pedestal and drill the pilot holes for the pedestal-mounting bolts, which work much in the same way as the sink-mounting bolts. Drill guide and pilot holes then drive the mounting bolts, leaving about 1¼" of the bolt end exposed.

6

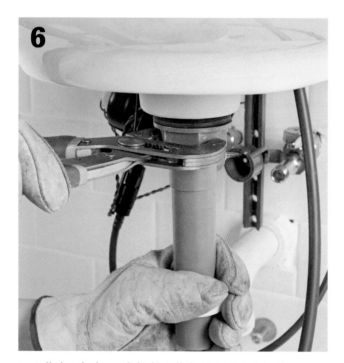

Install the drain and drain tailpiece on the sink. Also mount the faucet body to the sink deck if you have not done so already. Also attach the drain trap arm to the drain stub out in the wall and attach shutoff valves to the drain supply lines. You'll find instructions for doing all of these jobs elsewhere in this book.

7

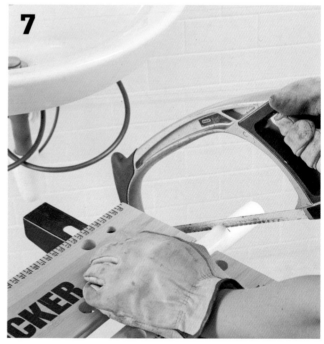

Complete the drain connection by installing a P-trap assembly that connects the tail piece and the trap arm. Also connect the drain pop-up rod that projects out of the tailpiece to the pop-up plunger mechanism you've already installed.

8

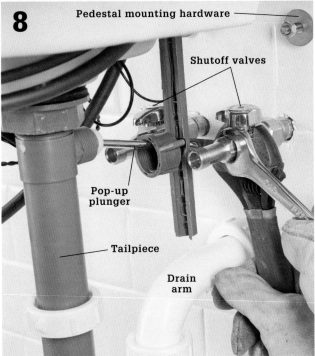

Pedestal mounting hardware

Shutoff valves

Pop-up plunger

Tailpiece

Drain arm

Make sure the shutoff valve fittings are tight and oriented correctly, and then hook up the faucet supply risers to the shutoff valves. Turn on the water supply and test.

Leak Finder ▶

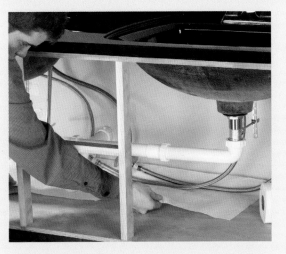

To quickly and easily find an undersink leak, lay bright white paper or paper towels under the pipes and drain connections. Open the water supply valves and run water in the sinks. It should be clear exactly where the water dripped from by the location of the drip on the paper.

9

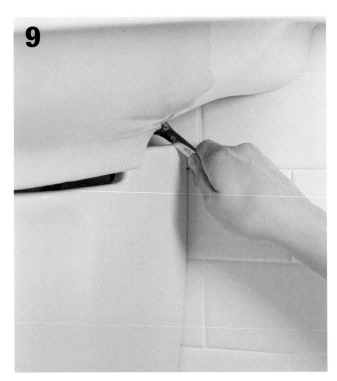

Slide the pedestal into place on the mounting studs. Working through the access space under the sink, use a wrench to tighten the mounting nut over the washer on the stud. Carefully tighten the nut until the pedestal is held securely in place. Be careful not to overtighten the nut.

10

Attach the towel bar to the sink by first pushing the well nuts into the holes on the underside of the sink rim. Set the bar in place, and screw in the attachment screws on both sides, just until snug.

Vessel Sinks

The vessel sink harkens back to the days of washstands and washbowls. Whether it's round, square, or oval, shallow or deep, the vessel sink offers great opportunity for creativity and proudly displays its style. Vessel sinks are a perfect choice for a powder room, where they will have high visibility.

Most vessel sinks can be installed on any flat surface—from a granite countertop to a wall-mounted vanity to an antique dresser. Some sinks are designed to contact the mounting surface only at the drain flange. Others are made to be partially embedded in the surface. Take care to follow the manufacturer's instructions for cutting holes for sinks and faucets.

A beautiful vessel sink demands an equally attractive faucet. Select a tall spout mounted on the countertop or vanity top or a wall-mounted spout to accommodate the height of the vessel. To minimize splashing, spouts should direct flow to the center of the vessel, not down the side. Make sure your faucet is compatible with your vessel choice. Look for a centerset or single-handle model if you'll be custom drilling the countertop—you only need to drill one faucet hole.

Tools & Materials ▶

Pliers	Pop-up drain
Wrench	P-trap and drain kit
Vanity or countertop	Faucet
Vessel sink	

Vessel sinks are available in countless styles of materials, shapes, and sizes. Their one commonality is that they all need to be installed on a flat surface.

Vessel Sink Options

This glass vessel sink embedded in a "floating" glass countertop is a stunning contrast to the strong and attractive wood frame anchoring it to the wall.

Vessel sinks come in many forms, including the dramatic sloped version here. The modern style fits perfectly with a custom glass counter and sophisticated glass wall tiles.

Vessel sinks don't have to be shaped like a bowl. This rectangular tray sink is a cool alternative to a more common bowl shape and accents the chic, light wood vanity and cabinets in the room.

Vitreous china with a glazed enamel finish is an economical and durable choice for a vessel sink (although it is less durable than stone). Because of the flexibility of both the material and the glaze, the design options are virtually unlimited with vitreous china.

How to Install a Vessel Sink

1

Secure the vanity cabinet or other countertop that you'll be using to mount the vessel sink.

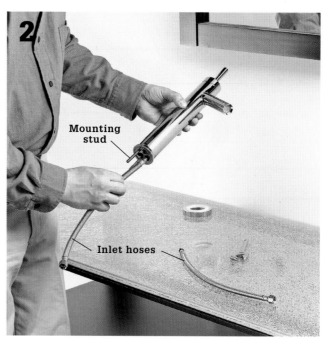

2

Mounting stud

Inlet hoses

Begin hooking up the faucet. Insert the brass mounting stud into the threaded hole in the faucet base with the slotted end facing out. Hand tighten, and then use a slotted screwdriver to tighten another half turn. Insert the inlet hoses into the faucet body and hand tighten. Use an adjustable wrench to tighten another half turn. Do not overtighten.

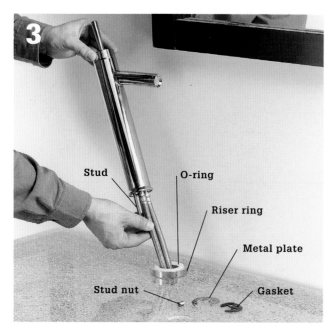

3

Stud   O-ring

Riser ring

Metal plate

Stud nut   Gasket

Place the O-ring on top of the riser ring over the faucet cutout in the countertop. From underneath, slide the rubber gasket and the metal plate over the mounting stud. Thread the mounting stud nut onto the mounting stud and hand tighten. Use an adjustable wrench to tighten another half turn.

4

To install the sink and pop-up drain, first place the small metal ring between two O-rings and place over the drain cutout.

Place the vessel bowl on top of the O-rings. In this installation, the vessel is not bonded to the countertop.

Put the small rubber gasket over the drain hole in the vessel. From the top, push the pop-up assembly through the drain hole.

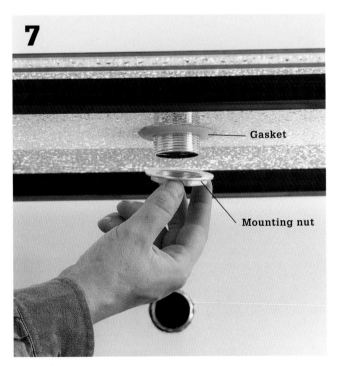

From underneath, push the large rubber gasket onto the threaded portion of the pop-up assembly. Thread the nut onto the pop-up assembly and tighten. Use an adjustable wrench or basin wrench to tighten an additional half turn. Thread the tailpiece onto the pop-up assembly.

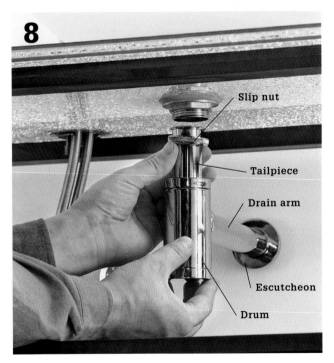

Install the drum trap. Loosen the rings on the top and outlet of the drum trap. Slide the drum trap top hole over the tailpiece. Slide the drain arm into the side outlet, with the flat side of the rubber gasket facing away from the trap. Insert the drain arm into the wall outlet. Hand tighten the rings.

Traditional Vanity

Simple vanity bases are stages upon which much of the drama in a bathroom can play out. Because there are now so many sink and counter styles and materials, and ways of incorporating the two, a stable base that can be attractive in its own right is more important than ever.

Although vanity cabinet styles vary, the basic structure—such as incorporating a toe kick—is common to the majority of them. The process outlined here covers the basic way that most vanities are secured in place to provide ample storage and sturdy foundation for sinks and countertops.

Tools & Materials ▸

Pencil
Carpenter's level
Screwdriver
Basin wrench
Cardboard
Masking tape
Plumber's putty

Lag screws
Tub & tile caulk
Studfinder
4-ft. level
Shims
3" drywall screws
Drill

A simple, traditional, white vanity base serves a supporting role for a stunning recycled-glass countertop.

How to Install a Vanity Cabinet

1

Measure and mark the top edge of the vanity cabinet on the wall, then use a 4-ft. level to mark a level line at the cabinet height mark. Use an electronic stud finder to locate the framing members, then mark the stud locations along the line.

2

Slide the vanity into position so that the back rail of the cabinet can later be fastened to studs at both corners and in the center. The back of the cabinet should also be flush against the wall. (If the wall surface is uneven, position the vanity so it contacts the wall in at least one spot, and the back cabinet rail is parallel with the wall.)

3

Using a 4-ft. level as a guide, shim below the vanity cabinet until the unit is level.

Variation: To install two or more cabinets, set the cabinets in position against the wall, and align the cabinet fronts. If one cabinet is higher than the other, shim under the lower cabinet until the two are even. Clamp the cabinet faces together, then drill countersunk pilot holes spaced 12" apart through the face frames so they go at least halfway into the face frame of the second cabinet. Drive wood screws through the pilot holes to join the cabinets together.

4

5

At the stud locations marked on the wall, drive 3" drywall screws through the rail on the cabinet back and into the framing members. The screws should be driven at both corners and in the center of the back rail.

Run a bead of caulk along small gaps between the vanity and wall, and between the vanity and floor. For larger gaps, use quarter-round molding between the vanity and wall. Between the vanity and floor, install the same baseboard material used to cover the gap between the wall and floor.

Plumbing a Double-Bowl Vanity

Side-by-side sinks are a bathroom luxury, especially for busy couples (which accounts for why they are called "his-and-her" sinks) or busy bathrooms. Although the basics of installing a vanity for a double sink are structurally the same as a single-bowl vanity, the plumbing requires modification to accommodate the extra fixture.

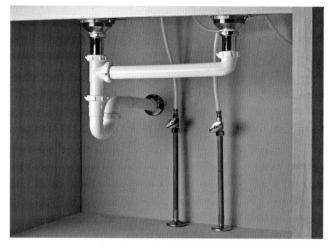

Double-bowl vanities have drain plumbing that's very similar to double-bowl kitchen sinks. In most cases, the drain tailpieces are connected beneath one of the tailpieces at a continuous waste T. The drainline from the second bowl must slope downward toward the T. From the T, the drain should have a trap (usually a P-Trap) that connects to the trap arm coming out of the wall.

Tools & Materials ▸

Carpenter's level
Screwdrivers
Drill and bits
Basin wrench
Stud finder
Adjustable wrench
Hacksaw

Silicone caulk
Dual outlet valves
Braided steel
  supply lines
P-trap
PVC connections
Plumber's putty

How to Plumb a Double Sink

1

Shut off the supply valves located under the sink. Disconnect and remove the supply lines connecting the faucet to the valves. Loosen the P-trap nuts at both ends and remove the P-trap.

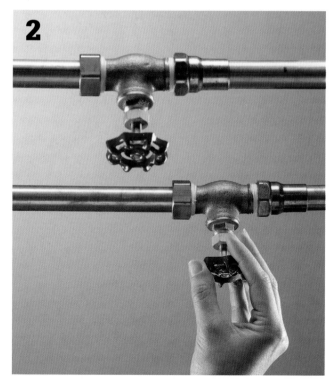

2

Remove the existing countertop and vanity. Turn off the house water supply at the main shut-off valve. Drain the remaining water by opening the faucet at the lowest point in the house. Use a hacksaw to remove existing undersink shut-off valves.

Slide the new dual-outlet valve onto the hot water supply line, pass the nut and compression washer over the pipe, and tighten with a wrench. Install the dual-outlet valve on the cold supply line in the same way.

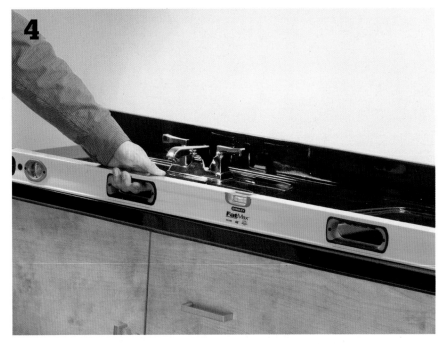

Secure the new vanity in place by screwing it to the wall. Lay a bead of caulk along the underside and back edge of the countertop, where it will contact the vanity and wall. Set the countertop in place and check it for level. If your sinks are not integral, install them according to the type of sink you're using.

Seat the faucets for the double sinks as you would for a single sink, by applying a bead of putty on the underside of the bases (unless they are to be used with gaskets instead of putty). Secure them in place by tightening the locking nuts on the underside of the faucets.

Connect a new PVC P-trap to the undersink drain pipe, and attach a T-connector to the trap. Extend PVC connections to the drain assemblies of both sinks.

Connect the pop-up stopper linkage. Connect the cold water supply lines to the appropriate faucet tailpieces and repeat with the hot water supply lines. Turn on the main water supply, remove the faucet aerator, and run the water in the sinks. Check for leaks and replace the aerator.

Lavatory Faucets

Bathroom faucets come in four basic mounting styles: centerset, single hole, wall mounted, and widespread. The type you choose depends largely on the sink or faucet body you are using—the new faucet may need to match the existing fixture. But in any case, the range of designs available in all mounting styles is astounding.

Widespread faucets have a clean, sophisticated look. They come in three pieces instead of one: a hot tap, a cold tap, and a spout. Each piece is mounted separately in its own hole in the sink. The hot and cold taps (valves) are connected to the spout with reinforced flexible hoses. If your lavatory doesn't have a predrilled flange, the great advantage to the widespread configuration is that you gain flexibility in locating your spout and handles (probably a bigger advantage for tubs than for lavatories). Even models made for bathroom lavatories, like the one you see here, offer many creative configuration options.

Single-body and centerset faucets are designed to fit into standard hole configurations. Make sure you know your sink's dimensions before buying the faucet: the most important dimension is the hole spread: 4 inches on center and 8 inches on center are most common.

An increasingly popular subset of single-hole faucets are touch faucets or motion-sensing faucets, such as the one shown here. Easy to install, these are also less challenging for anyone with motor-skill difficulties or serious disabilities to use.

Widespread faucets allow you to customize the locations and orientation of the faucets and spout in your sink deck.

Single-body faucets are faster and easier to install and are extremely reliable.

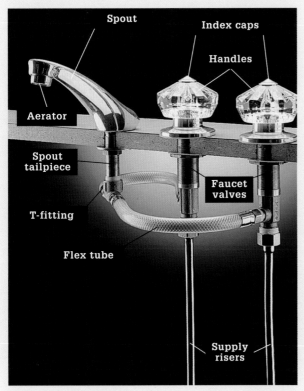

Widespread faucets come in three pieces, a spout and two valves. Supply risers carry hot and cold water to the valves, which are turned to regulate the amount of water going to the spout, where the water is mixed. Water travels from the valves to the spout through flex tubes, which in turn attach to the spout tailpiece via a T-fitting. Three-piece faucets designed to work with a pop-up stopper have a clevis and a lift rod. The handles attach with handle screws that are covered with index caps. An aerator is screwed on the faucet spout after debris is flushed from the faucet.

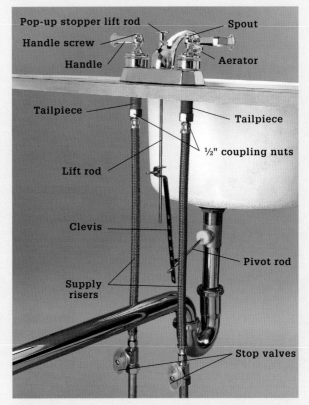

The tailpieces of a standard deck-mounted, one-piece bathroom sink faucet are 4" apart on center. As long as the two outside holes in the back of your sink measure 4" from center to center, and you have a middle hole for a pop-up stopper, you can put in any standard one-piece bathroom faucet with a pop-up stopper. The faucet is secured to the sink with mounting nuts that screw onto the tailpieces from below. Also get two flexible stainless steel supply risers for sinks, long enough to replace the old tubes. These typically attach to the stop valves with ⅜" compression-sized coupling nuts and to the faucet with standard faucet coupling nuts. But take your old tubes and the old compression nuts from the stop valves to the store to ensure a match. The clevis, lift rod, and pivot rod are parts of the pop-up stopper assembly. The handles attach with handle screws that are covered with index caps.

How to Install a Lavatory Faucet

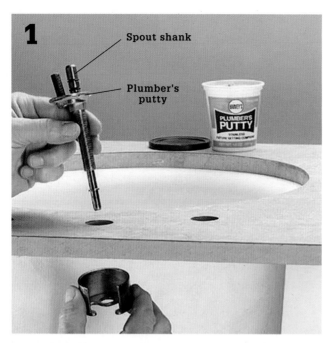

1

Spout shank

Plumber's putty

PLUMBER'S PUTTY

Insert the shank of the faucet spout through one of the holes in the sink deck (usually the center hole but you can offset it in one of the end holes if you prefer). If the faucet is not equipped with seals or O-rings for the spout and handles, pack plumber's putty on the undersides before inserting the valves into the deck. *Note: If you are installing the widespread faucet in a new sink deck, drill three holes of the size suggested by the faucet manufacturer.*

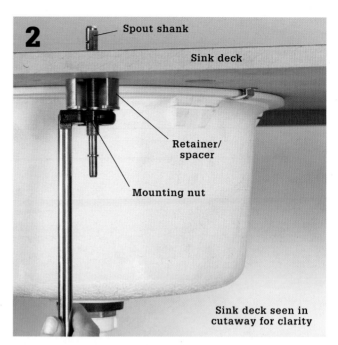

2

Spout shank

Sink deck

Retainer/ spacer

Mounting nut

Sink deck seen in cutaway for clarity

In addition to mounting nuts, many spout valves for widespread faucets have an open retainer fitting that goes between the underside of the deck and the mounting nut. Others have only a mounting nut. In either case, tighten the mounting nut with pliers or a basin wrench to secure the spout valve. You may need a helper to keep the spout centered and facing forward.

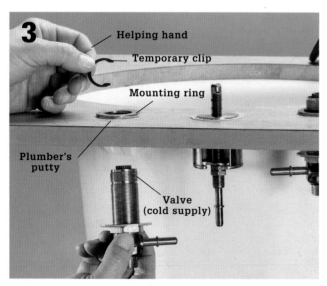

3

Helping hand

Temporary clip

Mounting ring

Plumber's putty

Valve (cold supply)

Mount the valves to the deck using whichever method the manufacturer specifies (it varies quite a bit). In the model seen here, a mounting ring is positioned over the deck hole (with plumber's putty seal) and the valve is inserted from below. A clip snaps onto the valve from above to hold it in place temporarily (you'll want a helper for this).

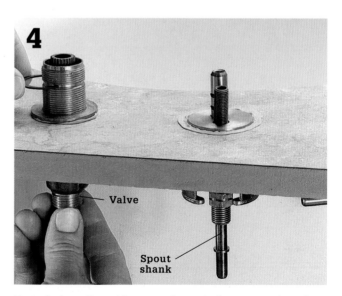

4

Valve

Spout shank

From below, thread the mounting nuts that secure the valves to the sink deck. Make sure the cold water valve (usually has a blue cartridge inside) is in the right hole (from the front) and the hot water valve (red cartridge) is in the left hole. Install both valves.

5

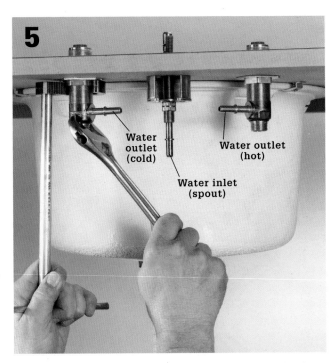

Water outlet (cold)

Water outlet (hot)

Water inlet (spout)

Once you've started the nut on the threaded valve shank, secure the valve with a basin wrench squeezing the lugs where the valve fits against the deck. Use an adjustable wrench to finish tightening the lock nut onto the valve. The valves should be oriented so the water outlets are aimed at the inlet on the spout shank.

6

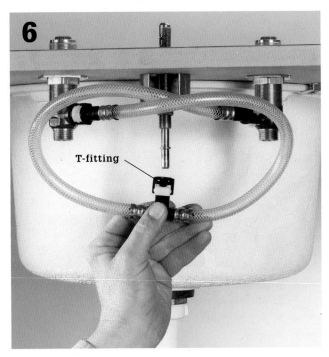

T-fitting

Attach the flexible supply tubes (supplied with the faucet) to the water outlets on the valves. Some twist onto the outlets, but others (like the ones above) click into place. The supply hoses meet in a T-fitting that is attached to the water inlet on the spout.

7

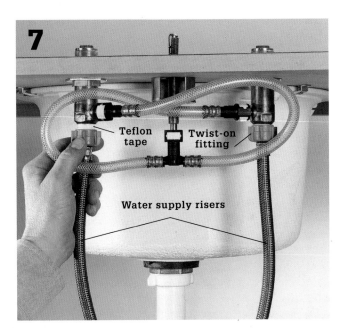

Teflon tape

Twist-on fitting

Water supply risers

Attach flexible braided metal supply risers to the water stop valves and then attach the tubes to the inlet port on each valve (usually with Teflon tape and a twist-on fitting at the valve end of the supply riser).

8

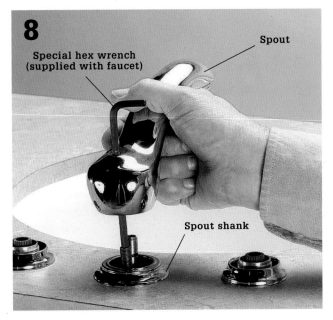

Special hex wrench (supplied with faucet)

Spout

Spout shank

Attach the spout. The model shown here comes with a special hex wrench that is threaded through the hole in the spout where the lift rod for the pop-up drain will be located. Once the spout is seated cleanly on the spout shank you tighten the hex wrench to secure the spout. Different faucets will use other methods to secure the spout to the shank.

(continued)

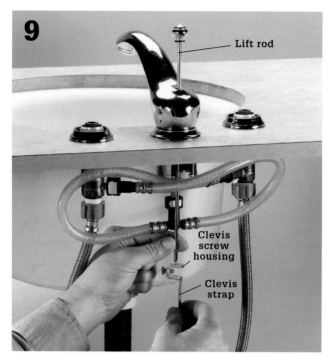

9 Lift rod

Clevis screw housing

Clevis strap

If your sink did not have a pop-up stopper, you'll need to replace the sink drain tailpiece with a pop-up stopper body (often supplied with the faucet). Insert the lift rod through the hole in the back of the spout and, from below, thread the pivot rod through the housing for the clevis screw.

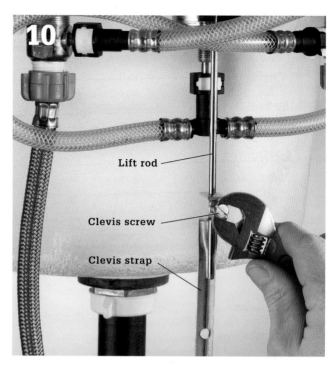

10 Lift rod

Clevis screw

Clevis strap

Attach the clevis strap to the pivot rod that enters the pop-up drain body and adjust the position of the strap so it raises and lowers properly when the lift rod is pulled up. Tighten the clevis screw at this point. It's hard to fit a screwdriver in here, so you may need to use a wrench or pliers.

11

Attach the faucet handles to the valves using whichever method is required by the faucet manufacturer. Most faucets are designed with registration methods to ensure that the handles are symmetrical and oriented in an ergonomic way once you secure them to the valves.

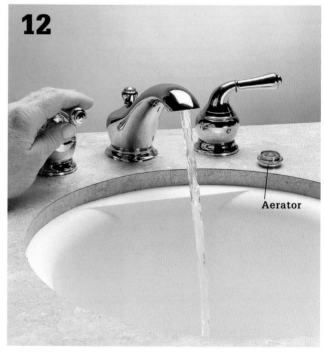

12

Aerator

Remove the faucet aerator, turn on the water supply, and test the faucet so any debris in the lines can clear the spout. Check the supply and drain connections under the sink for leaks, then replace the aerator.

Variation: Centerset Faucets

1

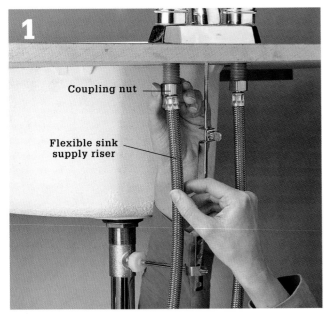

Coupling nut

Flexible sink
supply riser

Insert the faucet tailpieces through the holes in the sink. From below, thread washers and mounting nuts over the tailpieces, then tighten the mounting nuts with a basin wrench until snug. Put a dab of pipe joint compound on the threads of the stop valves and thread the metal nuts of the flexible supply risers to these. Wrench tighten about a half turn past hand tight. Overtightening these nuts will strip the threads. Now tighten the coupling nuts to the faucet tailpieces with a basin wrench.

2

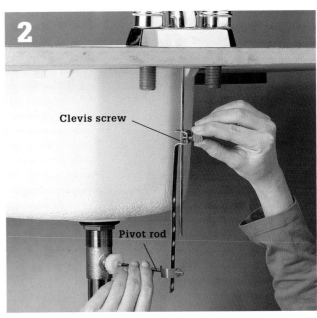

Clevis screw

Pivot rod

Slide the lift rod of the new faucet into its hole behind the spout. Thread it into the clevis past the clevis screw. Push the pivot rod all the way down so the stopper is open. With the lift rod also all the way down, tighten the clevis to the lift rod.

3

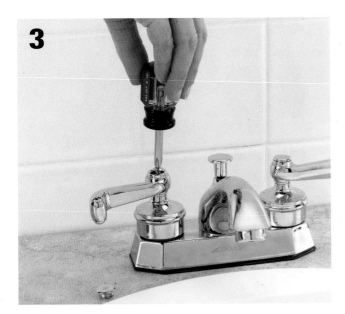

Install the handles on the faucet according to the manufacturer's directions. Cover each handle screw with the appropriate cap—"H" or "C".

4

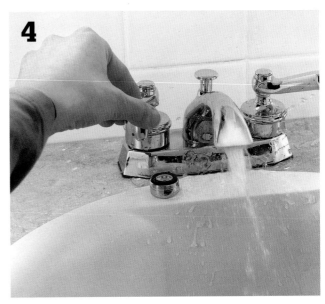

Unscrew the aerator from the end of the spout. Turn the hot and cold water taps on full. Turn the water back on at the stop valves and flush out the faucet for a couple of minutes before turning off the water at the faucet. Check the riser connections for drips. Tighten a compression nut only until the drip stops. Replace the aerator.

Hands-Free Bathroom Faucets

If you've ever washed your hands in an airport bathroom, chances are you've already come across a hands-free faucet. Developed to conserve water and stop the spread of disease, these faucets have quickly become ubiquitous in commercial facilities across the country and around the world.

But now homeowners can enjoy the benefits of hands-free faucets in their own bathrooms. Although not as widely available as standard faucets, different hands-free units are beginning to appear in the aisles of large home centers and hardware stores nationwide. These feature varying technologies depending on the manufacturer.

The most common type of commercial hands-free bathroom faucet relies on an infrared motion sensor, much like those in home security systems. When something solid passes within the sensor's range, the faucet turns on for a predetermined period of time. Home units operate a little differently. They include motion sensing and "touch-on, touch-off" units. The model we selected for this installation project uses an electrical field sensor that reacts to the stored charge in every human body, called *capacitance*. Whether motion- or touch-activated, these home faucets rely on an electrical field created by a solenoid connected to the faucet body. When a human hand disrupts the electrical field, the faucet turns on or off. Touch faucets operate the same, but the faucet body itself is the electrical field.

For most of these types of faucets, water temperature and flow rate are set manually before the faucet is "programmed." Then it's a case of tapping the faucet body or waving a hand near it to start or stop the flow.

Although these faucets are pricier than standard manual models, they represent a leap forward for people with motor-skill difficulties, or for preventing disease spread between family members using a busy bathroom in a crowded house. The good news is that they are not much more challenging to install than a standard faucet—with the exception of units that are hardwired into the home's electrical system. Hardwired units should be installed by a licensed professional.

Tools & Materials ▸

Faucet and hardware
Adjustable wrenches
Channel-type pliers
Teflon tape
Flashlight

A touch-on, touch-off faucet such as this can save water, make life easier for children and physically challenged users, and they come in a nice selection of style and finish options.

How to Install a Hands-Free Faucet

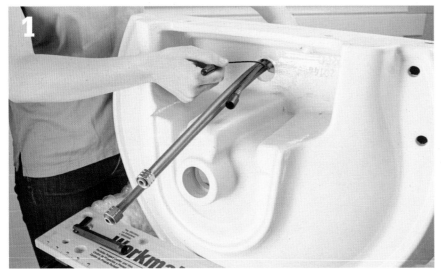

Check the parts in the box against the instruction sheet part list. Remove the center from the base gasket as necessary and thread the base's LED wire through the hole in the gasket. Seat the gasket into the groove in the insulator base and ensure that is snug and level. *Note: If your vanity deck has multiple holes, you'll need to use the supplied escutcheon plate. Run the LED wire through the escutcheon hole and seat the insulator base on top of the escutcheon (make sure the LED light is facing forward).*

Slide the mounting bracket into place under the sink, on the mounting post. Be sure that the LED wire and supply lines are not crimped by the bracket. The mounting bracket needs to be oriented correctly; check the manufacturer's instructions to ensure it's situated in the right way, and secured with the metal side down.

Ensure the LED wire is not crimped and thread the mounting post nut on the mounting post. Hand tighten. Check again that the faucet body is positioned correctly on the top of the sink and the LED light is facing forward. Tighten the mounting nut with a wrench, or with the tool supplied by the manufacturer, as shown here.

(continued)

4

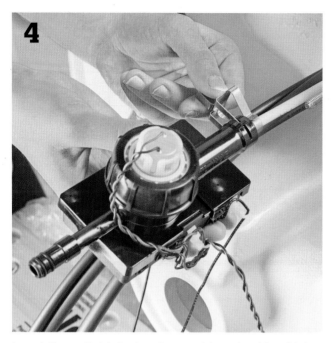

Insert the outlet tube into the top of the solenoid until it is snugly attached. Secure the tube in place with the metal clip provided. These clips can often be attached more than one way, so check the instructions to make sure you've installed the clip correctly. Then lightly pull on the solenoid to ensure the tube is firmly attached and won't come free under pressure.

5

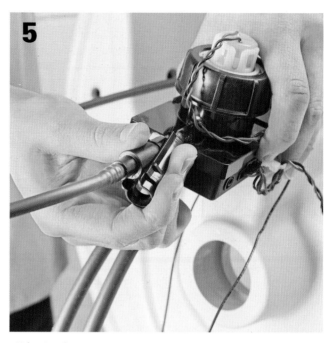

Slide the feeder hose into the bottom of the solenoid until it is snug. Snap the attachment clip in place to secure the hose, and again pull gently on the hose to make sure the clip is secure.

6

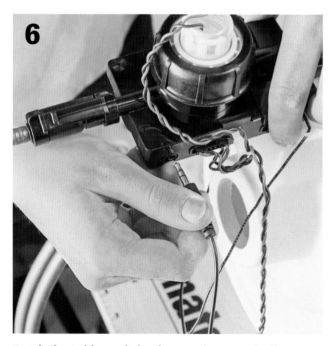

Touch the cold supply knob or another ground with your hand to dissipate any residual static charge. Remove the protective cap or endpiece from the end of the LED wire hanging from the faucet. Plug the prong of the wire into the hole in the solenoid. Make sure it is all the way in (on this model, you push until you hear a click).

7

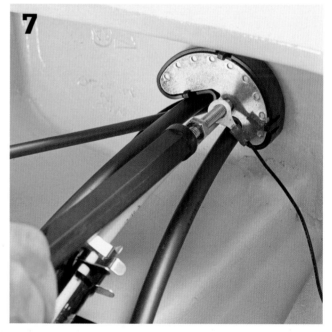

Slide the solenoid ground wire onto the mounting post and secure it in place with a nut. Tighten the nut with a wrench, ensuring that the wires don't twist together. Put the batteries in the battery box and then connect the wire from the solenoid to the connection on the battery box. Secure the battery box to the cabinet floor, wall, or underside of the sink according to the manufacturer's directions, and the type of vanity you have.

Hook up and test the faucet ▸

Connect the water lines for your hands-free faucet as you would with any faucet, using the supplied ferrules and check valves in place of the existing hardware on the stops. Insert the new ferrule and screw the check valve in place, hand tight. Then tighten the nut just one turn with a wrench. Attach the cold and hot lines to the proper check valves on the cold and hot stops—they must be connected to the appropriate stop (the ends of the faucet body supply lines will usually be marked as they are in this case—either with a color or other designation to signify which stop the supply line goes to). Attach the cold supply line to the check valve first, then repeat with the hot supply line. Snug to hand tight and then use a wrench to tighten one full turn more. Loop supply lines rather than cutting them.

Turn the faucet handle to the closed position and remove the aerator (use the manufacturers supplied tool for this). Turn on both water supplies. Turn on the water for about 1 minute. Turn off the water and reinstall the aerator. Check the solenoid, stops, and faucet for leaks.

To set and test the touch feature, turn the handle on and leave it in the position that gives you the preferred temperature and flow rate. Touch the faucet body firmly and deliberately to turn the flow off. And then try tapping to turn it on. Tap at different areas around the body to turn the faucet on and off. If you've installed a motion-sensor faucet, you should be able to perform these functions just by moving your hand close to the faucet.

Wall-Mount Faucets

A wall-mounted faucet adds a touch of elegance to your bathroom. It's perfect for vessel sinks and hanging vanities, because the hoses and shut-off valves are out of view.

A wall-mounted sink faucet is similar to a shower or bathtub faucet. The main difference is that the handles and faucet are usually in a line, rather than at a distance from each other. Like the shower or bathtub faucet, you will need to have an access door behind the sink, or have the plumbing easily accessible in the basement for a first floor bathroom.

The valve unit and the faucets and spout will likely need to be made by the same manufacturer, because the parts are generally not interchangeable.

Tools & Materials ▸

Tubing cutter
Tape measure
Level
Torch
Channel-type pliers
Allen wrench
Wallboard
   finishing tools

Lead-free solder
Flux
2 × 4 lumber
#10, 1" wood screws
Two-handle valve
Wall-mount faucet
Plumber's putty
Wallboard

Wall-mounted faucets have a spare, futuristic appeal that many high-end designers prefer. Functionally, they have the added advantage of keeping the sink deck clear.

How to Install a Wall-Mounted Sink Faucet

1

Determine the location for the faucet. Make reference marks for the faucet location on walls that will not be removed or create a cardboard template. Remove the wallboard between the studs at the faucet location and where necessary to run supply and drain lines. Install 2 × 4 bracing according to the faucet manufacturer's instructions.

2

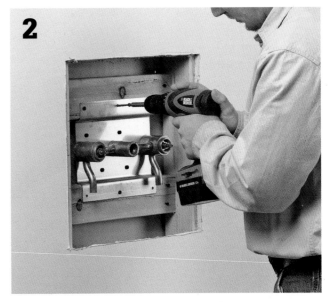

Attach the wall plate from the faucet kit to the studs with #10, 1" wood screws. Check the installation for level and correct it if necessary. Solder the lines from the valve assembly to ½" copper supply lines using couplings (left is hot, right is cold). Turn the water on and check for leaks.

3

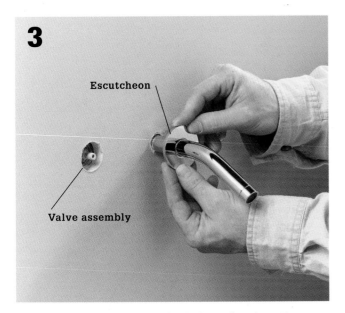

Escutcheon

Valve assembly

Replace the wallboard and finish the wall surface. The circular cutouts for the handles and spout should be no more than 1½" in diameter. Remove the plaster guards from the valve. Thread the spout into the spout stub until tight. Back off the spout until it faces downward and tighten the screws. Apply plumber's putty to the back of the escutcheon and slide it into place.

4

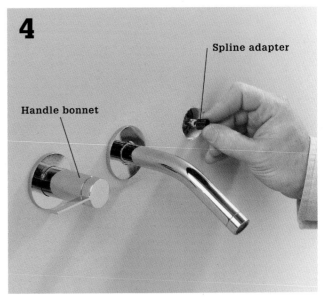

Spline adapter

Handle bonnet

Thread the handle assemblies onto the valve bodies and tighten. If the handles are not horizontal when closed, remove them. Remove the spline adapter and give it a quarter turn. Repeat until the handles are horizontal when closed. Remove the handles. Apply plumber's putty to the back of the escutcheons and slide over the handle bonnets. Securely hand tighten the handles and slide escutcheons into place. Remove excess putty from escutcheons.

Lavatory Drains

Pop-up stoppers are chrome-plated, long-legged plugs in bathroom sinks that are opened and closed with a knob behind the spout. The stopper itself is just the visible part of a behind-the-scenes assembly that makes sure the stopper sits and stands on cue. New faucets come with their own pop-up stopper assemblies, assuming they use one, but you may also purchase one by itself. This will include everything from the stopper to the pipe that drops into the trap. Choose a pop-up stopper assembly that's heavy brass under the chrome finish. This will hold up better to time and abuse than a plastic or light-gauge metal model.

Installing a lavatory drain is a bit trickier than installing a kitchen sink drain because most have a pop-up stopper with linkage.

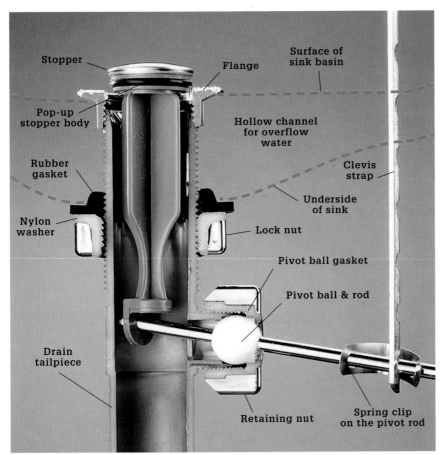

Stopper
Flange
Surface of sink basin
Pop-up stopper body
Hollow channel for overflow water
Rubber gasket
Clevis strap
Underside of sink
Nylon washer
Lock nut
Pivot ball gasket
Pivot ball & rod
Drain tailpiece
Retaining nut
Spring clip on the pivot rod

Pop-up stoppers keep objects from falling down the drain, and they make filling and draining the sink easy. When you pull up on the lift rod, the clevis strap is raised, which raises the pivot rod, which seesaws on the pivot ball and pulls the pop-up stopper down against the flange. This blocks water through the sink drain, but water may still overflow into the overflow channel drain through overflow ports in the pop-up body. This is a nice feature if you leave the water running in a plugged basin by mistake.

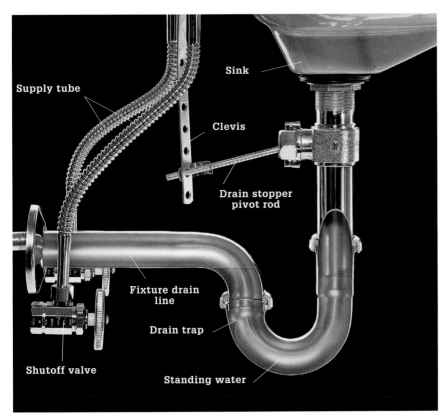

Supply tube
Sink
Clevis
Drain stopper pivot rod
Fixture drain line
Drain trap
Shutoff valve
Standing water

The lavatory drain trap holds water that seals the drain line and prevents sewer gases from entering the home. Each time a drain is used, the standing trap water is flushed away and replaced by new water. The shape of the trap and fixture drain line resembles the letter P, and sink traps are called P-traps.

How to Replace a Pop-up Stopper

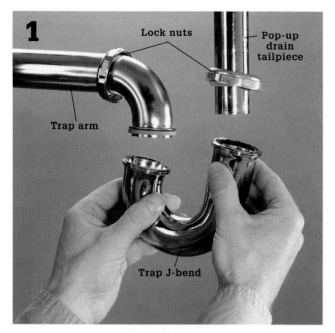

Put a basin under the trap to catch water. Loosen the nuts at the outlet and inlet to the trap J-bend by hand or with channel-type pliers and remove the bend. The trap will slide off the pop-up body tailpiece when the nuts are loose. Keep track of washers and nuts and their up/down orientation by leaving them on the tubes.

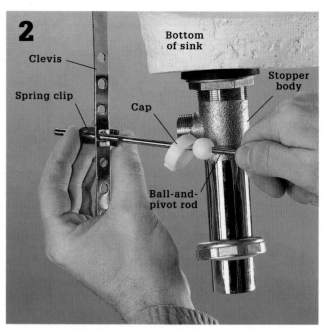

Unscrew the cap holding the ball-and-pivot rod in the pop-up body and withdraw the ball. Compress the spring clip on the clevis and withdraw the pivot rod from the clevis.

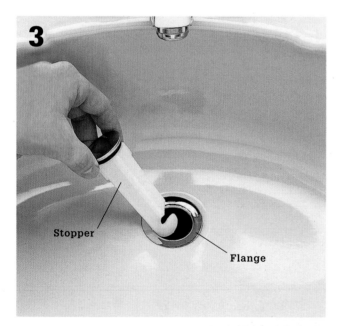

Remove the pop-up stopper. Then, from below, remove the lock nut on the stopper body. If needed, keep the flange from turning by inserting a large screwdriver in the drain from the top. Thrust the stopper body up through the hole to free the flange from the basin, and then remove the flange and the stopper body.

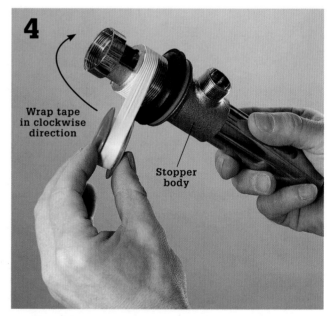

Clean the drain opening above and below, and then thread the locknut all the way down the new pop-up body followed by the flat washer and the rubber gasket (beveled side up). Wrap three layers of Teflon tape clockwise onto the top of the threaded body. Make a ½"-dia. snake from plumber's putty, form it into a ring, and stick the ring underneath the drain flange.

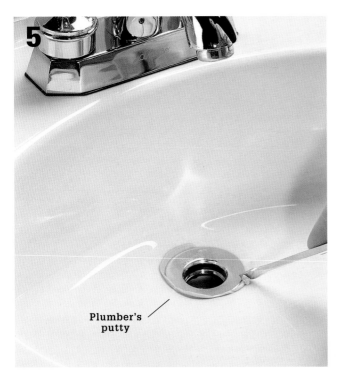

5

From below, face the pivot rod opening directly back toward the middle of the faucet and pull the body straight down to seat the flange. Thread the locknut/washer assembly up under the sink, then fully tighten the locknut with channel-type pliers. Do not twist the flange in the process, as this can break the putty seal. Clean off the squeezeout of plumber's putty from around the flange.

Plumber's putty

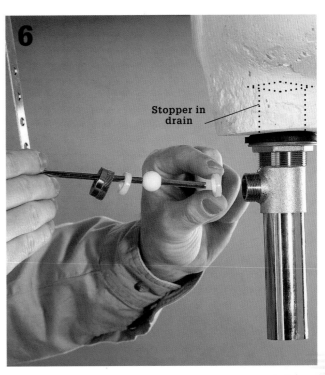

6

Stopper in drain

Drop the pop-up stopper into the drain hole so the hole at the bottom of its post is closest to the back of the sink. Put the beveled nylon washer into the opening in the back of the pop-up body with the bevel facing back.

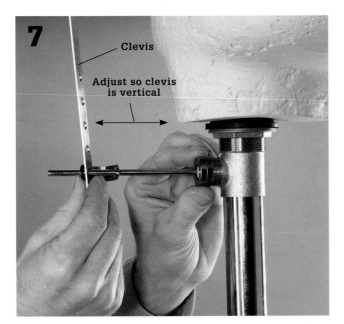

7

Clevis

Adjust so clevis is vertical

Put the cap behind the ball on the pivot rod as shown. Sandwich a hole in the clevis with the spring clip and thread the long end of the pivot rod through the clip and clevis. Put the ball end of the pivot rod into the pop-up body opening and into the hole in the the stopper stem. Screw the cap onto the pop-up body over the ball.

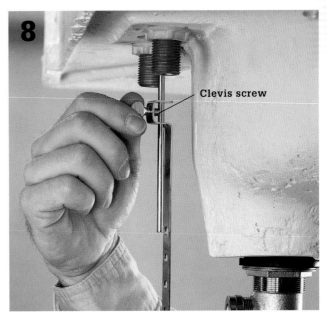

8

Clevis screw

Loosen the clevis screw holding the clevis strap to the lift rod. Push the pivot rod all the way down (which fully opens the pop-up stopper). With the lift rod also all the way down, tighten the clevis screw to the rod. If the clevis runs into the top of the trap, cut it short with your hacksaw or tin snips. Reassemble the J-bend trap.

Toilets & Bidets

Advancing technology has given us toilets that perform more reliably and more efficiently than ever, but it is still estimated that toilets are responsible for as many as half of all home plumbing repair calls. It is worth installing a quality fixture and taking the time to do it right.

The toilet has a close European relative in the bidet. This longtime Old World standard is increasingly finding its way into remodeled or newly built American bathrooms. A bidet is installed right next to the toilet and is used in place of toilet paper for personal hygiene.

The latest evolution of bidets and toilets include an increasing number of wall-mounted models. This reflects a larger trend toward Universal Design—because the units can be positioned at whatever height is best for the user—and sleek, sophisticated bathroom styles. When used together, bidets and toilets are almost always purchased as a matched set.

As water scarcity becomes a more pressing issue throughout the U.S., water-conserving bidets and toilets have become ubiquitous. A 1.6-gallon flush amount has been mandated by federal law since 1992, but many of today's units are even more stingy with the water they use—even as flush technology has improved in answer to early low-flow toilet problems. Installing a urinal is another way some homeowners have discovered to conserve water. While a bit unconventional in a home setting, they use just a fraction of the water consumed by a toilet flush.

In this chapter:

- Toilets
- Bidets
- Urinals

Toilets

You can replace a poorly functioning toilet with a new high-efficiency, high-quality toilet for a couple hundred dollars, an investment that will lead to savings in water usage and frustration—especially if you have a very old toilet. All toilets made since 1996 have been required to use 1.6 gallons or less per flush, which initially presented something of a challenge to the industry. Technology has evolved so that most new toilets have wide passages behind the bowl and wide (3") flush valve openings—features that facilitate short, powerful flushes. Manufacturers have also developed new alternatives, such as dual-flush technology that allows you to choose between two flushing options depending on what needs to be flushed.

All this technological advancement means fewer second flushes and fewer clogged toilets, which were the common complaints about the first generation of 1.6-gallon "low flow" toilets. Unfortunately, these problems still exist in some lower-end inferior models. Do your research when shopping for a new toilet and don't necessary look for the cheapest model you can find; a time-tested model with few customer complaints will be the better bargain in the long run.

Your criteria in selecting a new toilet should include ease of installation, proven flush performance, and reliability. With a little research, you should be able to find a highly efficient and economical gravity-flush toilet that will serve you for years to come.

Sleek new toilet options like this unibody model combine super-efficient function with incredibly sophisticated form.

Buy a toilet that will fit the space. Measure the distance from the floor bolts back to the wall (if your old toilet has two pairs of bolts, go by the rear pair). This is your rough-in distance and will be either 10" or approximately 12". Make note of the bowl shape, round or oval (long). Oval bowls (also called elongated bowls) are a few inches longer for greater comfort, but may be too big for your space. The safest bet is to buy a replacement with the same bowl shape. You can also opt for a wall-mounted unit. Although the installation is more involved, you can save up to a foot of floor space in front of the toilet—with the added bonus of being able to mount the toilet at whatever height works best for the primary users of the room.

Round front

Rough-in distance 10", 12", or 14" (12" is most common)

Floor bolt (cap on)

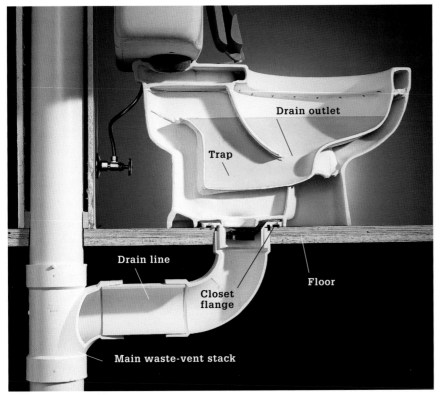

Knowing how a toilet works isn't essential to successful installation, but it helps. This cutaway photo features a pre-1.6-gal. law model, so your new toilet will have a much smaller trap. When the flush handle on the tank is depressed, the water in the tank rushes out through the hole in the underside of the bowl rim. The onrushing water forces the contents of the bowl and the trap out through the closet flange and into the drain line, while the fresh tank water refills the bowl and trap.

Drain outlet

Trap

Drain line

Closet flange

Floor

Main waste-vent stack

How to Install a Toilet

Clean and inspect the old closet flange. Look for breaks or wear. Also inspect the flooring around the flange. If either the flange or floor is worn or damaged, repair the damage. Use a rag and mineral spirits to completely remove residue from the old wax ring.

Insert new closet bolts (don't reuse old ones) into the openings in the closet flange. Make sure the heads of the bolts are oriented to catch the maximum amount of flange material.

Replacing a Flange ▸

If the old flange is solvent-welded to the closet pipe, cut the pipe flush with the floor. Dry-fit the new flange into the pipe. Turn the flange until the side cut-out screw slots are parallel to the wall. (Do not use the curved keyhole slots, as they are not as strong.) Attach the new flange with solvent glue.

Remove the wax ring and apply it to the underside of the bowl, around the horn. Remove the protective covering. Do not touch the wax ring. It is very sticky.

4

Lower the bowl onto the flange, taking care not to disturb the wax ring. The holes in the bowl base should align perfectly with the tank bolts. Add a washer and tighten a nut on each bolt. Hand tighten each nut and then use channel-type pliers to further tighten the nuts. Alternate back and forth between nuts until the bowl is secure. DO NOT OVERTIGHTEN.

5

Spud nut

Spud washer

Attach the toilet tank. Some tanks come with a flush valve and a fill valve preinstalled, but if yours does not, insert the flush valve through the tank opening and tighten a spud nut over the threaded end of the valve. Place a foam or rubber spud washer on top of the spud nut.

6

Adjust the fill valve as directed by the manufacturer to set the correct tank water level height and install the valve inside the tank. Hand-tighten the nylon lock nut that secures the valve to the tank (inset photo) and then tighten it farther with channel-type pliers.

7

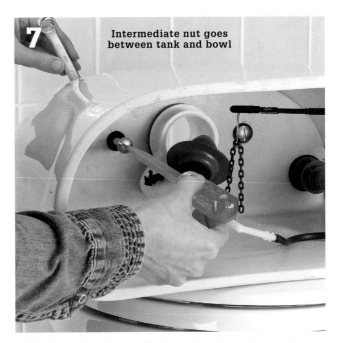

Intermediate nut goes between tank and bowl

With the tank lying on its back, thread a rubber washer onto each tank bolt and insert it into the bolt holes from inside the tank. Then, thread a brass washer and hex nut onto the tank bolts from below and tighten them to a quarter-turn past hand tight. Do not overtighten.

(continued)

8

Position the tank on the bowl, spud washer on the opening, bolts through bolt holes. Put a rubber washer followed by a brass washer and a wing nut on each bolt and tighten these up evenly.

Intermediate nut

9

You may stabilize the bolts with a large slotted screwdriver from inside the tank, but tighten the nuts, not the bolts. You may press down a little on a side, the front, or the rear of the tank to level it as you tighten the nuts by hand. Do not overtighten and crack the tank. The tank should be level and stable when you're done.

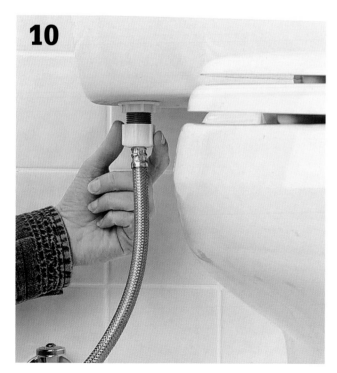

10

Hook up the water supply by connecting the supply tube to the threaded fill valve with the coupling nut provided. Turn on the water and test for leaks.

11

Attach the toilet seat by threading the plastic or brass bolts provided with the seat through the openings on the back of the rim and attaching nuts.

Toilet Height Extenders ▸

Although today's toilets are being made with higher seats than in the past, physically challenged and elderly people often find it difficult to use standard toilets, especially compact toilets (most of the more inexpensive toilets are compact). To address the problem of low toilet seats, you can retrofit your toilet with a seat riser or reinstall the toilet on a platform. See Resources, page 251.

Hinged Seat Risers: By replacing your old toilet seat with a riser seat, you can raise the functional height of the toilet by 3" to 4". Look for models that are hinged or removable for easy cleaning. This is the least expensive option.

Wall-Mounted Toilets: If you're willing to spend significantly more, you can install a wall-mounted unit to whatever height is most comfortable for the user. These are especially effective in bathrooms used by a wheelchair-bound person, or someone who uses a walker.

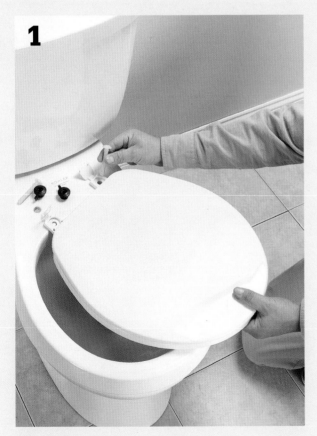

Remove the old seat. If the nuts for the seat bolts are corroded, slip a hack saw blade between the hinge plates and stool and cut the bolts.

Install the new height extender by bolting it to the stool through the seat bolt holes. Attach a standard toilet seat to the extender.

Bidets

Tools & Materials ▸

Tape measure
Drill
Adjustable wrench
Level
Silicone sealant
(2) ⅜" shut off valves
(2) ⅜" supply lines
P-trap

Tubing cutter
Plumber's putty
Thread tape
Bidet
Bidet faucet
Marker

Bidets are becoming ever more popular in the United States. Maybe that's because they can give a dream bath that European flare so many of us find alluring. Go to Europe, Asia, or South America and you'll see how much people can come to rely on bidets. Some fans of this bathroom fixture think those who don't use bidets are unhygienic.

With the trend moving toward larger and more luxurious bathrooms, many Americans are becoming intrigued by this personal hygiene appliance. The standard model features hot and cold faucets, and either a movable nozzle located by the faucet handles or a vertical sprayer located near the front of the bowl. Most bidets are outfitted with a pop-up drain. You can also buy a combination toilet and bidet if space is an issue.

Installing a bidet is very much like installing a sink. The only difference is that the bidet can have the waste line plumbed below the floor, like a shower. But like sinks, bidets may have single or multiple deck holes for faucets, so be certain to purchase compatible components.

A bidet is a useful companion to a toilet, and it is a luxury item you and your family will appreciate. For people with limited mobility, a bidet is an aide to independent personal sanitation.

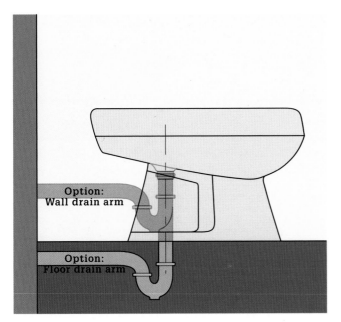

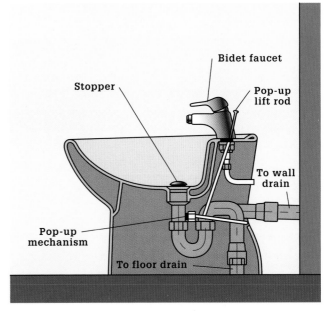

Bidet drains have more in common with sink drains than with toilet drains. Some even attach to a drain arm in the wall, with a P-trap that fits between the fixture drain tailpiece and the arm. Other bidets drain into a floor drain outlet with a trap that's situated between the tailpiece and the branch drain line.

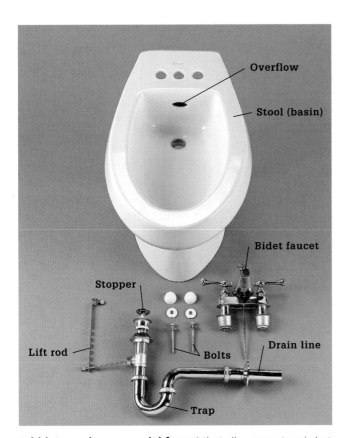

A bidet requires a special faucet that allows you to mix hot and cold water to a temperature you find comfortable. It has a third knob to control the water pressure. The aerator and spout pivot to allow you to adjust the spray to a comfortable height.

You can get all the features of a bidet on your existing toilet with a number of aftermarket bidet seats. These seats feature heaters, sprayers, and dryers in basic or deluxe versions. Installation takes less than an hour and no additional space is needed.

How to Install a Bidet

Rough-in the supply and drain lines according to the manufacturer's specifications. If you do not have experience installing home plumbing, hire a plumber for this part of the job. Apply a coil of plumber's putty to the base of the bidet faucet, and then insert the faucet body into the mounting holes. Thread the washers and locknut onto the faucet body shank and hand tighten. Remove any plumber's putty squeeze out.

Apply a coil of plumber's putty around the underside of the drain flange. Insert the flange in the drain hole, place the gasket and washer, and then thread the nut onto the flange. Do not fully tighten.

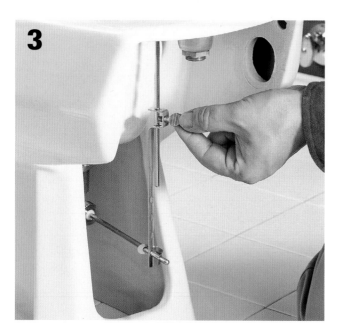

Install the pop-up drain apparatus according to the manufacturer's instructions.

Place the bidet in its final location, checking that supply and drain lines will be in alignment. Mark the locations of the two side-mounting holes through the predrilled holes on the stool and onto the floor.

5

Remove the bidet and drill ³⁄₁₆" pilot holes at the marks on the floor. Drive the floor bolts (included with the bidet basin) into the holes. Position the bidet so the floor bolts fit into the bolt holes in the base. Tighten nuts onto the floor bolts.

6

Connect the water supply risers to the bidet faucet using compression unions. Make sure to hook the hot and cold risers up to the correct ports on the faucet.

7

Hook up the drain line by attaching the P-trap to the drain tailpiece. The trap is then attached to a branch drain line coming out of the wall or floor in the same manner as a sink drain.

8

Remove the aerator so any debris in the supply line will clear and then turn on the water and open both faucets. Check for leaks in lines and fix, if found. Assemble the bolt caps and thread them onto the floor bolts. *Note: Do not dispose of paper in the bidet—return to the toilet to dry off after using the bidet for cleaning.*

Urinals

Most people consider a urinal to be a commercial or industrial bathroom accessory, so why would you want one in your home—and in your dream bathroom no less? The answer is in the many advantages a urinal has to offer and the fact that most major bathroom fixture manufacturers are now producing urinals designed for residential installation.

A urinal doesn't take up much space and it uses much less water per flush than a standard toilet: .5 to 1.0 gallon of water per flush for the urinal, as opposed to the low-flow toilet's 1.6 gallons of water per flush. You also have the option of a waterless urinal, a real boon in water-scarce areas. A urinal also has the emotional benefit of ending the "up versus down" toilet seat debate. Finally, a urinal is generally easier to keep clean than a toilet because splashing is minimized.

In today's homes with large multiple bathrooms and his and hers master baths, there are plenty of places you can choose to install a urinal. Of course, the perfect place is where it will get used the most: in the bathroom closest to the TV if the guys congregate at your house to watch sporting events; or in the bathroom closest to boys' bedrooms if you've got a passel of them.

Urinals are great water savers and are becoming increasingly popular in today's dream bathroom.

Tools & Materials ▸

Tape measure	Urinal flushometer
Adjustable wrench	Emery cloth
Pencil	Wire brush
Level	Allen wrench
Sealant tape	Drywall
Utility knife	Drywall tape
Drywall saw	Drywall compound
Tubing cutter	2 × 6 lumber
Hacksaw	PVC 2" drainpipe
Miter box	PVC 2" male threaded
Hex wrenches	drain outlet
Smooth-jawed	½" copper pipe
spud wrench	Urinal
Slotted screwdriver	Sealant tape

Waterless Urinals ▸

For the ultimate in water-conservation, you can now purchase a home urinal that uses zero water. A waterless urinal is never flushed, so you'll save about a gallon of water per usage. Naturally, waterless urinals are plumbed into your drain line system. But where typical plumbing fixtures rely on fresh water to carry the waste into the system, the waterless system relies simply on gravity for the liquid waste to find its way out of the fixture and into the drain. The secret is a layer of sealing liquid that is lighter than the water and forms a skim coat over the urine. When the urine enters the trap it displaces the sealing liquid, which immediately reforms on the surface to create a layer that seals in odors. The Kohler fixture seen here (see Resources, page 251) is an example of the sealing liquid system. Other waterless urinals use replaceable cartridges.

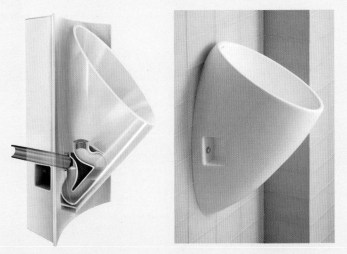

A layer of sealing liquid forms a skim coat that floats on top of the liquid to trap odors.

Flushing Options for Urinals

A manual flush handle is still the most common and least expensive flushing mechanism for urinals. It is reliable but not as sanitary as touchless types such as the flushometer on page 179.

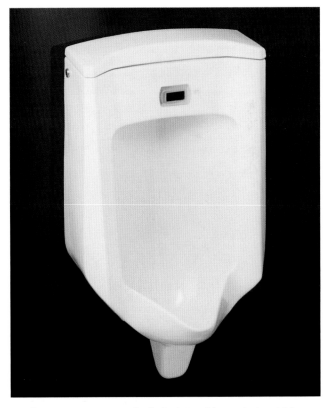

Motion sensors automatically flush touchless urinals, which is a great improvement in sanitation. These tend to be more expensive, however, and are more likely to develop problems. Also, because they flush automatically when users step away from the fixture, they don't allow you to conserve water by limiting flushing.

How to Install a Urinal

Remove the drywall or other surface coverings between the urinal location and the closest water supply and waste lines. Remove enough wall surface to reveal half of the stud face on each side of the opening to make patch work simpler.

Following the manufacturer's directions for the urinal and flushometer, determine the mounting height of the urinal, and mark the location of the supply and waste lines. For this installation, the 2" waste line is centered 17½" above the finished floor. Cut 5½" × 1½" notches in the wall studs centered at 32" above the finished floor surface, then attach a 2 × 6 mounting board.

Install the copper cold water supply line according to the manufacturer's specifications. Here, it is 4¾" to the side of the fixture centerline and 45" from the finished floor (11½" from the top of the fixture). Cap the stub-out 3" from the finished wall surface.

Install the 2" drainpipe and vent pipe, making sure that the centerline of the drain outlet is positioned correctly (here, 17½" above the finished floor and 4¾" to the side of the supply line). Attach the male threaded waste outlet to the drain pipe. It should extend beyond the finished wall surface. Replace the wall covering and finish as desired.

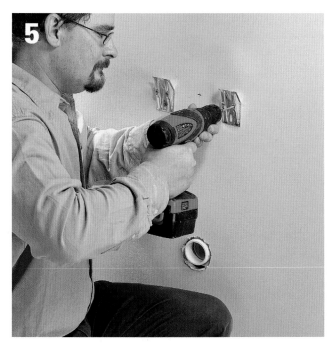

Attach the mounting brackets 32" above the floor, 3¼" to the sides of the centerline of the waste outlet.

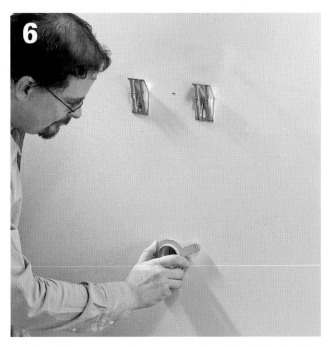

Apply Teflon tape to the waste outlet. Thread the female collar onto the waste outlet until it is firmly seated and the flanges are horizontally level. Place the gasket onto the female collar. The beveled surface of the gasket faces toward the urinal.

Hang the urinal on the brackets, being careful not to bump the porcelain as it chips easily. Thread the screws through the washers, the holes in the urinal, and into the collar. Tighten the screws by hand, then one full turn with an adjustable wrench. Do not overtighten.

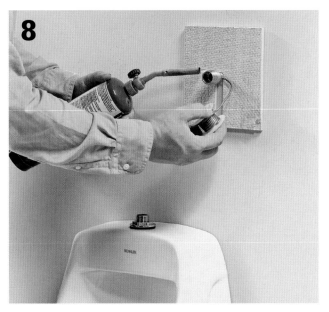

Determine the distance from the centerline of the water inlet on the top of the urinal, called the spud, to the finished wall. Subtract 1¼" from this distance and cut the water supply pipe to that length using a tubing cutter. Turn off the water before cutting. After cutting, deburr the inside and outside diameter of the supply pipe. Attach the threaded adapter to the cut pipe.

(continued)

9

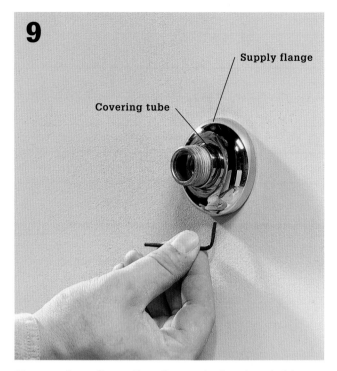

Covering tube

Supply flange

Measure from the wall surface to the first thread of the adapter. Using a hacksaw and a miter box or a tubing cutter, cut the covering tube to this length. Slide the covering tube over the water supply pipe. Slide the supply flange over the covering tube until it rests against the wall. Tighten the setscrew on the flange with an Allen wrench.

10

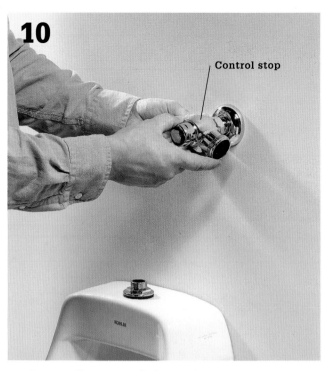

Control stop

Apply a small amount of pipe sealant to the adapter threads, then thread the control stop onto the adapter threads. Position the outlet toward the urinal so that it is horizontally level.

11

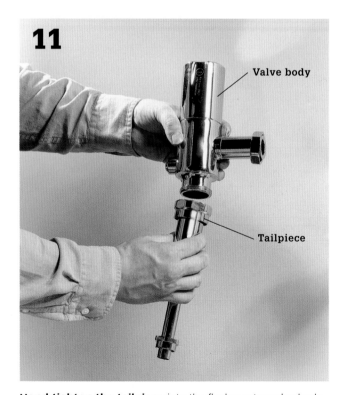

Valve body

Tailpiece

Hand tighten the tailpiece into the flushometer valve body.

12

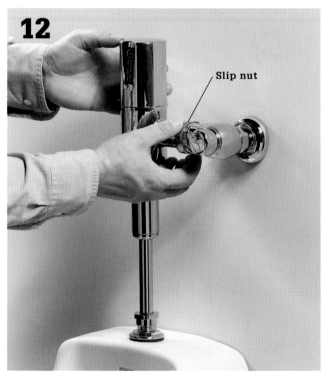

Slip nut

Hand tighten the slip nut that connects the valve body to the control stop.

13

Use a smooth-jawed spud wrench to securely tighten the tailpiece, vacuum breaker, and spud couplings.

The flushometer ▸

For maximum sanitation, choose a urinal flush mechanism with an electronic sensor, like the Kohler flushometer being installed here. The electronic eye on this type of flush mechanism senses when a user approaches the fixture and then commands the fixture to flush when the user steps away. This eliminates the need to touch the handle before the user has the opportunity to wash his hands.

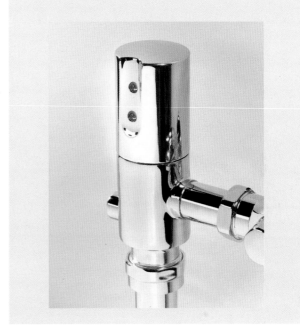

While testing the flush, adjust the supply stop screw counter-clockwise until adequate flow is achieved.

14

Lighting & Ventilaton

Lighting plays an important role in every bathroom. Without good lighting placed in strategic areas, we wouldn't be able to conduct most of our bathroom business. Many different types of lighting and a seemingly infinite array of styles are available to light up your dream bath. Unless you're starting from scratch or tearing down the walls is part of your bathroom remodel, be sure to choose fixtures designed for retrofit installations.

Ventilation is also crucial in a properly outfitted bathroom of any size. It's so important that most building codes require a vent fan in any bathroom lacking natural ventilation. Remodeling your bathroom gives you the perfect opportunity to add a new vent fan or upgrade to a quieter, more efficient model, maybe even one with a built-in heat lamp.

In this chapter:

- Vanity Lights
- Ceiling Lights
- Vent Fans
- Skylights
- Tubular Skylights

Vanity Lights

Many bathrooms have a single fixture positioned above the vanity, but a light source in this position casts shadows on the face and makes grooming more difficult. Light fixtures on either side of the mirror is a better arrangement.

For a remodel, mark the mirror location, run cable, and position boxes before drywall installation. You can also retrofit by installing new boxes and drawing power from the existing fixture.

The light sources should be at eye level; 66" is typical. The size of your mirror and its location on the wall may affect how far apart you can place the sconces, but 36 to 40" apart is a good guideline.

Tools & Materials ▸

Drywall tools	Electrical boxes
Drill	and braces
Combination tool	Vanity light fixtures
Circuit tester	NM cable
Screwdrivers	Wire connectors
Hammer	Drywall

Vanity lights on the sides of the mirror provide ideal lighting for shaving, applying makeup, and other grooming tasks.

How to Replace Vanity Lights in a Finished Bathroom

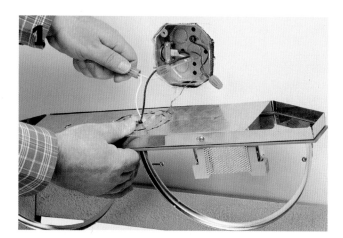

Turn off the power at the service panel. Remove the old fixture from the wall and test to make sure that the power is off. Then remove a strip of drywall from around the old fixture to the first studs beyond the approximate location of the new fixtures. Make the opening large enough that you have room to route cable from the existing fixture to the boxes.

Mark the location for the fixtures and install new boxes. Install the boxes about 66" above the floor and 18 to 20" from the centerline of the mirror (the mounting base of some fixtures is above or below the bulb, so adjust the height of the bracing accordingly). If the correct location is on or next to a stud, you can attach the box directly to the stud, otherwise you'll need to install blocking or use boxes with adjustable braces (shown).

3

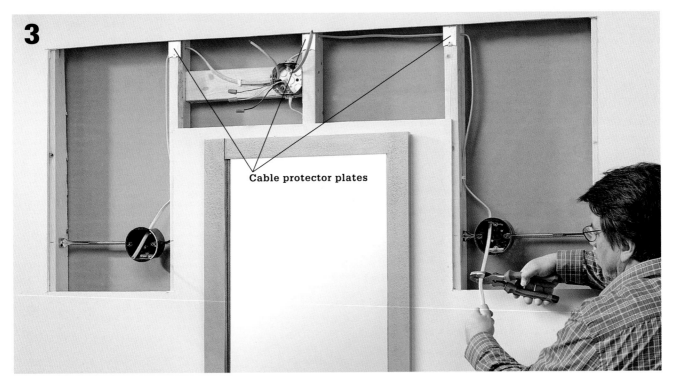

Cable protector plates

Open the side knockouts on the electrical box above the vanity. Then drill ⅝" holes in the centers of any studs between the old fixture and the new ones. Run two NM cables from the new boxes for the fixtures to the box above the vanity. Protect the cable with metal protector plates. Secure the cables with cable clamps, leaving 11" of extra cable for making the connection to the new fixtures. Remove sheathing and strip insulation from the ends of the wires.

4

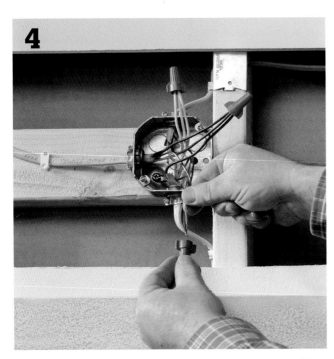

Connect the white wires from the new cables to the white wire from the old cable, and connect the black wires from the new cables to the black wire from the old cable. Connect the ground wires. Cover all open boxes and then replace the drywall, leaving openings for the fixture and the old box. (Cover the old box with a solid junction box cover plate.)

5

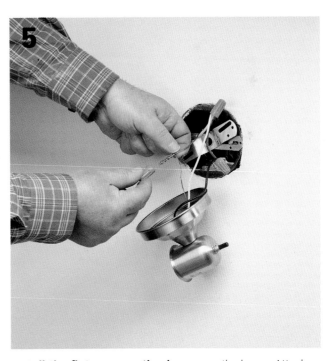

Install the fixture mounting braces on the boxes. Attach the fixtures by connecting the black circuit wire to the black fixture wire, and connecting the white circuit wire to the white fixture wire. Connect the ground wires. Position each fixture over each box, and attach with the mounting screws. Restore power and test the circuit.

Ceiling Lights

Ceiling fixtures don't have any moving parts and their wiring is very simple, so, other than changing bulbs, you're likely to get decades of trouble-free service from a fixture. This sounds like a good thing, but it also means that the fixture probably won't fail and give you an excuse to update a room's look with a new one. Fortunately, you don't need an excuse. Upgrading a fixture is easy and can make a dramatic impact on a room. You can substantially increase the light in a room by replacing a globe-style fixture with one that has separate spot lights, or you can simply install a new fixture that matches the room's décor.

Tools & Materials ▶

Replacement
   light fixture
Combination tool
Voltage sensor
Insulated
   screwdrivers
Wire connectors

It's a fairly unusual bathroom that has room for a fancy ceiling light fixture, but even modest bathrooms should have a bright, pleasant overhead light for general illumination and safety.

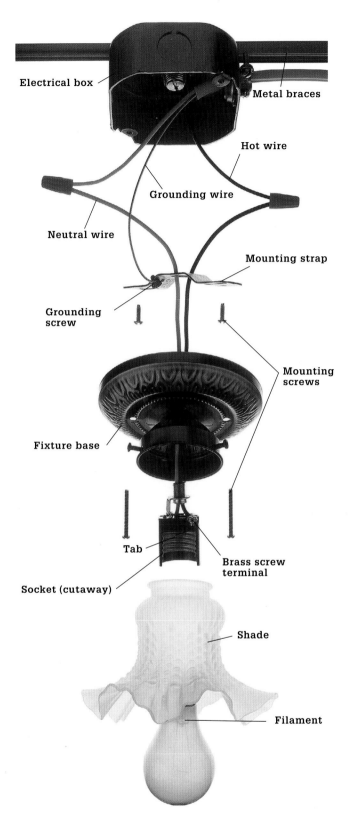

Electrical box

Metal braces

Hot wire

Grounding wire

Neutral wire

Mounting strap

Grounding screw

Mounting screws

Fixture base

Tab

Brass screw terminal

Socket (cutaway)

Shade

Filament

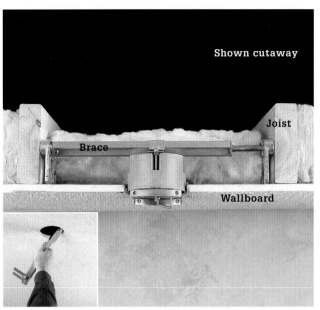

Shown cutaway

Joist

Brace

Wallboard

If the new fixture is much heavier than the original fixture, it will require additional bracing in the ceiling to support the electrical box and the fixture. The manufacturer's instructions should specify the size and type of box. If the ceiling is finished and there is no access from above, you can remove the old box and use an adjustable remodeling brace appropriate for your fixture (shown). The brace fits into a small hole in the ceiling (inset). Once the bracing is in place, install a new electrical box specified for the new fixture.

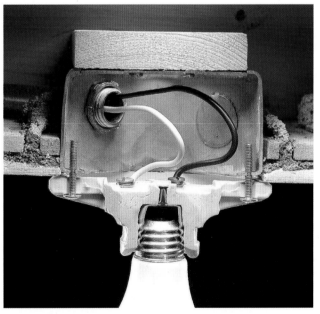

No matter what a ceiling light fixture looks like on the outside, they all attach in basically the same way. An electrical box in the ceiling is fitted with a mounting strap, which holds the fixture in place. The bare wire from the ceiling typically connects to the mounting strap. The two wires coming from the fixture connect to the black and the white wires from the ceiling.

Inexpensive light fixtures have screw terminals mounted directly to the back side of the fixture plate. Often, as seen here, they have no grounding terminal. Some codes do not allow this type of fixture, but even if your hometown does approve them, it is a good idea to replace them with a better quality, safer fixture that is UL-approved.

How to Replace a Ceiling Light

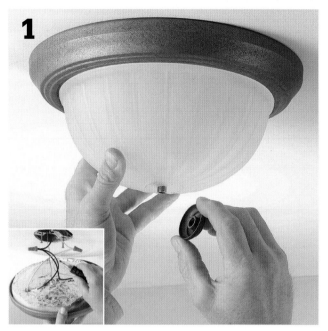

Shut off power to the ceiling light and remove the shade or diffuser. Loosen the mounting screws and carefully lower the fixture, supporting it as you work (do not let light fixtures hang by their electrical wires alone). Test with a voltage sensor to make sure no power is reaching the connections.

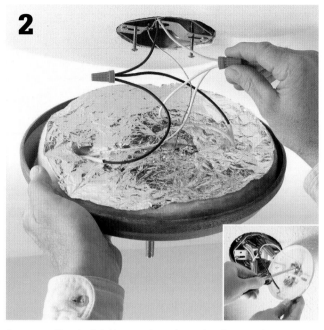

Remove the twist connectors from the fixture wires or unscrew the screw terminals and remove the white neutral wire and the black lead wire (inset).

Before you install the new fixture, check the ends of the wires coming from the ceiling electrical box. They should be clean and free of nicks or scorch marks. If they're dirty or worn, clip off the stripped portion with your combination tool. Then strip away about ¾" of insulation from the end of each wire.

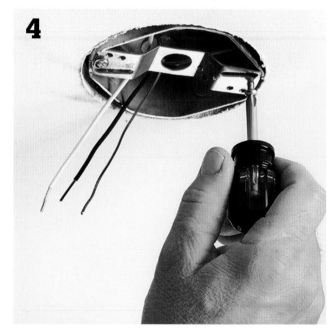

Attach a mounting strap to the ceiling fixture box if there is not one already present. Your new light may come equipped with a strap, otherwise you can find one for purchase at any hardware store.

5

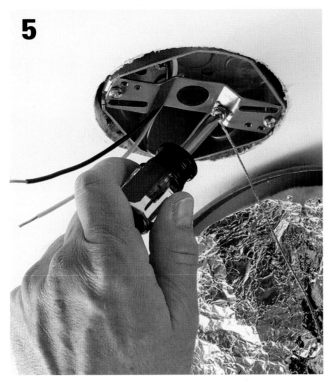

Lift the new fixture up to the ceiling (you may want a helper for this) and attach the bare copper ground wire from the power supply cable to the grounding screw or clip on the mounting strap. Also attach the ground wire from the fixture to the screw or clip.

6

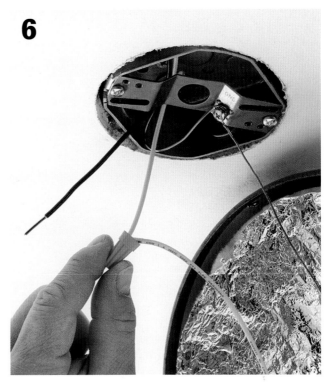

With the fixture supported by a ladder or a helper, join the white wire lead and the white fixture wire with a wire connector (often supplied with the fixture).

7

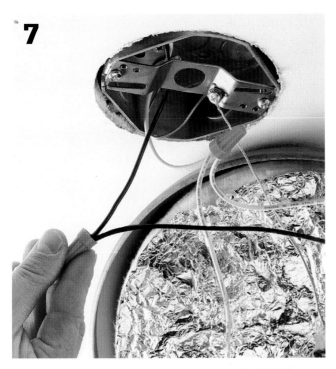

Connect the black power supply wire to the black fixture wire with a wire connector.

8

Position the new fixture mounting plate over the box so the mounting screw holes align. Drive the screws until the fixture is secure against the ceiling.

Vent Fans

Tools & Materials ▸

Phillips and straight
  screwdrivers
Jigsaw or drywall saw
Reciprocating saw
Drill
Electrical tester
Exhaust fan unit
Drywall screws
Wire connectors
Flexible dryer
  vent duct

Dryer vent clamps
Vent cover
Drywall
4" hole saw

For most of us, a dream bathroom does not include foggy mirrors or unpleasant odors. Opening a window, if your bathroom is equipped with one, can help, but vent fans do the best job of clearing the air.

Most vent fans are installed in the center of the bathroom ceiling or over the toilet area. A fan installed over the tub or shower area must be GFCI protected and rated for use in wet areas. You can usually wire a fan with a light fixture into a main bathroom electrical circuit, but units with built-in heat lamps or blowers require separate circuits.

If the fan you choose doesn't come with a mounting kit, purchase one separately. A mounting kit should include a vent hose (duct), a vent tailpiece, and an exterior vent cover.

Venting instructions vary among manufacturers, but the most common options are attic venting and soffit venting. Attic venting routes fan ductwork into the attic and out through the roof. Always insulate ducting in this application to keep condensation from forming and running down into the motor. Carefully install flashing around the outside vent cover to prevent roof leaks.

Soffit venting involves routing the duct to a soffit (roof overhang) instead of through the roof. Check with the vent manufacturer for instructions for soffit venting.

To prevent moisture damage, always terminate the vent outside your home—never into your attic or basement.

You can install a vent fan while the framing is exposed or as a retrofit, as shown in this project.

A combination light/vent fan is a great product in powder rooms and smaller baths that to do not generate excessive amounts of air moisture. In larger baths with tubs and showers, install a dedicated vent fan with a CFM rating that's at least 5 CFM higher than the total square footage of the bathroom (inset photo).

How to Replace an Overhead Light with a Light/Fan

1

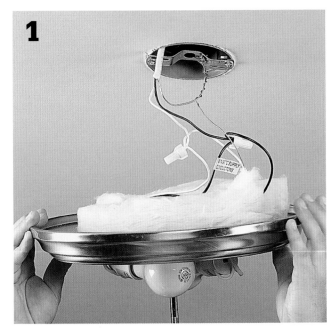

Shut off power to the ceiling light at the electrical service panel. Remove the globe and bulb from the overhead ceiling light, and then disconnect the mounting screws that hold the light fixture to the ceiling box.

2

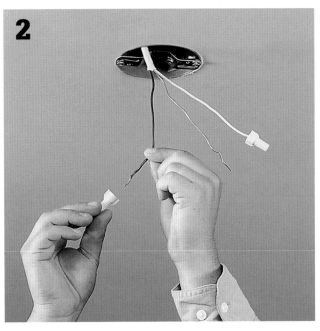

Test the wire connections with a current tester to make sure they are not live, and then disconnect the wires and remove the light fixture. Cap the wire ends.

3

Joist bay

Duct location

Plan your exhaust pipe route. In most cases, this means determining the shortest distance between the fan and the outdoors. If the room is located at the top living level, venting through the roof is usually smartest. On lower levels and in basements, you'll need to go through an exterior wall. If you need to route through a wall in a room with a finished ceiling, choose a route that runs through a single ceiling joist bay.

4

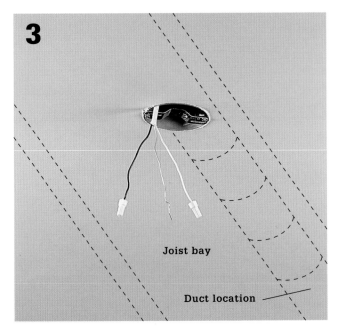

Remove ceiling covering in the fan unit installation area and between the joists at the end of the run, next to the wall. You'll need at least 18" of access. If you are running rigid vent pipe or the joist bay is insulated, you'll need to remove ceiling material between the joists for the entire run. Make cuts on the centerlines of the joists.

(continued)

5

Insert flexible vent tubing into one of the ceiling openings and expand it so the free end reaches to the ceiling opening at the wall. A fish-tape for running cable through walls can be a useful aid for extending the tubing.

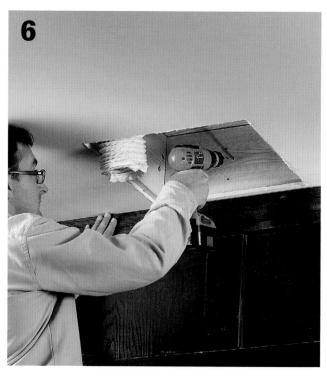

6

Draw a 4"-dia. circle on the wall framing at the end of the joist bay, marking the exit point for the duct. Choose a long, ¼"-dia. drill bit and drill a hole at the center of the circle. Drill all the way through the wall so the bit exits on the exterior side. This will mark your hole location outside.

7

On the exterior, draw a 4"-dia. circle centered on the exit point of the drill bit. Cut out the opening for the vent cover with a reciprocating saw or a 4" hole saw.

8

Insert the vent cover assembly into the opening, following the manufacturer's directions for fastening and sealing it to the house.

9

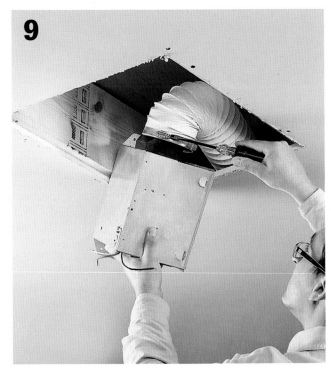

Attach the end of the vent tubing to the outlet on the vent cover unit and secure it with a large pipe clamp.

10

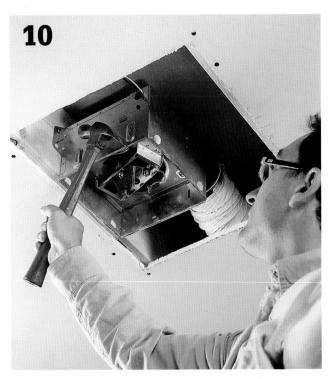

Nail the housing for the light/fan unit to the ceiling joist so the bottom edges of the housing are flush with the ceiling surface.

11

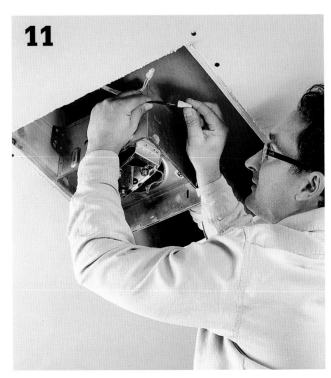

Make the wiring connections in the housing box according to the manufacturer's instructions. In just about every case you should be able to use the existing wires from the original light switch. Once you have connected the wires, restore the power and test the fan.

12

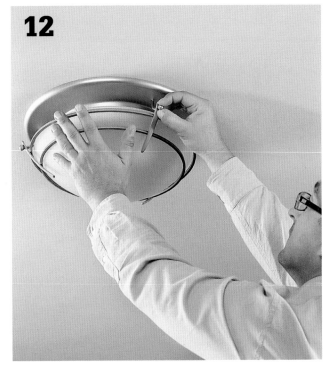

Patch and paint the wall and ceiling in the project area. Mount the light (the model we installed plugs into a receptacle in the fan box), grille, globe, and any other fixture parts.

Skylights

Skylights can bring an amazing amount of natural light into a bathroom, and can be an impressive architectural feature in their own right. You can choose from many shapes, including round, square, and flared (bigger at the bottom than the top). All of these are available as fixed skylights or operable openings—with manual or motorized opening mechanisms. There are even special "tubular" skylights that provide natural light even in bathrooms that are a long way from the roof.

Choosing one for your bathroom is a matter of matching size and exposure. An operable skylight is usually worth the extra money because venting is always in issue in a bathroom. But beyond that, you'll want to select a size that doesn't overwhelm the space. Be aware of exposure: a large skylight, or several skylights, facing south may experience hot sun during that day that can make the room uncomfortably hot. Even if your bathroom is on the bottom floor of a multi-story home, you can still have the beauty and warmth of a skylight by using a tubular unit that bounces the light from a lens in the roof down a reflective tunnel to a lens in the bathroom ceiling.

Once you've chosen a skylight, you'll face the bigger challenge of installing it. If the skylight is installed above an unfinished attic space, this may entail building a shaft in addition to installing the

skylight itself. In any case, the installation process usually involves cutting two or more rafters, reinforcing them to create a frame for the skylight, and creating the opening in the roof. All the work must be done carefully to ensure that the roof structure is not compromised, and to meet prevailing codes. It must also be done with little or no margin for error to avoid potentially troublesome leaks. All that is why most homeowners turn to professionals to install bathroom skylights.

A skylight can be the perfect addition to a luxury master bath. Here, the round, sunken jetted tub is perfectly matched to a matching round skylight that washes the room in sunlight. The skylight is large enough that at night, bathers can stare up at the stars.

A flared shaft such as the one in this bathroom helps disperse the natural light over a wider area than the skylight itself. The feature adds to the look of the room while providing abundant sunlight throughout the day.

Tubular Skylights

Any interior room, including a bathroom, can be brightened with a tubular skylight. Tubular skylights are quite energy-efficient and are relatively easy to install, with no complicated framing involved.

The design of tubular skylights varies among manufacturers, with some using solid plastic reflecting tubes and others using flexible tubing. Various diameters are also available. Measure the distance between the framing members in your attic before purchasing your skylight to be sure it will fit.

This project shows the installation of a tubular skylight on a sloped, asphalt-shingled roof. Consult the dealer or manufacturer for installation procedures on other roof types.

A tubular skylight is an economical way to introduce more sunlight into a room without embarking on a major framing project.

Tools & Materials ▸

Pencil	Reciprocating saw	Wire cutters	Stiff wire
Drill	Pry bar	Utility knife	2" roofing nails or
Tape measure	Screwdriver	Chalk	flashing screws
Wallboard saw	Hammer	Tubular skylight kit	Roofing cement

How to Install a Tubular Skylight

Drill a pilot hole through the ceiling at the approximate location for your skylight. Push a stiff wire up into the attic to help locate the hole. In the attic, make sure the space around the hole is clear of any insulation. Drill a second hole through the ceiling at the centerpoint between two joists.

Center the ceiling ring frame over the hole and trace around it with a pencil. Carefully cut along the pencil line with a wallboard saw or reciprocating saw. Save the wallboard ceiling cutout to use as your roof-hole pattern. Attach the ceiling frame ring around the hole with the included screws.

In the attic, choose the most direct route for the tubing to reach the roof. Find the center between the appropriate rafters and drive a nail up through the roof sheathing and shingles.

4

Use the wallboard ceiling cutout, centered over the nail hole, as a template for the roof opening. Trace the cutout onto the roof with chalk. Drill a starter hole to insert the reciprocating saw blade, then cut out the hole in the roof. Pry up the lower portion of the shingles above the hole. Remove any staples or nails around the hole edge.

5

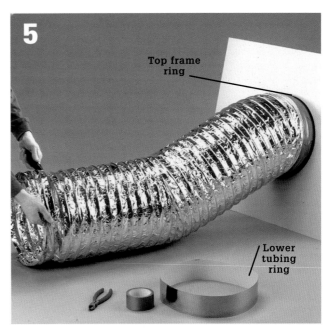

Top frame ring

Lower tubing ring

Pull the tubing over the top frame ring. Bend the frame tabs out through the tubing, keeping two or three rings of the tubing wire above the tabs. Wrap the junction three times around with included PVC tape. Then, in the attic, measure from the roof to the ceiling. Stretch out the tubing and cut it to length with a utility knife and wire cutters. Pull the loose end of tubing over the lower ring and wrap it three times with PVC tape.

6

Lower the tubing through the roof hole and slide the flashing into place with the upper portion of the flashing underneath the existing shingles. This is easier with two people, one on the roof and one in the attic.

7

Secure the flashing to the roof with 2" roofing nails or flashing screws. Seal under the shingles and over all the nail heads with roofing cement. Attach the skylight dome and venting to the frame with the included screws.

8

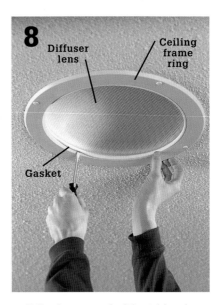

Diffuser lens

Ceiling frame ring

Gasket

Pull the lower end of the tubing down through the ceiling hole. Attach the lower tubing ring to the ceiling frame ring and fasten it with screws. Attach the gasket to the diffuser lens and work the gasket around the perimeter of the ceiling frame. Repack any insulation around the tubing in the attic.

Wall & Floor Projects

Bathroom walls and floors are easy to ignore because we tend to believe that only practical (and boring) surfaces can be used in bathrooms. After all, they need to be water resistant and easy to clean, right? Well, it's not that clear cut.

Yes, bathroom walls and floors should be water resistant, but that doesn't mean they have to be utterly impervious to moisture (unless, of course, they are in a shower stall). That said, you'll obviously want to avoid delicate or absorbent materials such as wallpaper, flat paint, or carpeting.

Even with those options out of the mix, though, you can pick from a growing list of wall and floor surfaces for your bathroom. Traditional choices such as ceramic or stone tile remain popular and present lots of looks, but you can also consider more contemporary alternatives, such as quartz composite surfaces and other solid surface materials.

In this chapter:

- Hanging Cementboard
- Wall Tile
- Toilet Enclosure
- Radiant Heat Floor
- Ceramic Tile Floor
- Sheet Vinyl Floor

Hanging Cementboard

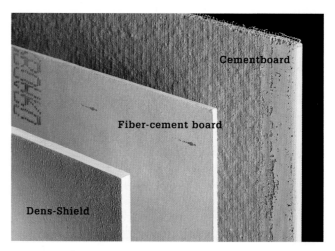

Use tile backer board as the substrate for tile walls in wet areas. Unlike drywall, tile backer won't break down and cause damage if water gets behind the tile. The three basic types of tile backer are cementboard, fiber-cement board, and Dens-Shield.

Though water cannot damage either cementboard or fiber-cement board, it can pass through them. To protect the framing members, install a water barrier of 4-mil plastic or 15# building paper behind the backer.

Dens-Shield has a waterproof acrylic facing that provides the water barrier. It cuts and installs much like drywall, but requires galvanized screws to prevent corrosion and must be sealed with caulk at all untaped joints and penetrations.

Common tile backers are cementboard, fiber-cement board, and Dens-Shield. Cementboard is made from portland cement and sand reinforced by an outer layer of fiberglass mesh. Fiber-cement board is made similarly, but with a fiber reinforcement integrated throughout the panel. Dens-Shield is a water-resistant gypsum board with a waterproof acrylic facing.

Tools & Materials ▸

Work gloves	Small masonry bits	Stapler	Latex-portland
Eye protection	Hammer	4-mil plastic sheeting	cement mortar
Utility knife or carbide-tipped cutter	Jigsaw with a carbide grit blade	Cementboard	15# building paper
T-square	Taping knives	1¼" cementboard screws	Spacers
		Cementboard joint tape	Screwgun

How to Hang Cementboard

Staple a water barrier of 4-mil plastic sheeting or 15# building paper over the framing. Overlap seams by several inches, and leave the sheets long at the perimeter. *Note: Framing for cementboard must be 16" on center; steel studs must be 20-gauge.*

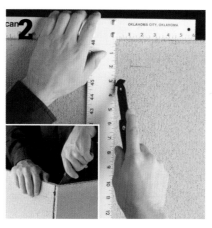

Cut cementboard by scoring through the mesh just below the surface with a utility knife or carbide-tipped cutter. Snap the panel back, then cut through the back-side mesh (inset). *Note: For tile applications, the rough face of the board is the front.*

Make cutouts for pipes and other penetrations by drilling a series of holes through the board, using a small masonry bit. Tap the hole out with a hammer or a scrap of pipe. Cut holes along edges with a jigsaw and carbide grit blade.

4

Install the sheets horizontally. Where possible, use full pieces to avoid butted seams, which are difficult to fasten. If there are vertical seams, stagger them between rows. Leave a ⅛" gap between sheets at vertical seams and corners. Use spacers to set the bottom row of panels ¼" above the tub or shower base. Fasten the sheets with 1¼" cementboard screws, driven every 8" for walls and every 6" for ceilings. Drive the screws at least ½" from the edges to prevent crumbling. If the studs are steel, don't fasten within 1" of the top track.

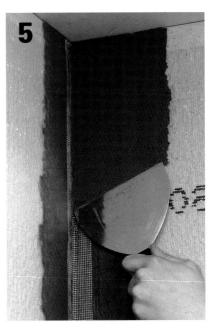

5

Cover the joints and corners with cementboard joint tape (alkali-resistant fiberglass mesh) and latex-portland cement mortar (thin-set). Apply a layer of mortar with a taping knife, embed the tape into the mortar, then smooth and level the mortar.

Finishing Cementboard

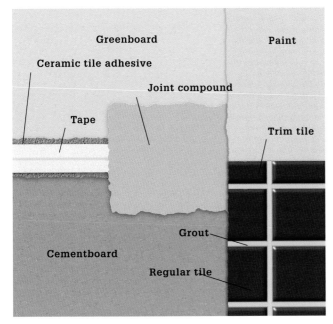

Greenboard Paint
Ceramic tile adhesive
Joint compound
Tape
Trim tile
Grout
Cementboard
Regular tile

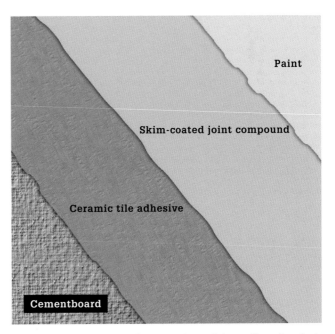

Paint
Skim-coated joint compound
Ceramic tile adhesive
Cementboard

To finish a joint between cementboard and greenboard, seal the joint and exposed cementboard with ceramic tile adhesive, a mixture of four parts adhesive to one part water. Embed paper joint tape into the adhesive, smoothing the tape with a taping knife. Allow the adhesive to dry, then finish the joint with at least two coats of all-purpose drywall joint compound.

To finish small areas of cementboard that will not be tiled, seal the cementboard with ceramic tile adhesive, a mixture of four parts adhesive to one part water, then apply a skim-coat of all-purpose drywall joint compound using a 12" drywall knife. Then prime and paint the wall.

Wall Tile

Beautiful, practical, and easy to clean and maintain, tile walls are well suited to bathrooms. When shopping for tile, keep in mind that tiles that are at least 6" × 6" are easier to install than small tiles, because they require less cutting and cover more surface area. Larger tiles also have fewer grout lines that must be cleaned and maintained. Check out the selection of trim, specialty tiles, and accessories available to help you customize your project.

Most wall tile is designed to have narrow grout lines (less than ⅛" wide) filled with unsanded grout. Grout lines wider than ⅛" should be filled with sanded floor-tile grout. Either type will last longer if it contains, or is mixed with, a latex additive. To prevent staining, it's a good idea to seal your grout after it fully cures, then once a year thereafter.

You can use standard drywall or water-resistant drywall (called "greenboard") as a backer for walls in dry areas. In wet areas, install tile over cementboard. Made from cement and fiberglass, cementboard cannot be damaged by water, though moisture can pass through it. To protect the framing, install a waterproof membrane, such as roofing felt or polyethylene sheeting, between the framing members and the cementboard. Be sure to tape and finish the seams between cementboard panels before laying the tile.

Tile is a practical, easy-to-maintain choice for bathroom walls. The variety of colors, shapes, patterns, and styles is nearly endless. Ceramic tile remains a low-cost, versatile, and attractive option, but glass tile adds shimmer to a room. Glass tiles can also offer a stunning contemporary edge with brilliant colors and patterns unlike any other material (below).

Tiling Bathroom Walls

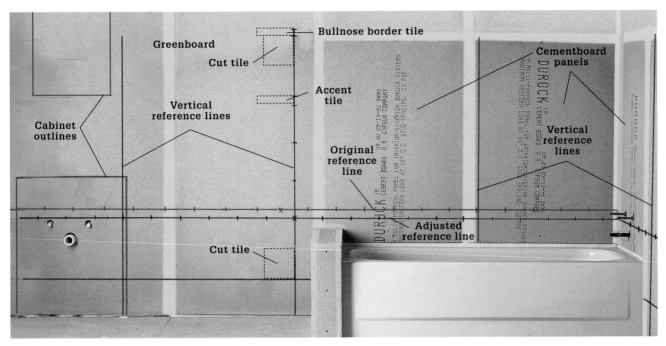

The key to a successful wall-tile project is the layout. Mark the wall to show the planned location of all wall cabinets, fixtures, and wall accessories, then locate the most visible horizontal line in the bathroom, which is usually the top edge of the bathtub. Use a story stick to see how the tile pattern will run in relation to the other features in the room. After establishing the working reference lines, mark additional vertical reference lines on the walls every 5 to 6 tile spaces along the adjusted horizontal reference line to split large walls into smaller, workable quadrants, then install the tile. *Note: Premixed, latex mastic adhesives are generally acceptable for wall tile in dry areas.*

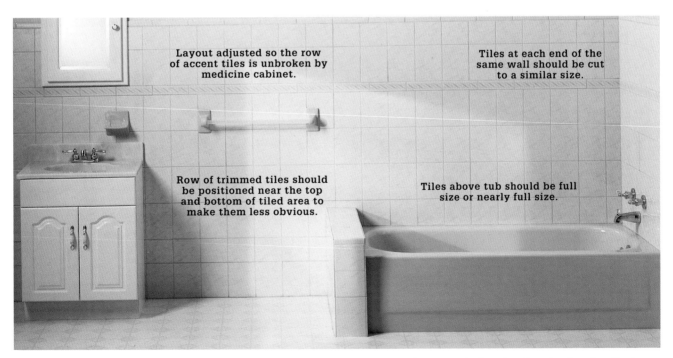

Tiling an entire bathroom requires careful planning. The bathroom shown here was designed so that the tiles directly above the bathtub (the most visible surface) are nearly full height. To accomplish this, cut tiles were used in the second row up from the floor. The short second row also allows the row of accent tiles to run uninterrupted below the medicine cabinet. Cut tiles in both corners should be of similar width to maintain a symmetrical look in the room.

How to Set Wall Tile

Design the layout and mark the reference lines. Begin installation with the second row of tiles above the floor. If the layout requires cut tiles for this row, mark and cut the tiles for the entire row at one time.

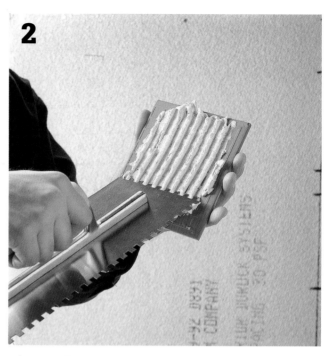

Mix a small batch of thinset mortar containing a latex additive. (Some mortar has additive mixed in by the manufacturer and some must have additive mixed in separately.) Cover the back of the first tile with adhesive, using a ¼" notched trowel.

Variation: Spread adhesive on a small section of the wall, then set the tiles into the adhesive. Thinset adhesive sets fast, so work quickly if you choose this installation method.

Beginning near the center of the wall, apply the tile to the wall with a slight twisting motion, aligning it exactly with the horizontal and vertical reference lines. When placing cut tiles, position the cut edges where they will be least visible.

4

Continue installing tiles, working from the center to the sides in a pyramid pattern. Keep the tiles aligned with the reference lines. If the tiles are not self-spacing, use plastic spacers inserted in the corner joints to maintain even grout lines. The base row should be the last row of full tiles installed. Cut tile as necessary.

5

As small sections of tile are completed, set the tile by laying a scrap of 2 × 4 wrapped with carpet onto the tile and rapping it lightly with a mallet. This embeds the tile solidly in the adhesive and creates a flat, even surface.

6

Spacers

Tile marked
for cutting

To mark tiles for straight cuts, begin by taping ⅛" spacers against the surfaces below and to the side of the tile. Position a tile directly over the last full tile installed, then place a third tile so the edge butts against the spacers. Trace the edge of the top tile onto the middle tile to mark it for cutting.

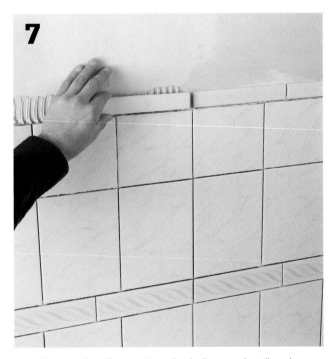

7

Install any trim tiles, such as the bullnose edge tiles shown above, at border areas. Wipe away excess mortar along the top edges of the edge tiles. Use bullnose and corner bullnose tiles (with two adjacent bullnose edges) at outside corners to cover the rough edges of the adjoining tiles.

(continued)

8

Let mortar dry completely (12 to 24 hrs.), then mix a batch of grout containing latex additive. Apply the grout with a rubber grout float, using a sweeping motion to force it deep into the joints. Do not grout joints adjoining bathtubs, floors, or room corners. These will serve as expansion joints and will be caulked later.

9

Wipe a damp grout sponge diagonally over the tile, rinsing the sponge in cool water between wipes. Wipe each area only once; repeated wiping can pull grout from the joints. Allow the grout to dry for about 4 hours, then use a soft cloth to buff the tile surface and remove any remaining grout film.

10

When the grout has cured completely, use a small foam brush to apply grout sealer to the joints, following the manufacturer's directions. Avoid brushing sealer on the tile surfaces, and wipe up excess sealer immediately.

11

Seal expansion joints at the floor and corners with silicone caulk. After the caulk dries, buff the tile with a soft, dry cloth.

How to Install Wall Tile in a Bathtub Alcove

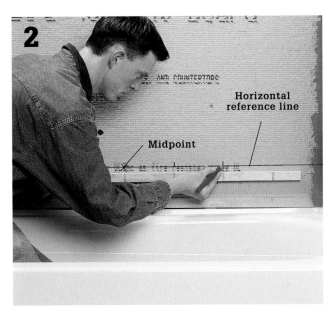

Beginning with the back wall, measure up and mark a point at a distance equal to the height of one ceramic tile (if the tub edge is not level, measure up from the lowest spot). Draw a level line through this point, along the entire back wall. This line represents a tile grout line and will be used as a reference line for making the entire tile layout.

Measure and mark the midpoint on the horizontal reference line. Using a story stick, mark along the reference line where the vertical grout joints will be located. If the story stick shows that the corner tiles will be less than half of a full tile width, move the midpoint half the width of a tile in either direction and mark (shown in next step).

Use a level to draw a vertical reference line through the adjusted midpoint from the tub edge to the ceiling. Measure up from the tub edge along the vertical reference line and mark the rough height of the top row of tiles.

Use the story stick to mark the horizontal grout joints along the vertical reference line, beginning at the mark for the top row of tiles. If the cut tiles at the tub edge will be less than half the height of a full tile, move the top row up half the height of a tile. *Note: If tiling to a ceiling, evenly divide the tiles to be cut at the ceiling and tub edge, as for the corner tiles.*

(continued)

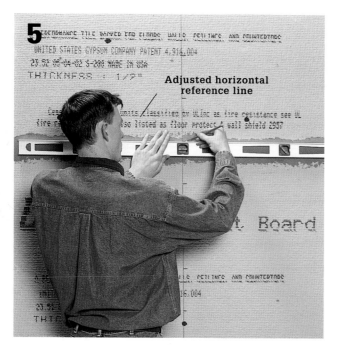

Use a level to draw an adjusted horizontal reference line through the vertical reference line at a grout joint mark close to the center of the layout. This splits the tile area into four workable quadrants.

Use a level to transfer the adjusted horizontal reference line from the back wall to both side walls, then follow Step 3 through Step 6 to lay out both side walls. Adjust the layout as needed so the final column of tiles ends at the outside edge of the tub. Use only the adjusted horizontal and vertical reference lines for ceramic tile installation.

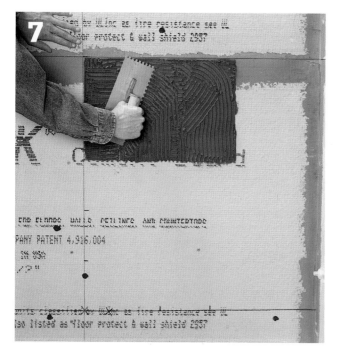

Mix a small batch of thinset mortar containing a latex additive. (Some mortar has additive mixed in by the manufacturer and some must have additive mixed separately.) Spread adhesive on a small section of the wall, along both legs of one quadrant, using a ¼" notched trowel.

Use the edge of the trowel to create furrows in the mortar. Set the first tile in the corner of the quadrant where the lines intersect, using a slight twisting motion. Align the tile exactly with both reference lines. When placing cut tiles, position the cut edges where they will be least visible.

9

10

Continue installing tiles, working from the center out into the field of the quadrant. Keep the tiles aligned with the reference lines and tile in one quadrant at a time. If the tiles are not self-spacing, use plastic spacers inserted in the corner joints to maintain even grout lines (inset). The base row against the tub edge should be the last row of tiles installed.

Install trim tiles, such as the bullnose tiles shown above, at border areas. Wipe away excess mortar along the top edges of the edge tiles.

11

12

Mark and cut tiles to fit around all plumbing accessories or plumbing fixtures.

Install any ceramic accessories by applying thinset mortar to the back side, then pressing the accessory into place. Use masking tape to support the weight until the mortar dries (inset). Fill the tub with water, then seal expansion joints around the bathtub, floor, and corners with silicone caulk.

Toilet Enclosure

One of the best ways to make a busy family bathroom more usable is to enclose the toilet in a room of its own. Toilet enclosures—originally called "water closets" after the cistern they enclosed—make a privacy compartment within the bathroom. This allows one person to shower while the other uses the toilet. It also effectively hides the fixture that most people think is the sore thumb of the bathroom.

Although toilet enclosures are basic structures comprised of framed walls and a pre-hung door, they must be built to maintain adequate spacing around the toilet for maximum comfort and to meet local codes. As a general rule of thumb, you want to leave at least 15" from the center of the toilet bowl to the wall surface on either side, and at least 21" from the front of the bowl to the door. You may also want to add baffles or soundproofing inside the walls, to make the space as private as possible.

The enclosure shown here includes a combination lighting/ventilation fixture. Both are absolute musts for appropriate hygiene and comfort, even if they are not mandated by local codes. (A window can serve the ventilation function, but you'll still need to install lighting for nighttime use.)

When it comes to toilet enclosures, more room is always better. If you can dedicate extra space to the enclosure, you'll not only make the space more comfortable, you'll be able to add nice finishing touches such as a magazine rack or shelves for candles.

Tools & Materials ▸

Prehung door unit	Circular saw
Hammer	Drill
16d nails	Drywall
Screwdriver	Handsaw
2 × 4 lumber	Utility knife
Drywall tape	Wall compound
Prehung door	Interior door lockset
Wood shims	Door trim
Quarter-round molding	Silicone caulk
Stud finder	Fiberglass insulation

A full enclosure with a door offers the maximum in privacy, but it may be a more extreme solution than you require. A simple partition wall next to the toilet creates a sense of privacy without any claustrophobia.

How to Build a Toilet Enclosure

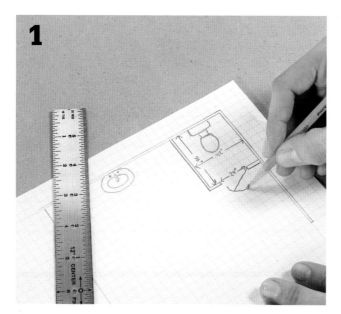

1

Carefully plan out the enclosure. Sketch your plans with exact dimensions to ensure that you allow proper space between toilet and walls, and to ensure door swing won't impede the shower, vanity drawers, or other fixtures.

2

Run wiring and ducting for lighting and ventilation as necessary. Install a box for an overhead fixture and run wire for the switch. We installed a combination light/vent fan (see page 188) connected to an interior wall switch placed just on the latch-side of the enclosure wall. The fixture can be run off the light switch circuit for the entire bathroom if that circuit has the capacity.

3

Check existing connection walls for plumb and square. Cut the sole and top plates accordingly, compensating as needed for any variances. Place top and sole plates side by side and mark stud locations, 16" on center.

4

Secure sole plates to the floor. Plates installed over resilient flooring as shown here, can be nailed through to subfloor. When installing over a tile floor, use a masonry bit to drill pilot holes and then screw through to subfloor. (Over mosaic floors, it's best to remove the tiles from under the sole plate and secure the plate directly to subfloor.)

5

Use a stud finder to locate ceiling joists, and then nail the top plates into place. Frame out the walls by toe-nailing studs between top and sole plates as marked. Frame L-corner for walls, as shown (inset).

6

Frame the doorway with header, cripple studs, and jack studs (you should purchase your prehung door first, so that you can double-check the opening measurements against the actual door unit).

7

Hang drywall on the framed walls, inside and out. The enclosure here was clad with standard drywall rather than greenboard, because the walls won't be subjected to any direct moisture contact. If the enclosure abuts a shower or bath, use greenboard or cementboard.

(continued)

8

Position the prehung door in place. Check that it is oriented correctly, to open out from the enclosure and against a wall, rather than blocking the central space or opening against the vanity.

9

Shim all around the jamb (specifically, behind hinges and lockset location) until the door unit is plumb and square in the opening, and the door opens smoothly. Nail through the door jambs into the framing at the shim points.

10

Saw the shims off flush. Measure, cut, and nail the trim for the door in place. Putty and sand over the nail heads on jambs and casework.

Use the Wall Cavity ▶

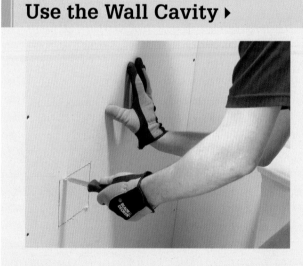

Because the partition wall you've built is essentially empty, it is a good candidate for installing niche fittings that are recessed into the wall. A recessed toilet tissue holder is one easy-to-install fitting. Space will be fairly tight in your enclosure, so using the wall space makes a lot of sense. A wall-niche magazine rack or niche shelving are just two additional ways you may use the wall cavity space.

11

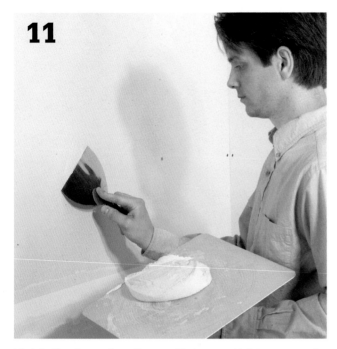

Finish the drywall surfaces with tape and joint compound. Work as neatly as you can to minimize sanding. Seal the new drywall with drywall primer before you paint.

12

Paint the enclosure walls and add any additional elements, including paper holders, grab bars, and shelves or cabinets. The wall area behind the toilet tank is a good spot for installing shallow shelving, but keep it at least 3 ft. above the tank lid.

13

Attach base quarter-round molding on bottom of walls, inside and out (or cove molding if you prefer). Apply a coat of silicone caulk to the bottom of molding before nailing it in place.

Radiant Heat Floor

Floor-warming systems require very little energy to run and are designed to heat ceramic or stone tile floors only; they generally are not used as sole heat sources for rooms.

A typical floor-warming system consists of one or more thin mats containing electric resistance wires that heat up when energized like an electric blanket. The mats are installed beneath the tile and are hardwired to a 120-volt GFCI circuit. A thermostat controls the temperature, and a timer turns the system off automatically.

The system shown in this project includes two plastic mesh mats, each with its own power lead that is wired directly to the thermostat. Radiant mats may be installed over a plywood subfloor, but if you plan to install floor tile you should put down a base of cementboard first, and then install the mats on top of the cementboard.

A crucial part of installing this system is to use a multimeter to perform several resistance checks to make sure the heating wires have not been damaged during shipping or installation.

Tools & Materials ▸

Vacuum cleaner	Trowel or rubber float
Multimeter	Conduit
Tape measure	Thinset mortar
Scissors	Thermostat with sensor
Router/rotary tool	Junction box(es)
Marker	Tile or stone
Electric wire fault	floorcovering
indicator (optional)	Drill
Hot glue gun	Double-sided
Radiant floor mats	carpet tape
12/2 NM cable	Cable clamps

Electrical service required for a floor-warming system is based on size. A smaller system may connect to an existing GFCI circuit, but a larger one will need a dedicated circuit; follow the manufacturer's requirements.

To order a floor-warming system, contact the manufacturer or dealer. In most cases, you can send them plans and they'll custom-fit a system for your project area.

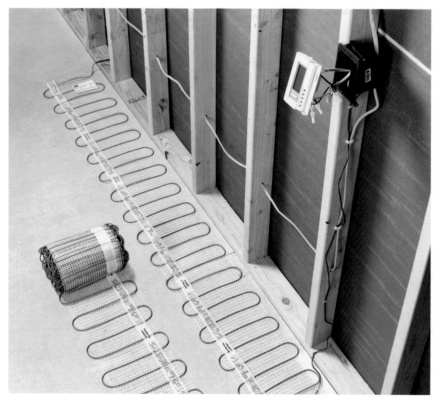

A radiant floor-warming system employs electric heating mats that are covered with floor tile to create a floor that's cozy underfoot.

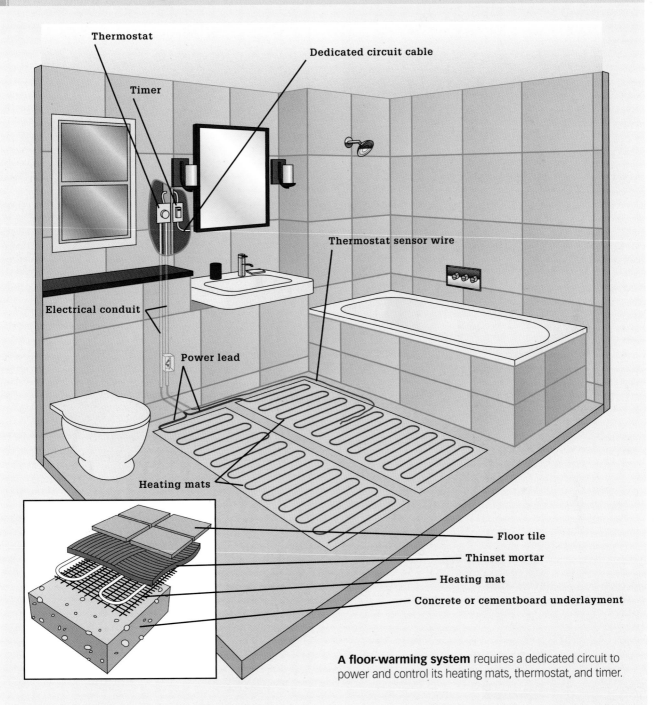

Thermostat

Timer

Dedicated circuit cable

Thermostat sensor wire

Electrical conduit

Power lead

Heating mats

Floor tile

Thinset mortar

Heating mat

Concrete or cementboard underlayment

A floor-warming system requires a dedicated circuit to power and control its heating mats, thermostat, and timer.

- Each radiant mat must have a direct connection to the power lead from the thermostat, with the connection made in a junction box in the wall cavity. Do not install mats in series.
- Do not install radiant floor mats under shower areas.
- Do not overlap mats or let them touch.
- Do not cut heating wire or damage heating wire insulation.
- The distance between wires in adjoining mats should equal the distance between wire loops measured center to center.

Installing a Radiant Floor-Warming System

Floor-warming systems must be installed on a circuit with adequate amperage and a GFCI breaker. Smaller systems may tie into an existing circuit, but larger ones need a dedicated circuit. Follow local building and electrical codes that apply to your project.

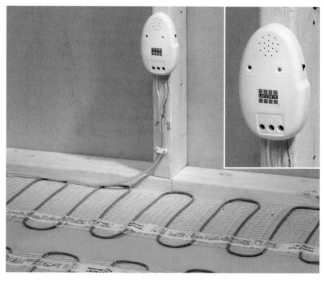

An electric wire fault indicator monitors each floor mat for continuity during the installation process. If there is a break in continuity (for example, if a wire is cut) an alarm sounds. If you choose not to use an installation tool to monitor the mat, test for continuity frequently using a multimeter.

How To Install a Radiant Floor-Warming System

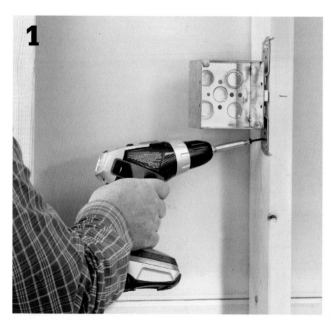

Install electrical boxes to house the thermostat and timer. In most cases, the box should be located 60" above floor level. Use a 4"-deep × 4"-wide double-gang box for the thermostat/timer control if your kit has an integral model. If your timer and thermostat are separate, install a separate single box for the timer.

Drill access holes in the sole plate for the power leads that are preattached to the mats (they should be over 10 ft. long). The leads should be connected to a supply wire from the thermostat in a junction box located in a wall near the floor and below the thermostat box. The access hole for each mat should be located directly beneath the knockout for that cable in the thermostat box. Drill through the sill plate vertically and horizontally so the holes meet in an L-shape.

3

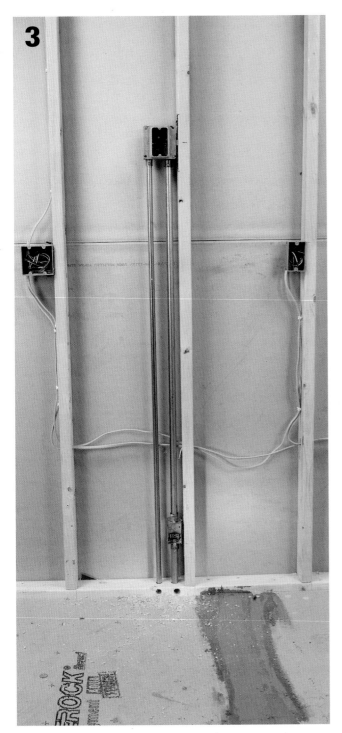

Clean the floor surface thoroughly to get rid of any debris that could potentially damage the wire mats. A vacuum cleaner generally does a more effective job than a broom.

4

Run conduit from the electrical boxes to the sill plate. The line for the supply cable should be ¾" conduit. If you are installing multiple mats, the supply conduit should feed into a junction box about 6" above the sill plate and then continue into the ¾" hole you drilled for the supply leads. The sensor wire needs only ½" conduit that runs straight from the thermostat box via the thermostat. The mats should be powered by a dedicated 20-amp GFCI circuit of 12/2 NM cable run from your main service panel to the electrical box (this is for 120-volt mats—check your instruction manual for specific circuit recommendations).

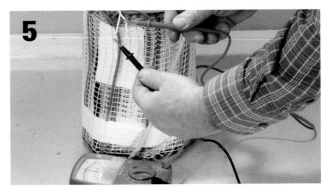

5

Test for resistance using a multimeter set to measure ohms. This is a test you should make frequently during the installation, along with checking for continuity. If the resistance is off by more than 10% from the theoretical resistance listing (see manufacturer's chart in installation instructions), contact a technical support operator for the kit manufacturer. For example, the theoretical resistance for the 1 × 50 ft. mat seen here is 19, so the ohms reading should be between 17 and 21.

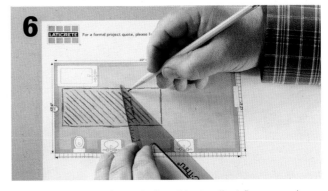

6

Finalize your mat layout plan. Most radiant floor warming mat manufacturers will provide a layout plan for you at the time of purchase, or they will give you access to an online design tool so you can come up with your own plan. This is an important step to the success of your project, and the assistance is free.

(continued)

7

Unroll the radiant mat or mats and allow them to settle. Arrange the mat or mats according to the plan you created. It's okay to cut the plastic mesh so you can make curves or switchbacks, but do not cut the heating wire under any circumstances, even to shorten it.

8

Finalize the mat layout and then test the resistance again using a multimeter. Also check for continuity in several different spots. If there is a problem with any of the mats, you should identify it and correct it before proceeding with the mortar installation.

9

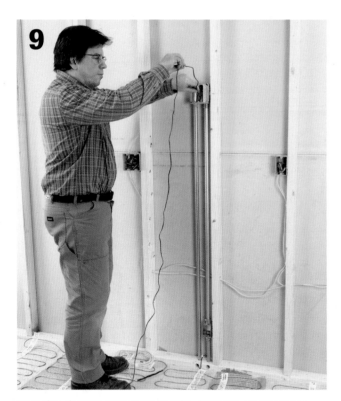

Run the thermostat sensor wire from the electrical box down the ½" conduit raceway and out the access hole in the sill plate. Select the best location for the thermostat sensor and mark the location onto the flooring. Also mark the locations of the wires that connect to and lead from the sensor.

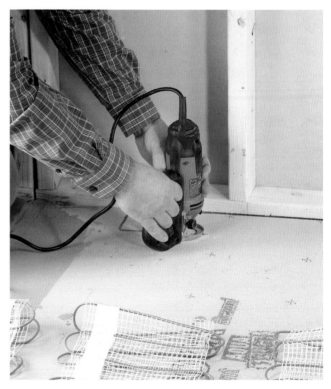

Variation: If your local codes require it, roll the mats out of the way and cut a channel for the sensor and the sensor wires into the floor or floor underlayment. For most floor materials, a spiral cutting tool does a quick and neat job of this task. Remove any debris.

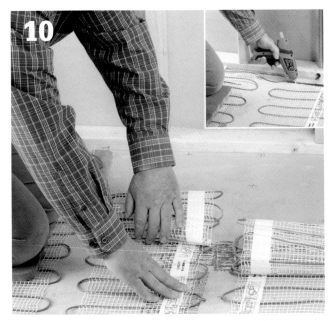

Bond the mats to the floor. If the mats in your system have adhesive strips, peel off the adhesive backing and roll out the mats in the correct position, pressing them against the floor to set the adhesive. If your mats have no adhesive, bind them with strips of double-sided carpet tape. The thermostat sensor and the power supply leads should be attached with hot glue (inset photo) and run up into their respective holes in the sill plate if you have not done this already. Test all mats for resistance and continuity.

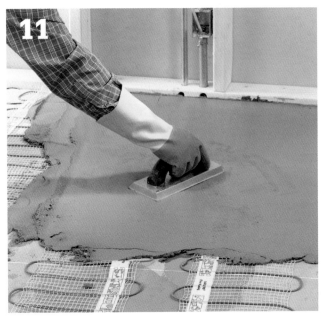

Cover the floor installation areas with a layer of thinset mortar that is thick enough to fully encapsulate all the wires and mats (usually around ¼" in thickness). Check the wires for continuity and resistance regularly and stop working immediately if there is a drop in resistance or a failure of continuity. Allow the mortar to dry overnight.

Connect the power supply leads from the mat or mats to the NM cable coming from the thermostat inside the junction box near the sill. Power must be turned off. The power leads should be cut so about 8" of wire feeds into the box. Be sure to use cable clamps to protect the wires.

Connect the sensor wire and the power supply lead (from the junction box) to the thermostat/timer according to the manufacturer's directions. Attach the device to the electrical box, restore power, and test the system to make sure it works. Once you are convinced that it is operating properly, install floor tiles and repair the wall surfaces.

Ceramic Tile Floor

Ceramic tile installation starts with determining the best layout. You snap perpendicular reference lines and dry-fit tiles to ensure the best placement.

When setting tiles, work in small sections so the mortar doesn't dry before the tiles are set. Use spacers between tiles to ensure consistent spacing. Plan an installation sequence to avoid kneeling on set tiles. Be careful not to kneel or walk on tiles until the designated drying period is over.

Tools & Materials ▸

¼" square trowel	Thin-set mortar
Rubber mallet	Tile
Tile cutter	Tile spacers
Tile nippers	Grout
Hand-held tile cutter	Latex grout additive
Needlenose pliers	Wall adhesive
Grout float	2 × 4 lumber
Grout sponge	Grout sealer
Soft cloth	Tile caulk
Small paint brush	Sponge brush

Floor tile can be laid in many decorative patterns, but for your first effort stick to a basic grid. In most cases, floor tile is combined with profiled base tile (installed after flooring).

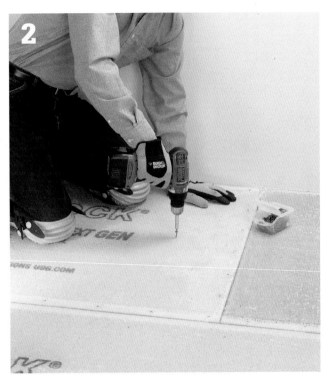

Make sure the subfloor is smooth, level, and stable. Spread thin-set mortar on the subfloor for one sheet of cementboard. Place the cementboard on the mortar, keeping a ¼" gap along the walls.

Fasten it in place with 1¼" cementboard screws. Place fiberglass-mesh wallboard tape over the seams. Cover the remainder of the floor.

Draw reference lines and establish the tile layout. Mix a batch of thin-set mortar, then spread the mortar evenly against both reference lines of one quadrant, using a ¼" square-notched trowel. Use the notched edge of the trowel to create furrows in the mortar bed.

Set the first tile in the corner of the quadrant where the reference lines intersect. When setting tiles that are 8" square or larger, twist each tile slightly as you set it into position.

(continued)

Using a soft rubber mallet, gently tap the central area of each tile a few times to set it evenly into the mortar.

Variation: For large tiles or uneven stone, use a larger trowel with notches that are at least ½" deep.

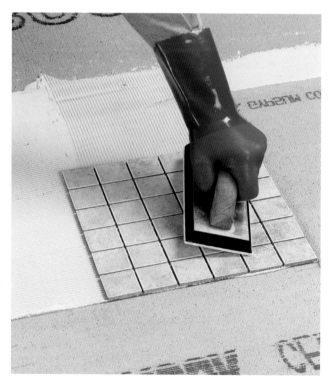

Variation: For mosaic sheets, use a ³⁄₁₆" V-notched trowel to spread the mortar and a grout float to press the sheets into the mortar. Apply pressure gently to avoid creating an uneven surface.

To ensure consistent spacing between tiles, place plastic tile spacers at the corners of the set tile. With mosaic sheets, use spacers equal to the gaps between tiles.

7

Position and set adjacent tiles into the mortar along the reference lines. Make sure the tiles fit neatly against the spacers.

8

To make sure the tiles are level with one another, place a straight piece of 2 × 4 across several tiles, then tap the board with a mallet.

9

Lay tile in the remaining area covered with mortar. Repeat steps 2 to 7, continuing to work in small sections, until you reach walls or fixtures.

10

Measure and mark tiles to fit against walls and into corners. Cut the tiles to fit. Apply thin-set mortar directly to the back of the cut tiles, instead of the floor, using the notched edge of the trowel to furrow the mortar.

(continued)

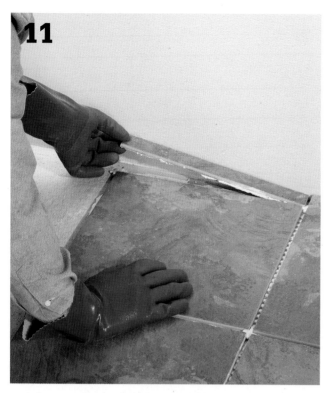

11

Set the cut pieces of tile into position. Press down on the tile until each piece is level with adjacent tiles.

12

Measure, cut, and install tiles that require notches or curves to fit around obstacles, such as exposed pipes or toilet drains.

13

Carefully remove the spacers with needlenose pliers before the mortar hardens.

14

Apply mortar and set tiles in the remaining quadrants, completing one quadrant before starting the next. Inspect all of the tile joints and use a utility knife or grout knife to remove any high spots of mortar that could show through the grout.

15

Install threshold material in doorways. If the threshold is too long for the doorway, cut it to fit with a jigsaw or circular saw and a tungsten-carbide blade. Set the threshold in thin-set mortar so the top is even with the tile. Keep the same space between the threshold as between tiles. Let the mortar set for at least 24 hours.

16

Prepare a small batch of floor grout to fill the tile joints. When mixing grout for porous tile, such as quarry or natural stone, use an additive with a release agent to prevent grout from bonding to the tile surfaces.

17

Starting in a corner, pour the grout over the tile. Use a rubber grout float to spread the grout outward from the corner, pressing firmly on the float to completely fill the joints. For best results, tilt the float at a 60° angle to the floor and use a figure eight motion.

18

Use the grout float to remove excess grout from the surface of the tile. Wipe diagonally across the joints, holding the float in a near-vertical position. Continue applying grout and wiping off excess until about 25 sq. ft. of the floor has been grouted.

(continued)

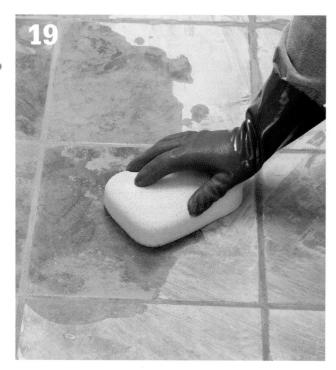

19

Wipe a damp grout sponge diagonally over about 2 sq. ft. of the floor at a time. Rinse the sponge in cool water between wipes. Wipe each area only once since repeated wiping can pull grout back out of joints. Repeat steps 15 to 18 to apply.

20

Allow the grout to dry for about 4 hours, then use a soft cloth to buff the tile surface and remove any remaining grout film.

21

Apply grout sealer to the grout lines, using a small sponge brush or sash brush. Avoid brushing sealer on tile surfaces. Wipe up any excess sealer immediately.

Variation: Use a tile sealer to seal porous tile, such as quarry tile or unglazed tile. Following the manufacturer's instructions, roll a thin coat of sealer over the tile and grout joints, using a paint roller and extension handle.

How to Install Bullnose Base Trim

1

Dry-fit the tiles to determine the best spacing. Grout lines in base tile do not always align with grout lines in the floor tile. Use rounded bullnose tiles at outside corners, and mark tiles for cutting as needed.

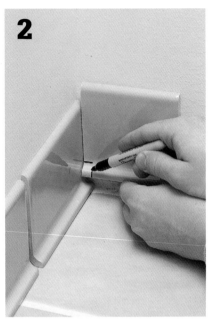

2

Leaving a ⅛" expansion gap between tiles at corners, mark any contour cuts necessary to allow the coved edges to fit together. Use a jigsaw with a tungsten-carbide blade to make curved cuts.

3

Begin installing base-trim tiles at an inside corner. Use a notched trowel to apply wall adhesive to the back of the tile. Place ⅛" spacers on the floor under each tile to create an expansion joint.

4

Press the tile onto the wall. Continue setting tiles, using spacers to maintain ⅛" gaps between the tiles and ⅛" expansion joints between the tiles and floor.

5

Use a double-bullnose tile on one side of outside corners to cover the edge of the adjoining tile.

6

After the adhesive dries, grout the vertical joints between tiles and apply grout along the tops of the tiles to make a continuous grout line. Once the grout hardens, fill the expansion joint between the tiles and floor with caulk.

Sheet Vinyl Flooring

Preparing a perfect underlayment is the most important phase of resilient sheet vinyl installation. Cutting the material to fit the contours of the room is a close second. The best way to ensure accurate cuts is to make a cutting template. Some manufacturers offer template kits, or you can make one by following the instructions on the opposite page. Be sure to use the recommended adhesive for the sheet vinyl you are installing. Many manufacturers require that you use their glue for installation. Use extreme care when handling the sheet vinyl, especially felt-backed products, to avoid creasing and tearing.

Tools & Materials ▶

Linoleum knife	Heat gun
Framing square	$\frac{1}{16}$" V-notched trowel
Compass	Straightedge
Scissors	Vinyl flooring
Non-permanent	Masking tape
felt-tipped pen	Heavy butcher
Utility knife	or brown
Straightedge	wrapping paper
$\frac{1}{4}$" V-notched trowel	Duct tape
J-roller	Flooring adhesive
Stapler	$\frac{3}{8}$" staples
Flooring roller	Metal threshold bars
Chalk line	Nails

Resilient sheet vinyl is a very popular choice for bathroom floors because it is resistant to moisture and easy to clean. It is also relatively inexpensive, but you will find that the style and design options are more limited than with some other floorcovering types.

How to Make a Cutting Template

1

Place sheets of heavy butcher paper or brown wrapping paper along the walls, leaving a ⅛" gap. Cut triangular holes in the paper with a utility knife. Fasten the template to the floor by placing masking tape over the holes.

2

Follow the outline of the room, working with one sheet of paper at a time. Overlap the edges of adjoining sheets by about 2" and tape the sheets together.

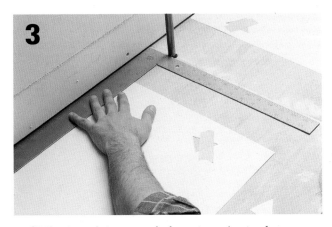

3

To fit the template around pipes, tape sheets of paper on either side. Measure the distance from the wall to the center of the pipe, then subtract ⅛".

4

Transfer the measurement to a separate piece of paper. Use a compass to draw the pipe diameter on the paper, then cut out the hole with scissors or a utility knife. Cut a slit from the edge of the paper to the hole.

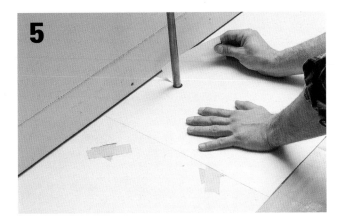

5

Fit the hole cutout around the pipe. Tape the hole template to the adjoining sheets.

6

When completed, roll or loosely fold the paper template for carrying.

How to Install Perimeter-bond Sheet Vinyl

Unroll the flooring on any large, flat, clean surface. To prevent wrinkles, sheet vinyl comes from the manufacturer rolled with the pattern-side out. Unroll the sheet and turn it pattern-side up for marking.

For two-piece installations, overlap the edges of the sheets by at least 2". Plan to have the seams fall along the pattern lines or simulated grout joints. Align the sheets so the pattern matches, then tape the sheets together with duct tape.

Make a paper template (see page 229) and position it. Trace the outline of the template onto the flooring using a non-permanent felt-tipped pen.

Remove the template. Cut the sheet vinyl with a sharp linoleum knife or a utility knife with a new blade. Use a straightedge as a guide for making longer cuts.

Cut holes for pipes and other permanent obstructions. Cut a slit from each hole to the nearest edge of the flooring. Whenever possible, make slits along pattern lines.

Roll up the flooring loosely and transfer it to the installation area. Do not fold the flooring. Unroll and position the sheet vinyl carefully. Slide the edges beneath undercut door casings.

Cut the seams for two-piece installations using a straightedge as a guide. Hold the straightedge tightly against the flooring, and cut along the pattern lines through both pieces of vinyl flooring.

Remove both pieces of scrap flooring. The pattern should now run continuously across the adjoining sheets of flooring.

Fold back the edges of both sheets. Apply a 3" band of multipurpose flooring adhesive to the underlayment or old flooring, using a ¼" V-notched trowel or wallboard knife.

Lay the seam edges one at a time onto the adhesive. Make sure the seam is tight, pressing the gaps together with your fingers, if needed. Roll the seam edges with a J-roller or wallpaper seam roller.

Apply flooring adhesive underneath flooring cuts at pipes or posts and around the entire perimeter of the room. Roll the flooring with the roller to ensure good contact with the adhesive.

If you're applying flooring over a wood underlayment, fasten the outer edges of the sheet with ⅜" staples driven every 3". Make sure the staples will be covered by the base molding.

Accessories & Upgrades

The accessories you include in a bathroom remodel or new design are the jewelry on the room's design. Although modest, these touches can not only make or break the look of the room, they also affect how easy it will be to use. Basically, you can choose from big-impact luxuries like towel warmers, or simpler functional elements like shelving.

Other accessories serve a more crucial role. Grab bars—whether standalone or built into other elements—are becoming not only thoughtful additions to new bathroom designs, they are more and more being included as a simple matter of course. We're all aging, and grab bars are a way to make the bathroom safe now, and for decades to come.

Grab bars have specific mounting requirements to support minimum weight, which usually means mounting them to studs or blocking. Other accessories should be mounted the same way whenever possible. However, if no studs or blocking are located in the area where a shelf or towel bar will be placed, use toggle or molly bolts to anchor accessories to the wall.

In this chapter:

- Medicine Cabinets
- Grab Bars
- Tilting Wall Mirror
- Glass Shelving
- Towel Warmers

Medicine Cabinets

Common bathroom cabinets include vanities, medicine cabinets, linen cabinets, and "tank topper" cabinets that mount over the toilet area.

When installing cabinets in a damp location, like a bathroom, choose the best cabinets you can afford. Look for quality indicators, like doweled construction, hardwood doors and drawers, and high-gloss, moisture-resistant finishes. Avoid cabinets with sides or doors that are painted on one side and finished with laminate or veneer on the other because these cabinets are more likely to warp.

Tools & Materials ▸

Electronic stud finder
Level
Pry bar
Hammer
Screwdriver
Drill
Circular saw
Reciprocating saw
Pencil

Bar clamp
Framing square
Duplex nails
10d common nails
Finish nails
1 × 4 lumber
2½" wood screws
Wood shims
Cabinet

Medicine cabinets don't have to be frumpy. This sleek version has a concealed finger grip and integral modular lights that are as useful as they are cool.

How to Install a Surface-Mounted Cabinet

1

Locate the wall studs and mark them clearly on the wall surface. Draw a level line at the desired top height of the cabinet body, then measure and mark a second line to indicate the bottom of the cabinet.

2

Attach a temporary ledger board (usually 1 × 4) just below the lower level line using duplex nails. Rest the base of the cabinet on the ledger and hold it in place or brace it with 2 × 4s.

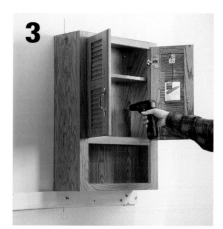

3

Attach the cabinet to the wall at the stud locations by drilling pilot holes and driving wood screws. Remove the ledger when finished, and patch the nail holes with drywall compound.

How to Install a Recessed Cabinet

1

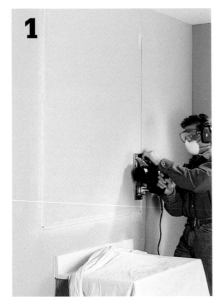

Locate the first stud beyond either side of the planned cabinet location, then remove the wall surface between the studs. (Removing the wall surface all the way to the ceiling simplifies patch work.) Cut along the center of the studs, using a circular saw with the blade depth set to the thickness of the wall surface.

2

Mark a rough opening ½" taller than the cabinet frame onto the exposed wall studs. Add 1½" for each header and sill plate, then cut out the studs in the rough opening area.

3

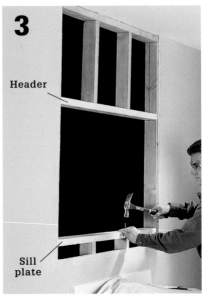

Header

Sill plate

Frame out the top and bottom of the rough opening by installing a header and a sill plate between the cut wall studs. Make sure the header and sill plate are level, then nail them in place with 10d common nails.

4

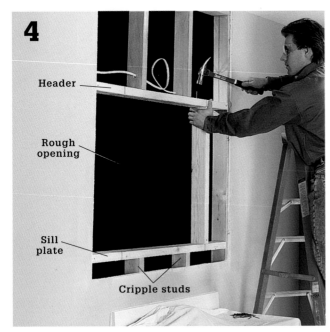

Header

Rough opening

Sill plate

Cripple studs

Mark the rough opening width on the header and sill plates, centering the opening over the sink. Cut and nail jack studs between the header and the sill plate, just outside the rough opening marks. Install any wiring for new light fixtures and receptacles, then patch the wall where necessary.

5

Position the cabinet in the opening. Check it for level with a carpenter's level, then attach the cabinet by drilling pilot holes and driving wood screws through the top and bottom of the cabinet sides and into the wall studs, header, and sill plate. Attach the doors, shelves, and hardware.

Special Section: Accessorizing for Universal Design

There are an increasing number of bathroom accessories that can make the room more usable for anyone with mobility limitations and other motor-skill impairments. These include traditional bathroom elements such as toilet paper holders that are now offered with integral grab bars.

These features are offered in a range of styles and finishes, making them design complements for any bathroom style. That means that there is really no reason not to include a set of grab bar accessories in your bathroom.

The trick is to make sure these extras are installed correctly. They should be secured to studs or blocking to reliably support minimum weight requirements. But they also need to be installed at the correct heights. The following are the Americans with Disabilities Acts (ADA) requirements for grab bar heights. The ADA is generally used as the basis for Universal Design in bathrooms.

- **Toilets:** Grab bars behind toilets (centered over the tank, or bowl if no tank is present) should be a minimum of 36" long, mounted between 33" and 36" up from the floor. Grab bars on a wall alongside the toilet should be mounted 12" out from the back wall, 33" to 36" from the floor, and should be a minimum of 45" long. Where there isn't a side wall, you can use a swing-up or swing-away independent grab bar unit with a supporting post and mounted with the same measurements as a wall-mounted bar.

- **Showers:** Back wall (main support) grab bars should be mounted 33" to 36" up from the shower floor, and can be between 38" and 48", depending on the space available in the stall. These can be used in conjunction with a permanent or fold-down seat mounted 18" up from the shower floor. Side-wall grab bars should be a length that fits on the side wall, mounted 33" to 36" up from the shower floor.

This handsome bathroom is an example of ultimate accessibility, with a curbless shower that allows a wheelchair or walker-bound individual to easily take a shower (fold down seat and grab bars assure stability). A roll-under sink is great for all users, and a toilet-side fold-down grab bar makes it simple for those with limited mobility to get on and off the essential fixture.

- **Bathtubs:** As with other locations, all grab bars in a tub area should be mounted between 33" and 36" up from the floor of the bathroom. A back-wall grab bar should be a minimum of 48" long, but should leave no more than 12" from the end of the grab bar to the head wall of the tub, and no more than 15" from the back end of the grab bar to the foot wall of the tub. Head-wall grab bars should be a minimum of 24" long and should be mounted with the outer end flush with the outside edge of the head wall. A back-wall grab bar should be installed in the same way, and should be a minimum of 12" long.

You can supplement these requirements with angled bars around shower stalls, offering variable heights at which the user can grab the bar. Use additional grab bars—such as those as part of a towel rack—to supplement these primary bars and make navigating the room easier.

A stylish accent ring around the faucet controls in this tub doubles as a grip bar that helps bathers safely get in and out of the tub.

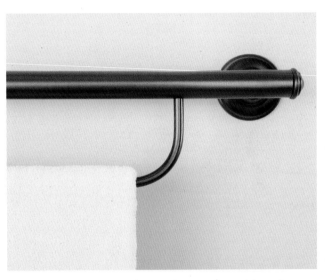

Why install just a towel bar, when you can add a safety feature with a combination towel-and-grab bar accessory. This one features a handsome rubbed bronze finish, but you'll find these in a range of surface styles.

Combine stability with convenience by adding a simple shelf holder-grab bar combo like this one. The sleek curving style of this unit is just one of many forms and finishes available in this type of accessory.

Small, handheld showerheads are ideal for anyone with grip-strength or coordination issues. A wall-mount makes this handy fixture even more usable and accessible.

Grab Bars

Bathrooms are beautiful with their shiny ceramic tubs, showers, and floors, but add water and moisture to the mix and you've created the perfect conditions for a fall. The good news is that many falls in the bathroom can be avoided by installing grab bars at key locations.

Grab bars help family members steady themselves on slippery shower, tub, and other floor surfaces. Plus, they provide support for people transferring from a wheelchair or walker to the shower, tub, or toilet.

Grab bars come in a variety of colors, shapes, sizes, and textures. Choose a style with a 1¼" to 1½" diameter that fits comfortably between your thumb and fingers. Then properly install it 1½" from the wall with anchors that can support at least 250 pounds.

The easiest way to install grab bars is to screw them into wall studs or into blocking or backing attached to studs. Blocking is a good option if you are framing a new bathroom or have the wall surface removed during a major remodel (see Illustration A). Use 2 × 6 or 2 × 8 lumber to provide room for adjustments, and fasten the blocks to the framing with 16d nails. Note the locations of your blocking for future reference.

As an alternative, cover the entire wall with ¾" plywood backing secured with screws to the wall framing, so you can install grab bars virtually anywhere on the wall (see Illustration B).

Grab bars can be installed in areas without studs. For these installations, use specialized heavy-duty hollow-wall anchors designed to support at least 250 pounds.

Tools & Materials ›

Measuring tape	Grab bar
Pencil	Hollow-wall
Stud finder	anchors
Level	#12 stainless steel
Drill	screws
Masonry bit	Silicone caulk

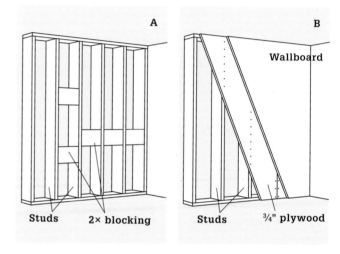

Blocking or backing is required for secure grab bars. If you know where the grab bars will be located, add 2× blocking between studs (Illustration A). You also can cover the entire wall with ¾" plywood backing, which allows you to install grab bars virtually anywhere on the wall.

Grab bars of different styles and configurations meet varied needs in any bathroom, and in different areas of the bathroom.

How to Install Grab Bars

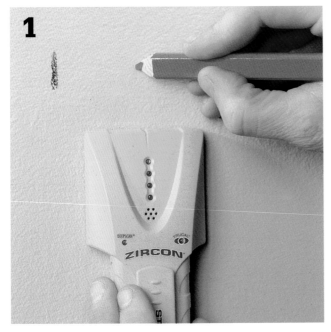

Locate the wall studs in the installation area using a stud finder. If the area is tiled, the stud finder may not detect studs, so try to locate the studs above the tile, if possible, then use a level to transfer the marks lower on the wall. Otherwise, you can drill small, exploratory holes through grout joints in the tile, then fill the holes with silicone caulk to seal them. Be careful not to drill into pipes.

Mark the grab bar height at one stud location, then use a level to transfer the height mark to the stud that will receive the other end of the bar. Position the grab bar on the height marks so at least two of the three mounting holes are aligned with the stud centers. Mark the mounting hole locations onto the wall.

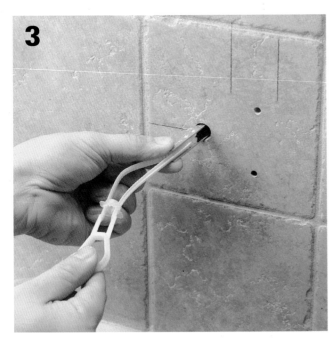

Drill pilot holes for the mounting screws. If you are drilling through tile, start with a small bit (about ⅛"), then redrill the hole with the larger bit. For screws that won't hit studs, drill holes for wall anchors, following the manufacturer's directions for sizing. Install anchors, if necessary.

Apply a continuous bead of silicone caulk to the back side of each bar end (inset). Secure the bar to the studs using #12 stainless steel screws (the screws should penetrate the stud by at least 1"). Install a stainless steel screw or bolt into the wall anchors. Test the bar to make sure it's secure.

Tilting Wall Mirrors

Tools & Materials ▶

Level
Drill
Flat-bladed
   screwdriver

Allen wrench
Tilting wall mirror
Extending
   arm mirror

A mirror is a necessity in any bathroom, but not every bathroom mirror has to be attached to a medicine cabinet. Tilting mirrors and telescoping makeup mirrors are only two of the nearly endless options available.

The most important part of mounting a mirror is accurate placement. A mirror over the vanity should be centered over the centerline of the sink. If you have an asymmetrical sink, center the mirror over the vanity.

Mirror height is also important, especially to those who are above or below average height. Tilting mirrors are useful if there is a dramatic difference between the tallest and the shortest person in the household.

A smaller tilting mirror can take the place of a large stationary mirror.

Extending arm mirrors are handy for shaving or applying makeup. These mirrors typically have two sides with one side providing magnification. Some come with lights and antifogging as well.

A tilting wall mirror adjusts to people of varying heights and should be centered over the sink or the vanity. Extending arm mirrors are installed off to the side, since the arm allows the mirror to be drawn closer when needed.

How to Install a Tilting Wall Mirror

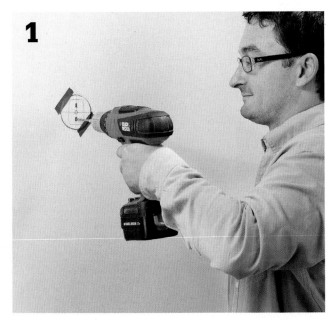

Determine the height of the mirror mounts by dividing the overall height of the mirror by two and adding the result to the number of inches above the vanity you want the bottom edge of the mirror to be placed. In this case, the mirror came with a mounting template. Tape the template to the wall and drill two $5/16$" holes at each of the mounting post locations.

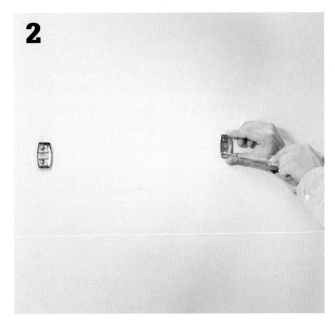

Insert the included wall anchors and tap into place. Remove the brackets from the mounting posts by loosening the setscrew. Attach the brackets to the wall at the wall anchor locations.

Assemble the mirror if necessary. Make sure the setscrews on the mounting posts are facing downward. Carefully lift the mirror, place the mounting posts over the brackets, and slide into place. Tighten the setscrews.

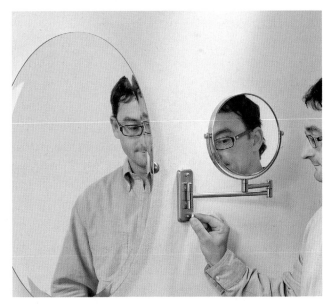

Variation: How to Hang an Extending Arm Mirror. Most extending wall mirrors are surface mounted. Next to the vanity mirror, use a level to mark a vertical line at the eye level of the mirror's main user. Make sure there is sufficient space for the mirror to fold back against the wall. Hold the mirror unit over the line and mark the screw hole locations. Drill two ¼" holes at the marks and insert the wall anchors. Hold the mirror in position and drive in the screws.

Glass Shelving

Tools & Materials ▶

Level   Pencil
Drill   Glass shelves

Glass shelving is unobtrusive so it can fit many styles of bathrooms—from sleek modern to elaborate Victorian. You can find a wide variety of shelving available in home stores and online.

Most glass shelves are held in place with metal mounts. How the shelves are secured to the mounts differs and how the mounts are attached to the wall also differs. Most shelves have a hidden bracket that is secured to the wall. The mount then slips over the bracket and is secured with a setscrew. The most basic models may have mounts that are screwed directly into the wall with exposed screws. The directions here are for shelving that uses hidden brackets.

If you are installing shelves on a tiled wall, mount the brackets in grout lines if at all possible to minimize the possibility of cracking the tiles. Many glass shelves have some flexibility in the distance between the mounts.

Glass shelves fit any style and size of bathroom. They are held in place with metal mounts, which can be decorative and attached to the wall.

How to Install Glass Shelves

Assemble the shelf and shelf holders (not the brackets). Hold the shelf against the wall in the desired location. On the wall, mark the center point of each holder, where the setscrew is.

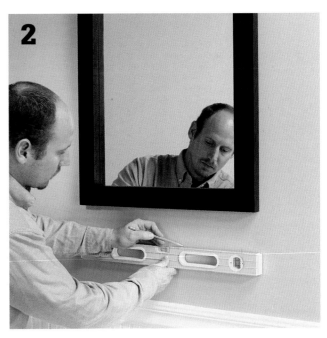

Remove the shelves and use the level to extend the mark into a 3" vertical line. Use the level to mark a horizontal line across the centers of these lines.

Center the middle round hole of the bracket over the intersection of the vertical and horizontal lines. Mark the center of each of the oblong holes. Put the bracket aside and drill a ¼" hole at each mark. Insert the included wall anchors in the holes. Replace the bracket, insert the screws into the wall anchors, and drive the screws. Repeat for the second bracket.

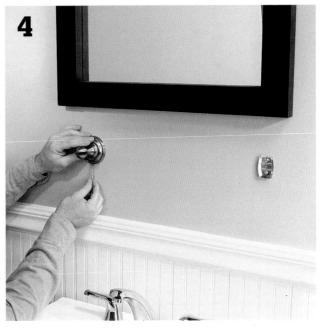

Remove the shelf from the holders. Slide a holder over a bracket, check that the shelf mount is level, and tighten the setscrew. Repeat with the other holder. Insert the shelf and fix in place. Check the shelf for level. If it's not level, remove one holder and loosen the bracket screws. Slide the bracket up or down to make the unit level. Replace the holder and shelf.

Towel Warmers

Here's a little bit of luxury that need not be limited to high-end hotel stays. You can have toasty towels in your own bathroom with an easy-to-install towel warmer. In a relatively cold room, this can make stepping out of the shower a much more pleasant experience.

Heated towel racks are available in a wide range of styles and sizes. Freestanding floor models as well as door- and wall-mounted versions can be plugged in for use when desired. Hardwired wall-mounted versions can be switched on when you enter the bathroom so your towels are warm when you step out of the shower. Although installing them requires some electrical skills, the hardwired models do not need to be located near wall receptacles and they do not have exposed cords or extension cords hanging on the wall. However, if you locate the

Tools & Materials ▶

Drill
Level
Keyhole saw
Wiring tools
Phillips screwdriver
Stud finder

Retrofit electrical
  outlet box
Wire connectors
NM cable
Towel warmer
Pencil
Masking tape

warmer directly above an existing receptacle, you can save a lot of time and mess by running cable up from the receptacle to the new electrical box for the warmer.

Before installing hardwired models, check your local electrical codes for applicable regulations. If you are not experienced with home wiring, have an electrician do this job for you or opt for a plug-in model.

A hard-wired towel warmer offers the luxury of heated towels without the safety concerns of a plug-in device.

How to Install a Hardwired Towel Warmer

Use a stud finder to locate the studs in the area you wish to place the towel warmer. Mark the stud locations with masking tape or pencil lines. Attach the wall brackets to the towel warmer and hold the unit against the wall at least 7" from the floor and 3" from the ceiling or any overhang. Mark the locations of the wall bracket outlet plate (where the electrical connection will be made) and the mounting brackets.

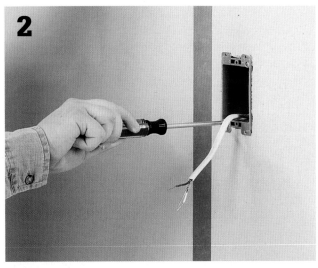

Shut off electrical power at the main service panel. At the mark for the wall bracket outlet, cut a hole in the wallcovering for a retrofit electrical box. Run NM cable from the opening to a GFCI-protected circuit (here, we ran cable down to a receptacle directly beneath it), or install a separate GFCI-protected circuit (you'll need to consult a wiring book or an electrician). Pull the cable through the hole in the retrofit box, and then tighten the cable clamp. Place the box in the hole flush with the wall surface and tighten the mounting screw in the rear of the box. Cut the wires so about 5" extends into the box and strip the insulation off at ⅜" from the end of each wire.

Position the towel warmer over the outlet box and mark the locations of the screw holes for the wall brackets. Make sure the appliance is level. Remove the warmer and drill ¼" pilot holes at the marked locations. If the marks are located over studs, drill ⅛" pilot holes. If not, push wall anchors into the holes. Thread the mounting screws through the brackets. Have a helper hold the towel rack in place and use wire connectors to connect the wires, including the ground wire, according to the instructions.

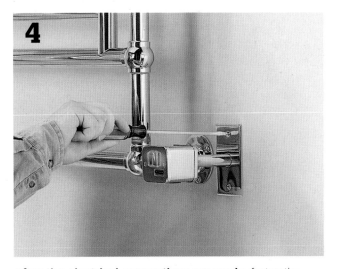

After the electrical connections are made, fasten the towel rack brackets to the wall. Turn on power and test the towel warmer. Finally, attach the electrical cover plate with integral on/off switch.

Appendix A: Plumbing Codes & Permits

The Plumbing Code is the set of regulations that building officials and inspectors use to evaluate your project plans and the quality of your work. Codes vary from region to region, but most are based on the National Uniform Plumbing Code, a highly technical, difficult-to-read manual. More user-friendly code handbooks are available at bookstores and libraries. These handbooks are based on the National Uniform Plumbing Code, but they are easier to read and include diagrams and photos.

Sometimes these handbooks discuss three different plumbing zones in an effort to accommodate state variations in regulations. Remember that local plumbing code always supersedes national code. Your local building inspector can be a valuable source of information and may provide you with a convenient summary sheet of the regulations that apply to your project.

As part of its effort to ensure public safety, your community building department requires a permit for most plumbing projects. When you apply for a permit, the building official will want to review three drawings of your plumbing project: a site plan, a water supply diagram, and a drain-waste-vent diagram. If the official is satisfied that your project meets code requirements, you will be issued a plumbing permit, which is your legal permission to begin work. As your project nears completion, the inspector will visit your home to check your work.

Note: These specifications may not conform to all building codes; check with your local building department regarding regulations in your area.

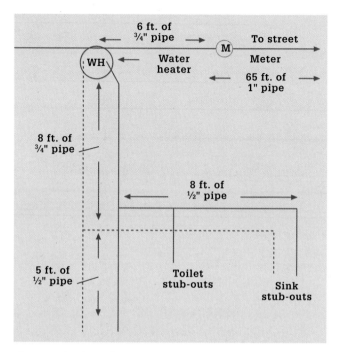

The supply riser diagram shows the length of the hot and cold water pipes and the relation of the fixtures to one another. The inspector will use this diagram to determine the proper size for the new water supply pipes in your system.

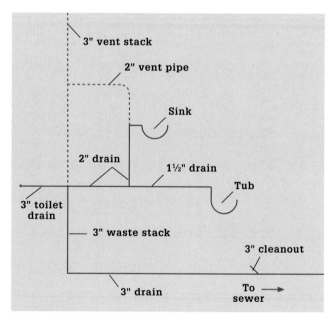

A DWV diagram shows the routing of drain and vent pipes in your system. Indicate the lengths of drain pipes and the distances between fixtures. The inspector will use this diagram to determine if you have properly sized the drain traps, drain pipes, and vent pipes.

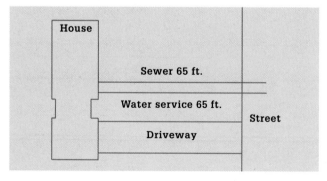

The site plan shows the location of the water main and sewer main with respect to your yard and home. The distances from your foundation to the water main and from the foundation to the main sewer should be indicated on the site map.

Fixture Supply Pipe & Trap Sizes

FIXTURE	UNIT RATING	MINIMUM BRANCH PIPE SIZE	MINIMUM SUPPLY TUBE SIZE	MINIMUM TRAP SIZE
Toilet	3	½"	⅜"	n/a
Vanity Sink	1	½"	⅜"	1¼"
Shower	2	½"	⅜"	2"
Bathtub	2	½"	½"	1½"

To determine the minimum size of supply pipes and fixture drain traps, you must know the fixture's unit rating, a unit of measure assigned by the plumbing code. *Note: Branch pipes are the water supply lines that run from the distribution pipes toward the individual fixtures. Supply tubes carry water from the branch pipes to the fixtures.*

Sizes for Horizontal & Vertical Drain Pipes

PIPE SIZE	MAXIMUM FIXTURE UNITS FOR HORIZONTAL BRANCH DRAIN	MAXIMUM FIXTURE UNITS FOR VERTICAL DRAIN STACKS
1¼"	1	2
1½"	3	4
2"	6	10
2½"	12	20
3"	20	30
4"	160	240

Drain pipe sizes are determined by the load on the pipes, as measured by the total fixture units. Horizontal drain pipes less than 3" in diameter should slope ¼" per foot toward the main drain. Pipes 3" or more in diameter should slope ⅛" per foot. *Note: Horizontal or vertical drain pipes for a toilet must be 3" or larger.*

Maximum Hole & Notch Sizes

FRAMING MEMBER	MAXIMUM HOLE SIZE	MAXIMUM NOTCH SIZE
2 × 4 loadbearing stud	1⁷⁄₁₆" diameter	⅞" deep
2 × 4 non-loadbearing stud	2½" diameter	1⁷⁄₁₆" deep
2 × 6 loadbearing stud	2¼" diameter	1⅜" deep
2 × 6 non-loadbearing stud	3⁵⁄₁₆" diameter	2³⁄₁₆" deep
2 × 6 joists	1½" diameter	⅞" deep
2 × 8 joists	2⅜" diameter	1¼" deep
2 × 10 joists	3¹⁄₁₆" diameter	1½" deep
2 × 12 joists	3¾" diameter	1⅞" deep

The maximum hole and notch sizes that can be cut into framing members for running pipes is shown above. Where possible, use notches rather than bored holes to ease pipe installation. When boring holes, there must be at least ⅝" of wood between the edge of a stud and the hole, and at least 2" between the edge of a joist and the hole. Joists can be notched only in the end one-third of the overall span; never in the middle one-third of the joist. When two pipes are run through a stud, the pipes should be stacked one over the other, never side by side.

Pipe Support Intervals

TYPE OF PIPE	VERTICAL SUPPORT INTERVAL	HORIZONTAL SUPPORT INTERVAL
Copper	6 ft.	10 ft.
ABS	4 ft.	4 ft.
CPVC	3 ft.	3 ft.
PVC	4 ft.	4 ft.
Galvanized Iron	12 ft.	15 ft.
Cast Iron	5 ft.	15 ft.

Minimum intervals for supporting pipes are determined by the type of pipe and its orientation in the system. Use only brackets and supports made of the same (or compatible) materials as the pipes. Remember that the measurements shown above are minimum requirements; many plumbers install pipe supports at closer intervals.

Wet Venting

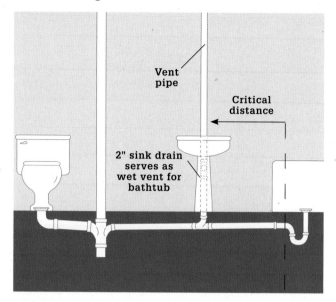

Vent pipe

Critical distance

2" sink drain serves as wet vent for bathtub

Wet vents are pipes that serve as a vent for one fixture and a drain for another. The sizing of a wet vent is based on the total fixture units it supports: a 3" wet vent can serve up to 12 fixture units; a 2" wet vent is rated for 4 fixture units; a 1½" wet vent, for only 1 fixture unit. *Note: The distance between the wet-vented fixture and the wet vent itself must be no more than the maximum critical distance.*

Auxiliary Venting

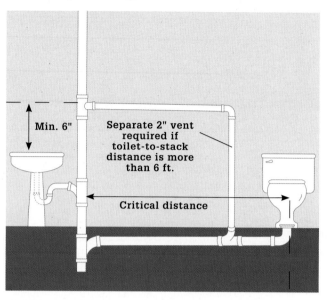

Min. 6"

Separate 2" vent required if toilet-to-stack distance is more than 6 ft.

Critical distance

Fixtures must have auxiliary vents if the distance to the main waste-vent stack exceeds the critical distance. A toilet, for example, should have a separate vent pipe if it is located more than 6 ft. from the main waste–vent stack. This secondary vent pipe should connect to the stack or an existing vent pipe at a point at least 6" above the highest fixture on the system.

Vent Pipe Sizes, Critical Distances

SIZE OF FIXTURE DRAIN	MINIMUM VENT PIPE SIZE	MAXIMUM TRAP-TO-VENT DISTANCE
1¼"	1¼"	2½ ft.
1½"	1¼"	3½ ft.
2"	1½"	5 ft.
3"	2"	6 ft.
4"	3"	10 ft.

Vent pipes are usually one pipe size smaller than the drain pipes they serve. Code requires that the distance between the drain trap and the vent pipe fall within a maximum *critical distance,* a measurement that is determined by the size of the fixture drain. Use this chart to determine both the minimum size for the vent pipe and the maximum critical distance.

Vent Pipe Orientation to Drain Pipe

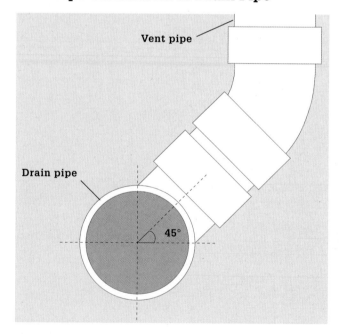

Vent pipe

Drain pipe

45°

Vent pipes must extend in an upward direction from drains, no less than 45° from horizontal. This ensures that waste water cannot flow into the vent pipe and block it. At the opposite end, a new vent pipe should connect to an existing vent pipe or main waste–vent stack at a point at least 6" above the highest fixture draining into the system.

Appendix B: Wiring Codes & Permits

To ensure public safety, every community requires that you get a permit to install new wiring and have the completed work reviewed by an appointed inspector. Electrical inspectors use the National Electrical Code (NEC) as the primary authority for evaluating wiring, but they also follow the local building code and electrical code standards.

As you begin planning new circuits, call or visit your local electrical inspector and discuss the project with him or her. The inspector can tell you which of the national and local code requirements apply to your job, and may give you a packet of information summarizing these regulations. Later, when you apply to the inspector for a work permit, he or she will expect you to understand the local guidelines as well as a few basic NEC requirements.

The NEC is a set of standards that provides minimum safety requirements for wiring installations. It is revised every three years.

In addition to being the final authority of code requirements, inspectors are electrical professionals with years of experience. Although they have busy schedules, most inspectors are happy to answer questions and help you design well-planned circuits.

As with any project, if you are uncomfortable working with electricity, hire a professional electrician to complete new wiring installations and connections.

The bathroom requirements listed below are for general information only. Contact your local electrical inspector for specific wiring regulations:

- A separate 20-amp receptacle circuit for small appliances is required.
- All receptacles must be GFCI protected.
- Light fixtures and switches must be on a separate circuit. (A minimum 15-amp circuit.)
- All fixture and appliance switches must be grounded.
- There must be at least one ceiling-mounted light fixture.
- Whirlpools and other large fixtures or appliances are required to be on a dedicated circuit.

The manufacturers of some home spa fixtures, such as saunas and whirlpools, may specify that a certified electrician make the electrical connections for their product. Make sure to follow these directions, as doing otherwise may result in the warranty being voided.

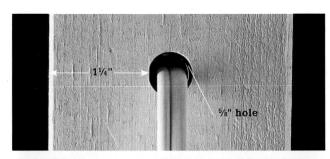

Cables must be protected against damage by nails and screws by at least 1¼" of wood (top). When cables pass through 2 × 2 furring strips (bottom), protect the cables with metal protector plates.

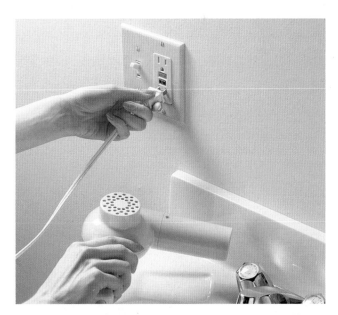

Kitchen and bathroom receptacles must be protected by a GFCI. Also, all outdoor receptacles and general use receptacles in an unfinished basement or crawlspace must be protected by a GFCI.

Measurement Conversions

Lumber Dimensions

NOMINAL - U.S.	ACTUAL - U.S. (IN INCHES)	METRIC
1 × 2	¾ × 1½	19 × 38 mm
1 × 3	¾ × 2½	19 × 64 mm
1 × 4	¾ × 3½	19 × 89 mm
1 × 5	¾ × 4½	19 × 114 mm
1 × 6	¾ × 5½	19 × 140 mm
1 × 7	¾ × 6¼	19 × 159 mm
1 × 8	¾ × 7¼	19 × 184 mm
1 × 10	¾ × 9¼	19 × 235 mm
1 × 12	¾ × 11¼	19 × 286 mm
1¼ × 4	1 × 3½	25 × 89 mm
1¼ × 6	1 × 5½	25 × 140 mm
1¼ × 8	1 × 7¼	25 × 184 mm
1¼ × 10	1 × 9¼	25 × 235 mm
1¼ × 12	1 × 11¼	25 × 286 mm

NOMINAL - U.S.	ACTUAL - U.S. (IN INCHES)	METRIC
1½ × 4	1¼ × 3½	32 × 89 mm
1½ × 6	1¼ × 5½	32 × 140 mm
1½ × 8	1¼ × 7¼	32 × 184 mm
1½ × 10	1¼ × 9¼	32 × 235 mm
1½ × 12	1¼ × 11¼	32 × 286 mm
2 × 4	1½ × 3½	38 × 89 mm
2 × 6	1½ × 5½	38 × 140 mm
2 × 8	1½ × 7¼	38 × 184 mm
2 × 10	1½ × 9¼	38 × 235 mm
2 × 12	1½ × 11¼	38 × 286 mm
3 × 6	2½ × 5½	64 × 140 mm
4 × 4	3½ × 3½	89 × 89 mm
4 × 6	3½ × 5½	89 × 140 mm

Metric Conversions

TO CONVERT:	TO:	MULTIPLY BY:
Inches	Millimeters	25.4
Inches	Centimeters	2.54
Feet	Meters	0.305
Yards	Meters	0.914
Square inches	Square centimeters	6.45
Square feet	Square meters	0.093
Square yards	Square meters	0.836
Ounces	Milliliters	30.0
Pints (U.S.)	Liters	0.473 (Imp. 0.568)
Quarts (U.S.)	Liters	0.946 (Imp. 1.136)
Gallons (U.S.)	Liters	3.785 (Imp. 4.546)
Ounces	Grams	28.4
Pounds	Kilograms	0.454

TO CONVERT:	TO:	MULTIPLY BY:
Millimeters	Inches	0.039
Centimeters	Inches	0.394
Meters	Feet	3.28
Meters	Yards	1.09
Square centimeters	Square inches	0.155
Square meters	Square feet	10.8
Square meters	Square yards	1.2
Milliliters	Ounces	.033
Liters	Pints (U.S.)	2.114 (Imp. 1.76)
Liters	Quarts (U.S.)	1.057 (Imp. 0.88)
Liters	Gallons (U.S.)	0.264 (Imp. 0.22)
Grams	Ounces	0.035
Kilograms	Pounds	2.2

Counterbore, Shank & Pilot Hole Diameters

SCREW SIZE	COUNTERBORE DIAMETER FOR SCREW HEAD (IN INCHES)	CLEARANCE HOLE FOR SCREW SHANK (IN INCHES)	PILOT HOLE DIAMETER HARD WOOD (IN INCHES)	SOFT WOOD (IN INCHES)
#1	.146 (⁹⁄₆₄)	⁵⁄₆₄	³⁄₆₄	¹⁄₃₂
#2	¼	³⁄₃₂	³⁄₆₄	¹⁄₃₂
#3	¼	⁷⁄₆₄	¹⁄₁₆	³⁄₆₄
#4	¼	⅛	¹⁄₁₆	³⁄₆₄
#5	¼	⅛	⁵⁄₆₄	¹⁄₁₆
#6	⁵⁄₁₆	⁹⁄₆₄	³⁄₃₂	⁵⁄₆₄
#7	⁵⁄₁₆	⁵⁄₃₂	³⁄₃₂	⁵⁄₆₄
#8	⅜	¹¹⁄₆₄	⅛	³⁄₃₂
#9	⅜	¹¹⁄₆₄	⅛	³⁄₃₂
#10	⅜	³⁄₁₆	⅛	⁷⁄₆₄
#11	½	³⁄₁₆	⁵⁄₃₂	⁹⁄₆₄
#12	½	⁷⁄₃₂	⁹⁄₆₄	⅛

Resources

Accessibility Resource Center (ARC)
Shower and wet room kits, Aging in Place and
    accessibility accessories
715-743-2771
www.arcfirst.net

American Standard
Bathroom and kitchen fixtures
800-442-1902
www.americanstandard-us.com

BLACK+DECKER
Power tools and accessories
800-544-6986
www.blackanddecker.com

Duravit
Bathtubs, sinks and bathroom furniture
www.duravit.us

Interstyle Glass and Ceramic
Ceramic and glass tiles
604-421-7229
www.interstyle.ca

Laticrete
Floor-warming mats and supplies
800-243-4788
www.laticrete.com

Moen
Bathroom faucets, shower fixtures, safety and
    accessibility accessories
800-289-6636
www.moen.com

MTI
Tubs, shower bases and enclosures, sinks, accessories
800-783-8827
mtibaths.com

National Kitchen and Bath Association
Industry association offering advice and connection
    to professionals
800-843-6522
www.nkba.org

**Plumbing, Heating, Cooling Contractors Association
    (PHCC)**
Producers of the National Standard Plumbing Code
www.phccweb.org
800-533-7694

Robern
Bathroom cabinets, lighting, vanities and mirrors
800-877-2376
www.robern.com

Photo Credits

Index

WHOLE HOME NEWS

A BLOG ABOUT...
Sustainable Living • Farming
DIY • Gardening • Home Improvement

For even more information on improving your own home or homestead, visit **www.wholehomenews.com** today! From raising vegetables to raising roofs, it's the one-stop spot for sharing questions and getting answers about the challenges of self-sufficient living.

Brought to you by two publishing imprints of Quarto Publishing Group USA Inc., Voyageur Press and Cool Springs Press, *Whole Home News* is a blog for people interested in the same things we are: self-sufficiency, gardening, home improvement, country living, and sustainability. Our mission is to provide you with information on the latest techniques and trends from industry experts and everyday enthusiasts.

In addition to regular posts written by our volunteer in-house advisory committee, you'll also meet others from the larger enthusiast community dedicated to "doing it for ourselves." Some of these contributors include published authors of bestselling books, magazine and newspaper journalists, freelance writers, media personalities, and industry experts. And you'll also find features from ordinary folks who are equally passionate about these topics.

Join us at **www.wholehomenews.com** to keep the conversation going.
You can also shoot us an email at wholehomenews@quartous.com.
We look forward to seeing you online, and thanks for reading!

 @wholehomenews